Valuing Technology

Drawing on insights from social studies of technology, gender studies and the sociology of consumption, *Valuing Technology* opens up new directions in the analysis of sociotechnical change within organisations. Based on a major research project focused upon the introduction of management information systems in health, higher education and retailing, it explores the active role of end-users in innovation.

This book argues that it is through the, often difficult, engagement between users and technology that new computer systems come to gain value within organisations. Key themes developed through analysis of case studies include:

- the valuing of technology via the on-going construction of needs, uses and utilities
- occupational identities, organisational inequalities and technological change
- the gendering of technological and organisational change
- the interplay of technological and organisational cultures
- the 'stabilisation' of technological systems and their 'incorporation' into the lives of people in organisations

A stimulating blend of the theoretical and substantive, this book demands a radical redefinition of 'technology acquisition'. Its highly original approach makes *Valuing Technology* essential reading for students, lecturers and researchers within the fields of organisation studies and the sociology of technology.

Janice McLaughlin is Research Fellow and Lecturer in Sociology and Women's Studies. **Paul Rosen** is Research Fellow in Social Studies of Technology. **David Skinner** is Senior Lecturer in Sociology and Deputy Director of the Science and Technology Studies Unit. **Andrew Webster** is Professor of Sociology and Director of the Science and Technology Studies Unit. All are based at Anglia Polytechnic University, UK.

The Management of Technology and Innovation

Edited by David Preece

University of Portsmouth, UK

The books in this series offer grounding in central elements of the management of technology and innovation. Each title will explain, develop and critically explore issues and concepts in a particular aspect of the management of technology/innovation, combining a review of the current state of knowledge with the presentation and discussion of primary material not previously published.

Each title is designed to be user-friendly, with an international orientation and key introductions and summaries.

Valuing Technology

Organisations, culture and change

Janice McLaughlin, Paul Rosen
David Skinner and Andrew Webster

London and New York

First published 1999
by Routledge
11 New Fetter Lane, London EC4P 4EE

Simultaneously published in the USA and Canada
by Routledge
29 West 35th Street, New York, NY 10001

Routledge is an imprint of the Taylor & Francis Group

Typeset in Garamond by
M Rules
Printed and bound in Great Britain by
Biddles Ltd, Guilford and King's Lynn

British Library Cataloguing in Publication Data
A catalogue record for this book is available from the British Library

Library of Congress Cataloging in Publication Data
Valuing technology: organisations, culture, and change / Janice
McLaughlin . . . [et al.].
    p. cm. – (The management of technology and innovation)
    Includes bibliographical references and index.
    1. Technological innovations – Social aspects. 2. Information
    technology – Social aspects. 3. Employees – Effect of
    technological innovations on.   I. McLaughlin, Janice, 1968-
    II. Series.
    HM221.V32 1999
    303.48'33–dc21   99-17599
                        CIP

ISBN 0-415-19210-2 (hbk)
ISBN 0-415-19211-0 (pbk)

For our parents, partners, progeny and pets

Contents

Illustrations

Figures

Tables

Acknowledgements

As with any book, there are many besides the authors who have contributed to this group project, though nobody but the four of us will have been as fully enrolled, nor will they have incorporated it into their daily lives to quite the extent that we have. We hope nobody has suffered too much as a result of us living, breathing, eating or sleeping what we have fondly come to know as 'the TA project', but we would like to break with tradition and acknowledge before all others our long-suffering families and companions for putting up with it. It would be nice to say we will now all have more free time, but of course there is now that other research project to begin, that other paper to write, or that other lecture course to prepare.

This book developed out of a research project entitled 'Technology Acquisition as a Process of Consumption: Negotiating Needs and Negotiating Uses'. It was funded by the ESRC, project number R000236105, and ran from 1995 to 1998. Special thanks go to Kathryn Packer for her role in developing the research proposal. We have benefited enormously too from discussions about substantive and theoretic issues with our other colleagues in and around SATSU – Brian Rappert, Sharon Tabberer, Annemiek Nelis, Nik Brown and Tom Ling – and in the Department of Sociology and Politics at APU. Our analysis has developed in part through discussion also with others in the wider community of science and technology studies, feminist social theory and critical theory, consumption studies, and social and political sciences more broadly. Our discussions with colleagues in these areas have all helped shape our ideas.

On the practical side, we have many reasons to thank Jacqueline Rose – for transcribing what must have seemed like endless interviews and then preparing them for NUD•IST, as well as a range of administrative work for the project. Nikki Robinson's help with the transcripts has also been much appreciated. Our editor at Routledge, Stuart Hay, deserves great credit for his speedy and efficient processing of the book from a proposal to a finished manuscript, as well as commiserations for having to deal with our repeated renegotiations of our deadlines. Our two reviewers, Ian McLoughlin and David Collins, have made a very positive contribution to the book in helping us shape and define its tone, clarify arguments and generally situate it as something which straddles several different academic fields.

Finally, the book could clearly not have been written without the cooperation and time given freely by those who helped us gain access to our three sites,
and those we interviewed there. Very grateful thanks, therefore, firstly to the
gatekeepers who allowed us access at Finlay, Brodies and Bancroft. For the
most part, we are unable to name these people, but Joe Hutcheon, Peter Ford
and Angela Crum Ewing helped us negotiate the background and context of
the MAC Initiative, whilst John Bray kindly lent us the MAC Blueprint
Document. Our greatest debt, though, is owed to 'the users' — our respondents from the Finlay Microbiology and Pathology labs; Head Office, Area
Office and the twelve stores we studied at Brodies; and the IT Steering Group
and staff at Bancroft. Many thanks to them all.

Parts of Chapter 4 have been published by Janice McLaughlin and Andrew
Webster as 'Rationalising knowledge: IT systems, professional identities and
power', *Sociological Review* 46, 4 (1998): 781–802.
   Parts of Chapter 6 will be published by Janice McLaughlin as 'Gendering
occupational identities and technology: IT in the retail sector', *New Technology,
Work and Employment* (forthcoming, 1999).

Cambridge, January 1999

Introduction

When someone buys or acquires a new piece of technology – a new car, PC, digital TV or any other device – it is usually presumed that it is to meet certain needs (for transport, information, leisure, and so on) and provide certain clear benefits. It is also assumed that those who design technologies do so to serve the well-defined needs of consumers. The image presented here is of the 'rational' consumer buying a new technology to satisfy clearly defined needs, and willing to complain when those needs are *not* being met in some way, and of producers seeking to exploit their knowledge of consumer needs in order to develop better products.

When we broaden our focus and consider large, complex organisations and the ways they go about acquiring new technologies, we might think that there, too, management buys in only those technologies that will meet well-defined organisational (financial, bureaucratic, technical or other) needs. Technology suppliers, for their part, will try to ensure they understand the sorts of requirement any particular organisation might have, and, in the light of this, design and provide technologies that do the job.

These views of, in the first instance, the individual consumer and, in the second, the organisation are both based on a perspective which assumes it is possible to identify user needs (at whatever scale), to develop appropriate technologies to meet them, and so to ensure that they are used 'successfully'. Yet there are other stories one comes across – of the collapse of a technological system because user needs had not been properly considered, such as the 'Taurus' software once acquired to run the UK stock exchange which crashed almost as soon as it went operational, of consumers questioning the value of the so-called 'built-in functionality' of the latest version PC, of the smart-card that refuses to recognise your credit-worthiness, of consumers reluctant to buy new products, such as Clive Sinclair's C5 electric bicycle. We can also find users – at both the individual and organisational level – redesigning the technologies they buy, customising machines, disabling certain functions, building in new capacities, or simply using the technologies in ways unforeseen by the original designers.

Here, then, whether it be through the experience of a troublesome and awkward technology, or through the desire to reshape or reposition technologies, it would seem that the relationship between technological design and user needs is both more problematic than it sometimes appears to be, and more open to reinterpretation, change and challenge, at both the individual and organisational levels.

This book argues that this more unstable, provisional relationship between technologies and user needs is, in practice, the norm. It shows how the acquisition of technology and its subsequent deployment by users are complex processes that *cannot* be fully anticipated by the designers of the technology. It shows how the value of a technology has to be *built* by users over time as they make sense of and embed it in their local settings. We do this by exploring a particular type of technology, management information systems (MIS), and describe how three types of MIS were acquired by and brought to life in three very different types of organisation.

Much of the distinctiveness of our approach is summed up by the phrase 'valuing technology'. Firstly, this relates to our central concern with how, over time and within particular settings, technologies come to have value. Secondly, it highlights the powerful imperatives underlying innovation that privilege new technology as a solution to organisational problems. Thirdly, it suggests that, although they are often represented as otherwise, both technologies and organisations are cultural phenomena (and thus embody values).

Our account is one which will be of particular interest to the reader familiar with 'change management' or organisational studies, for we explore a set of issues which is close to contemporary debates in such fields. Yet, as authors, we write from a *sociological* perspective and bring to the debate ideas that draw on very different conceptual frameworks. This we hope to do in a constructive, not imperialistic, manner, for we want to try to show how insights from within sociology, especially from the areas of 'social studies of technology' and the 'sociology of consumption', can contribute to management studies and help explain why and how new technologies come to have value and utility. At the same time, we hope also to contribute to the sociology of science and technology itself and to consumption studies, by developing, through the empirical enquiry described in this book, new ways of understanding technological systems and how they are embedded in different social contexts.

In building our argument there will be a need to draw on concepts and terms unfamiliar to those working in management or organisational studies. We have tried to develop our conceptual framework in a gradual way throughout the book, and in the earlier chapters we show how sociological concepts complement as well as challenge more recent work in management perspectives on new technology. It is quite clear that these perspectives have themselves shifted over recent years and have sought to address what many acknowledge as the more complex processes involved in acquiring and using technologies.

For example, the contributions by Badham (1995) and Orlikowski (1992) within management and organisational studies explore the process of 'sociotechnical change' and the introduction of MIS and 'smart' manufacturing techniques within organisations. Badham shows how, in order to manage the 'change process' associated with the introduction of new sociotechnical systems, such systems have to be adapted and customised through a process of sociotechnical 'configuration' to 'fit the context within which [they are] to operate' (1995: 77). Crucially, Badham argues that such a configuration 'includes a set of meanings or interpretations of the technology and its requirements that to a degree "constitute" the technology in a specific operating environment and undermine any *simple* view of the "non-human" character of such configurations' (ibid., emphasis in original). Such a view encourages us to see that the meaning and role of technological systems in organisational settings are not pre-given, laid down in advance and constant. Orlikowski in a similar vein argues that technology should be conceived of as 'the outcome of co-ordinated human action and hence as inherently social . . . technology is *interpretively flexible*' (1992: 403, emphasis in original).

These accounts point to the need to understand that technology itself is socially constituted and that the acquisition and implementation of a new MIS is not a single, bounded event, but a process that stretches over time. Why this should be so, what it tells us about the ways in which technologies come to have (changing) value, and what theoretical and practical lessons might be drawn from this in terms of understanding the 'success' of a technological system are the key questions which shape this book.

Key concepts and issues

As noted earlier, our argument will draw on a variety of conceptual terms to explain the dynamics of technology acquisition and its subsequent embedding in organisations. But it will help the reader to understand our approach if we recount in the first instance the inspiration for the book itself. The book is based on a research project undertaken by the authors which took as its starting point the question of what happens when organisations acquire new technologies, and how they use them and derive value from them. A similar question, but with its focus on the individual consumer, had already been posed by one of us (Skinner 1992) in a detailed study of the purchase and use of 'home computers': it was clear from that study that the enormous demand for this new technology that began in the mid-1980s could not be explained in terms of the satisfaction of pre-existing needs. In fact many consumers of early computers had little idea of the capabilities of their machines when they purchased them. Instead, users developed needs and utilities after purchase in a process a number of them termed 'finding a use for the computer'. The users related to their new computers in a variety of ways – sometimes hiding them away in cupboards! – that gave them meanings and value (both positive and negative) which neither the designers nor the retailers envisaged. It was also evident that the meaning and value of the new technology were actively constructed and reconstructed over time in relation to the user's wider home environment.

It seemed that the lessons from this study of the domestic setting might be deployed elsewhere, specifically in the rather different setting of organisations, where the relationships between provider and user(s) would be much more complex, but might also demonstrate similar processes of redefining, giving meaning to and valuing (or not) new technologies. This idea led to a three-year research project on which this book is based.

The lessons from the study of home computing and our deployment of ideas from social studies of science and technology and consumption studies have ensured that our approach is framed by a number of core concepts which we can sketch out briefly here, though all are, of course, developed more fully in later chapters.

1   We are concerned in this book about *processes of technology acquisition*. Typically, it is assumed that technologies are acquired to serve some clearly defined set of needs, and that the process of acquisition will – properly managed and implemented – ensure these needs are (subsequently) met. In many cases this seems perfectly straightforward – one buys a pen in order to write. Of course, this technically modest instrument could be used for other purposes (or 'needs') too – like cleaning your ears, removing bits of biscuit from the keyboard, stirring your coffee (but make sure you do these in the right order!) and so on. But it will always be the case – even with modest, everyday, technologies – that the needs they serve can be redefined over time as the setting in which they are used and the purposes they serve are themselves reconfigured. When more complex and novel technologies – such as the computer software and hardware on which MIS technologies depend – are acquired by complex and differentiated organisations, we should also expect that, while there are certain needs expressed that justify often exceedingly expensive systems, these needs can be redefined, be rearticulated, and even get 'lost' as different organisational actors, from senior managers to more junior staff, interact with and deploy the technologies in distinct ways. What makes this process particularly interesting with regard to MIS is that, compared with many other technological systems, we can expect acquirers to anticipate that the acquisition of new information systems will presuppose and require their uniform adoption and use across the organisation. After all, that is how they are supposed to add value to the organisation. Our stories in this book suggest things are very different indeed.

2   As our last point suggests, technologies gain part of their value within specific organisational settings. In our accounts in later chapters of the particular cases that form the substantive focus of this book, we point to some elements of *organisational culture* that are a key component of the settings in which technology acquires value – notably the *narratives* and *practices* fostered by management but always mediated and reinterpreted at a local level, the gendering of organisational 'skills', and the varied way these cultural forms are articulated and reshaped by different occupational groupings within an organisation. We attempt to map the varying stories

that organisational actors recount about their own organisation, how they see themselves as members of it, the ways these accounts help members make sense of and give an identity to their role within the organisation, and the sorts of activity and behaviour this gives rise to. These mediate the technology acquisition process but, like other aspects of the organisational setting, are themselves changed during the process.

3   Organisations are *regulated*: this includes the ways in which the members are managed and the way they themselves, at the subjective level, regulate their own action as organisational members. Again, it is our claim in the book that new technologies mediate and are in turn reshaped by these various forms of regulation. Of course, part of the managerial rationale for acquiring new MIS is to deploy it precisely in order to control staff movement, performance and efficiency: yet our case studies will show how this depends on the structure of the organisation, the character of and relation between its members, and the local forms of subjective regulation these members express.

4   We examine how new technologies are, over time, embedded in organisations: this issue is explored through the key concepts of the *stabilisation* of the technology and its place in the organisation, and its *incorporation* into the lives and projects of differently placed organisational actors. Crucially, we show how the same technology can be made stable and be seen to be 'working' in multiple ways. In management literature this multiplicity of meanings is regarded as a problem to be resolved by 'better' management. In contrast, we will argue that such plural patterns of stabilisation and incorporation are not only normal but the very basis on which systems come to have value and function within large organisations.

5   As is perhaps clear from the above, the processes associated with the acquisition of new information technology (IT) systems, their mediation by and stabilisation within an organisational setting, all depend on users constructing, in different ways and over time, their *usability* and *utility*. Users are not passive but active participants – or 'consumers' – in how technologies are given meaning and then 'envalued' or 'devalued'. User needs cannot simply be inscribed or built into a technology at a given point. Yet in practice many organisations appear to act as though this were the case: the whole notion of piloting and then 'rolling out' a new IT system across the sites of a large national corporation, such as a bank or retail company, is premised on the assumption that the pilot irons out technical wrinkles and identifies relevant needs which can then be assumed to be found and met across the organisation as a whole.

Moreover, such a strategy tends to ignore or at least glosses over the significant differences that can be found between organisational members in terms of power, status and identity. Users do not just use a particular piece of hardware or machine, but carry or share collective identities, ways of seeing themselves which reflect wider identities and inequalities. So our book tries to explore the ways in which new technologies are mediated by *identities* and *inequalities of power* – such as those associated with gender and claims to 'professionalism' found in our case studies. Differences here reveal how users are more, or less, able to negotiate the terms on which new technologies shape their organisational (and occupational) roles. Users have to be 'enrolled' by those acquiring the technology, and some may be more resistant than others precisely because of the position they enjoy as members of a specific group in the organisation.

Sociological perspectives

We can complement this outline of some of the core issues we will be addressing in the book with a few introductory words about the two main sociological perspectives from which they are drawn. These are developed much more fully in the following chapters (principally in Chapter 2). Here we can give some of the key ideas which we find most compelling.

First, our argument draws on *social studies of technology*, a perspective which encompasses a range of sociological and historical approaches that place technology – of whatever size, shape or scale – firmly within 'the social'. Technology is not 'outside' of society but a carrier and mediator of social relations, meanings and interests. This perspective goes against the conventional view that technology is 'merely' a collection of bits and pieces, components, design elements and so on. Instead it is to be regarded as a *sociotechnical ensemble*, whose component parts and their composition are shot through with and held together by social relations among people, as much as by more physical ties such as screws, bolts or electrons.

This perspective is especially important when it comes to exploring technologies such as large-scale MIS packages adopted by organisations, because these packages can be 'opened up' to reveal their sociotechnical constitution. Here, those working within social studies of technology speak of opening the 'black box' of (science and) technology, lifting the lid on the technological systems people use. In our case studies we show how, by doing this, things (in the box) are socially constructed, and so might have been different. Technologies are always in this sense 'in the making', and always open to more than one possible interpretation about what they do, how 'successful' they are in achieving this, whether they can be said to be 'working well' or not, and so on.

We also show how the process of stabilising a technological system involves considerable work to ensure that it is 'black-boxed', finalised, finished and 'working' or 'running' smoothly. We argue that this may succeed for some time but eventually new social relations in organisations may emerge to disturb the system: the black box of technology is then reopened, this time not by sociologists, but by the users themselves.

We want to combine ideas from social studies of technology with concepts drawn from a second perspective, the *sociology of consumption*. Consumption studies, not surprisingly, have focused their attention on the contemporary consumer culture that is said to dominate our society today: as Bauman has observed, unlike the past when one consumed in order to live, perhaps today we 'live in order to consume. That is, if we are still able, and feel the need, to tell apart the living from the consuming' (1998: 81). Recent work in sociology not only demonstrates the scale and impact of consumption on our lives, but also shows how, despite Bauman's rather weary observation, consumers play a central part in defining the meaning, significance and value of the 'goods' they consume. Such goods are part of and placed within users' local social worlds and only through that contextualising do they begin to take on a specific role, and serve the 'needs' of the consumer. It is this 'localisation' of technological goods that gives them their value.

These insights can be adapted to explore the consumption of technological goods by people in organisations, and indeed this is what we hope to show later in the book. But it is important to note that in organisational settings, there is considerable pressure by management to ensure that systems are 'delocalised', that is deployed in standardised ways, precisely because this is where *they* see the value of MIS technologies lying. This tension between localised and delocalised meanings given to a technology within organisations will be seen in all our case studies. Such a tension, along with other processes we shall discuss, indicates the ways in which technological change and organisational change are *mutual processes*: we should, therefore, speak of such stories of technology acquisition as stories of *techno-organisational* change.

The contribution we hope to make through this book can be seen as part of a small but growing literature within sociology that is exploring the ways in which new technologies are acquired by organisations, as well as ways in which the relationship between technology and user can be understood. For example, Pollock (1996) has explored the relationship between user 'needs' and the way these are perceived by programmers developing a proposal for a new computer system. He describes how over time these needs are constructed and reconstructed and to some degree translated through the negotiations over the design of the system, which, as we discuss in a later chapter, can act as a 'boundary object' through which the user/programmer relation develops. Thomas (1994) has described how new IT systems introduced into a variety of manufacturing companies could only be made workable when the organisational fabric of the firms was rewoven to accommodate technological change. At the level of the individual user of IT, Noble and Lupton have explored the ways in which people in a university setting construct their sense of self in the workplace, negotiating their relation to both the computer system and their co-workers. This negotiation may well lead to a redefinition of boundaries, as they note:

> As academics and administrators become more like secretaries and secretaries more like administrators and technicians in an increasingly technologised workplace, notions of skill and professional boundaries become open to negotiation.
>
> (1998: 825)

These and other studies (e.g. Silverstone *et al.* 1992; Grint and Woolgar 1997) point to the need to deconstruct the technology/user relationship and examine how the role and function of technologies are highly contextualised: as such, we should expect the new IT systems acquired by organisations to be similarly subject to a sociotechnical deconstruction and reconstruction. This is the story we want to relate, and the way we intend to do so is sketched out below.

Structure of the book

As noted above, the book is based on research conducted at a number of UK-based organisations that have recently acquired new information management systems. In order to evaluate the importance of setting, we followed the acquisition of technologies and techno-organisational change in three distinct environments – those of retailing, healthcare and higher education. The three systems which were examined were:

- a staff management system, which we call the 'Staff Organiser', introduced into a national retail store (which, to preserve anonymity, we have called 'Brodies');
- a clinical information system, which we call the 'Patient-Based System' (PBS), used to record and report tests on patient samples in the public health laboratories of a major UK hospital (which we have called 'Finlay Hospital');
- a management and administrative system, nationally known as 'MAC', used by a UK university (which we call 'Bancroft University').

The book itself is divided into three parts. Part I introduces the main conceptual ideas that provide the analytical framework for our subsequent discussion of our three principal case studies. In Chapter 1 we explore the ways in which technology and organisation are related. Our argument is that these two are interdependent and shape each other in ways that reflect not only local circumstances within the organisation but also wider social, economic and political processes within which organisations and their acquisitions of IT are located. The chapter provides a brief account of these wider processes. This internal/external dynamic affects the ways in which new technologies are acquired and implemented. An important aspect we discuss here is the rhetorical power of notions of instrumentality and of the power and neutrality of technology, claims often made on behalf of new technologies as ever-efficient drivers of change which organisations cannot ignore.

In Chapter 2 we open up our theoretical framework further to discuss the two main perspectives on which the argument of the book principally rests – social studies of technology and the sociology of consumption. We argue that we need to use these perspectives to show how sociotechnologies are shaped by structures of power and inequality, by the language and identities of gender, and crucially by the localised practices and meanings of users. The user is at the core of the book and as such is the principal locus for our subsequent accounts of the university, retail and hospital sectors. We discuss the ways in which we can understand how users construct value in technologies, and how this is to be understood through an analysis of the processes of stabilisation and incorporation. We close this chapter with an outline of the different MIS technologies that were introduced into each of these sectors, recounting the acquisition process up until the point when the IT systems went 'live'. This completes the first part of the book.

Part II contains the main substantive account of our research in each of the organisations. Each of the chapters focuses on one specific aspect or theme associated with the acquisition and use of new systems: these relate to organisational structure, patterns of professional control, organisational culture, and the gendering of IT systems. Thus, in Chapter 3 we use the case study of 'Bancroft University' to examine how the organisational structure of the university played a crucial role in determining the way in which the IT system was introduced and made to 'work'. As an externally acquired technology, the Management and Administrative Computing (MAC) system had embedded within it certain assumptions about organisational relations which did not fully match those held by Bancroft staff. We show how this meant that the system had to be deconstructed and rebuilt, but in such a way as to reflect the localised agendas and interests of a range of very different users located in distinct parts of the university. We suggest that without this localising of the meaning of MAC it would not have been possible to give it any value. However, as we also stress, there is always tension between the desire of management to delocalise and standardise practices, and the localisation practices in which users engage.

Chapter 4 takes us into the world of the hospital setting and the laboratories of 'Finlay Hospital', a large teaching hospital which has an extensive range of public health laboratories providing the pathology services that are crucial to identifying and controlling illness and disease. In the laboratories we find a range of groups – consultant pathologists, chief bacteriologists, medical laboratory scientific officers (MLSOs) and clerical staff – performing different roles relating to the receipt, logging, diagnosis and reporting of patient samples provided by hospital wards or general practitioners (GPs) in the community. Our account focuses on the claims to professional status and identity made by these groups – especially the doctors and MLSOs. Our interest here is whether the newly imported MIS disturbed or threatened the professional identities of such groups, and especially their claims to specialised forms of knowledge and expertise.

Chapter 5 brings us to our first detailed encounter with 'Brodies', the national retail store. In this chapter we relate some results from our study of Brodies to show how organisational culture shapes the terms on which new technologies come to be incorporated by users and gain value. The Brodies culture exhibited two quite distinct frames of meaning to which its members more or less subscribed. These are what we call the 'family' and the 'technicist' cultures, which engendered very different senses of organisational identity, practices and priorities for the members of the store. Most importantly, they were the cultural frames through which store members interpreted and gave value to the 'Staff Organiser', but they also conflicted with each other. We show how, over time, the family narrative was displaced by the logic of the technicist framework embodied in the Staff Organiser.

Gender provides our focus in Chapter 6, which discusses the strongly gendered organisational culture at Brodies, articulated through the 'family culture' noted above. We identify how the powerful paternalistic family discourse encouraged the notion that the predominantly female, middle-aged workforce in the stores would have difficulty using technology. Male managers adopted a highly paternalistic attitude towards store staff, paralleled by a maternalism among female supervisors on the shop floor: both declared a responsibility for 'looking after the girls', and protecting their needs, and merged this with wider social narratives of women's failings when confronted with technology. The Staff Organiser was the site through which gendered identities were constructed and reconstructed, such that eventually the longest-serving female supervisory staff were involved in new forms of 'self-regulation' which ensured that the new technology was eventually incorporated through an accommodation with the technical and instrumental discourses embodied in the new technology. We show too, however, that new, younger female supervisors, less constrained by conventional narratives of femininity and domesticity, took up the technical culture of the system from their arrival in the stores, but in such a way as to confirm the masculine attribution accorded to technical narratives and practices and the 'skills' associated with them.

Part III of the book provides a comparative and synthetic overview of the three different case studies, concentrating on the user–technology relation. Chapter 7 provides a systematic exploration of how the usability and utility of the different systems were constructed over time: we interviewed a core group of staff at each of our three organisations and mapped the changing notions of usability and utility expressed over a twelve-month period. We discuss how, for the different groups in each of our cases, the construction of value and need continued throughout the life of the technologies, and how these constructions reflected differences in the power and organisational 'space' enjoyed by different users.

Chapter 8 extends our argument to look at the ways in which new technologies are 'stabilised' within organisations. However, we question the value of using 'stabilisation' as a primarily technical term, to account for how the process of techno-organisational change comes to an end. The same technology stabilises for different users and groups in quite distinct ways: we cannot see stabilisation as involving the same process for each of them. Moreover, what becomes stable is not just the technology but also the users themselves and their relationship to the system and to the organisation, especially as this is expressed in the stabilisation of work routines, identities, skills and other

store chain is part of a wider division of enterprises owned by the company. The company as a whole employs approximately 77,000 staff. The store chain is at the heart of the company and represents a significant proportion of company profits (60 per cent in 1994). The company has recently expanded into new markets in the UK and abroad. At the same time its management has changed, with unprofitable areas sold off. A few years ago, the different divisions were separated into distinct business units which contract with each other and have their own profit and operations figures. The retail store division is representative of retailers at the higher end of the market, selling a range of goods and a 'shopping experience' which includes quality and customer service.

There are approximately 1200 Brodies stores. They vary in size and product range and are divided into two groupings of large and small stores. The scale, variety and geographical dispersal of the stores are dealt with via a quite rigid system of line management which runs from the departments of Head Office through Area Offices and finally to the local store managers.

The strict hierarchy in Brodies includes a visible gender division common to many retailers. Of the twelve stores in the study none had a female store manager, and the majority of key figures in Head Office were also male. The Area Offices did contain women in their management teams, but not as area managers. In the individual stores the store manager is supported by a management team made up of a deputy manager in large stores, a personnel officer, an accounts manager and sales managers. All of the store management teams which were interviewed – excluding the store manager – were female. The link between management teams and the shop floor are the supervisors, who, along with sales assistants, are mostly female. Of the twenty-one supervisors and assistant supervisors who were interviewed, two were male. Within the store each supervisor is responsible for one area of the sales floor. Their main role is to manage the day-to-day running of the department and negotiate between management and sales assistants. Stores are divided into departments according to product range on the shop floor, and all shopfloor support activity – stock room, accounting, staff cafeteria, maintenance, etc. – is carried out by Sales Support.

Apart from the Head Office, we visited twelve stores where we interviewed the store manager, the management team in the large stores and either the whole supervisory team in the case of small stores or a sample of supervisors in large stores. In Head Office we spoke to the key managers behind the purchase and design of the Organiser as well as computer specialists who worked on the Help Desk or on modifying the Organiser.

The Hospital

'Finlay' is a large teaching hospital linked to its local university. Within it are a collection of Pathology laboratories, alongside two laboratories under the administration of the Public Health Laboratory Service (PHLS). Pathology is made up of six laboratories: Haematology and Blood Transfusion, Biochemistry, Histopathology and Cytology, Tissue Typing, Clinical Immunology, Molecular Genetics and Cytogenetics. The PHLS laboratories are Bacteriology and Virology and are collectively known as Microbiology. The management structure of the PHLS laboratories has recently been through a series of changes, first, amalgamating the management of hospital and GP work, and then, in 1994, removing the dual management of the laboratories and making the PHLS nationally a distinct organisation separate from the hospitals within which it works. The PHLS laboratories now have a contract with the hospital to supply Bacteriology and Virology tests and results. Organisational change within these two laboratories was not complete when we did our research: the grouping of PHLS laboratories in the region was being reorganised such that throughout the region different laboratories would specialise in specific tests.

Microbiology and the six Pathology laboratories each have their own line management structure, with either a chief medical officer or scientist, or a chief technologist, at the helm. The PHLS laboratories at Finlay have a director, as does Pathology, which is run by an Executive Committee.

Microbiology provides clinical and other microbiological services principally associated with testing hospital and GP patients' blood, sputum, urine, faecal and other samples for bacterial or viral infection and disease. In addition, as a PHLS laboratory it performs a wider, more strategic, role at regional and national levels, in mapping the history and epidemiology of specific diseases such as diphtheria and AIDS. We interviewed a range of staff in Microbiology, including senior management, medical consultants, MLSOs, laboratory assistants and clerical staff. MLSOs and laboratory assistants make up the largest part of the forty laboratory staff, testing and interpreting specimens: the results of these tests are then confirmed by doctors and relayed to the wards or to GPs in the region.

Tissue Typing is a much smaller laboratory than Microbiology, made up of the head, four clinical scientists, one laboratory aid, one clerical assistant and one computer programmer. We interviewed the entire Tissue Typing staff. The function of this laboratory is focused on tissue typing potential transplant patients, keeping track of the condition of patients in need of transplant operations, and doing research on and monitoring the long-term success of transplant procedures. An aspect of this work involves being on call when donor organs become available so that the staff can attempt to match the organ to one of their patients.

Part I

Theorising techno-organisational change

1 The technology–organisation relation

Settings and contexts

Many careers in academia and in consultancy have been built speculating about the revolutionary impact of IT on organisations. Among commentators on and practitioners in the sphere of technological change there is, however, a growing awareness of the limitations of hyperbole. Prophecy is not enough. Clearly IT is implicated in some highly significant trends but to understand these requires a sophisticated account of technological development, organisational change and, crucially, the relationship between the two. This book's starting premise is that there is still much work to be done on technology when it enters an organisation: the acquisition of new IT is only the start of a process during which both the technology *and* the organisation change.

This chapter begins our exploration of the technology–organisation relation. It introduces issues that have figured in literature on innovation and organisations and lays the foundations of the approach we shall be taking throughout the rest of the book. A key argument is that detailed analysis of the introduction, or embedding, of IT into organisations is a necessary precursor to discussions of the role or importance of such technologies. A focus on acquisition and adoption reveals how the peculiarities of particular organisational settings influence the use, character and impact of ostensibly similar technologies. Thus, while there are wider patterns and constraints, acquisition and adoption are about the interplay between technological systems and organisational dynamics and between internal *settings* and external *contexts*. Seen in this light, acquisition is also recast as a long-running process in which the end-users of the system are active participants.

This chapter begins to address a set of questions that the remainder of the book explores more fully:

- How does technological innovation occur within and across organisations?
- How do organisational actors attempt to direct innovation?
- How does the internal organisational setting influence the course and consequences of technological change?
- What part do end-users play in this?
- How do external 'imperatives' influence organisational change?

The chapter is structured into four main sections. The first reviews some of the existing work on technological change and organisations, making the case for a more developed analysis of the innovation process and introducing the concept of 'techno-organisational change'. The next section places technology in a broader discussion of how organisations stay organised. As part of this, it considers the varied strategies and tactics employed by people in organisations to construct some sense of order and direction to change. In different ways, the next two sections examine external contexts of techno-organisational change. The first of these considers the wider cultural repertoire from which people within organisations construct meaning. IT comes into organisations strongly associated with images of inevitable progress through technology, and abstract notions of instrumental rationality; these general values exert a powerful influence over specific processes of innovation. The final section of the chapter discusses the assertion that 'imperatives' beyond the boundaries of the organisation are driving innovation. This is explored through a discussion of the sectoral environments (technological, economic and policy) of our three case studies – the National Health Service (NHS), higher education and retailing. It should be noted that in discussing technological culture and imperatives we do not wish to move our focus away from the organisation. Rather, our interest is in the way that these wider factors are articulated in and mediated by the organisational setting.

Information technology and organisational change

Claims that new computer systems are shaping tomorrow's organisations draw on an influential body of prophecy concerning IT. Discussions of the emergence of a 'post-industrial society' (Bell 1976), of the 'information society' (Lyon 1988, Webster 1995), of the compression of time and space (Harvey 1990), and of the 'knowledge society' (Stehr 1994) all, ultimately, centre on the claim that new technology in general and IT in particular are bringing about a qualitative shift in social conditions. Discussion of the 'knowledge-based organisation', 'the network organisation' (Goddard 1992), and the 'virtual' or 'cyber organisation' (Barnett 1995) feeds off these prophecies. They rest on a belief that new technology is not simply changing but transforming organisational possibilities. This can, in its most extreme forms, be manifested in hi-tech utopianism, such as the following:

> The computing and telecommunications technologies of the future will be wondrous. Finally we will be granted infinite freedom to walk and fly in the cyberspace realm of pure information, to create the physically impossible, to reach out to other human beings as never before, and to augment our own mental capacities as one with machines.
>
> (Barnett 1995: 29)

A common theme of much predictive writing is that IT alters relationships within organisations. Zuboff (1988), for example, suggests that the 'informating' qualities of IT can be the basis of a new type of organisation, decentred, flat and responsive to changing conditions. She is also aware, however, of the potential offered by IT for new forms of surveillance and control at a distance. This concern is developed further in a range of speculative (Poster 1990) and empirically based work (see for example Jackson 1997, Collinson and Collinson 1997). Zuboff and others undeniably raise important questions about the future of IT and organisations – ones we will return to later in the book – but there are dangers in a generalised account of the 'impact' of IT on organisations in which technological development has a life and momentum of its own.

During the 1990s many of the utopian and dystopian predictions about the information society have sounded increasingly hollow (Garnham 1994). Frank Webster suggests that the clearest clue to the inadequacy of many accounts of change is their neatness:

> it follows such a neat linear logic – technological innovation results in social change – that it is almost a pity to announce that it is simply the wrong point of departure for those embarking on a journey to see where informational trends, technological and other, are leading.

> (1995: 215)

Webster identifies a series of limitations in much of the predictive work on IT. The first is an over-emphasis on transformation: chronic patterns of organisational and economic structuring get lost in the quest to highlight the new and the discontinuous. Related to this is a tendency to misrepresent or simplify the previous conditions replaced by the new world of IT. Another limitation concerns indicators: quantitative measures of the diffusion of technology or the amount of information are taken as simple, obvious markers of qualitative change. Most fundamentally, prophecies rely on implied or explicit 'technological determinism': technological development is treated as an independent variable driving organisational change. This determinism usually side-steps the social processes involved in the development and adoption of new technology.

For the prophets of a computerised revolution the reasons why organisations should adopt IT and the uses to which it can be put are largely self-evident. If these issues are considered at all it is usually with reference to the inherent qualities of the technology and a generalised account of organisational needs: IT provides obvious benefits for and requires obvious changes to the organisation. Critics of IT prophecy (of which Webster is only an example) suggest, however, that the issues of why and how organisations might acquire and use IT are more complex and interesting than this. If we are to move beyond 'gee-whiz' accounts of an organisational future revolutionised by technology then a more developed and measured understanding of how organisations adopt and utilise IT is required.

Rethinking technology acquisition

In the past decade, writing on the acquisition and diffusion of IT and other new technologies has sought ways of transcending many of the assumptions that informed earlier work in the field. There is an often-expressed concern to move beyond viewing 'acquisition' as a one-off moment of capture when pre-existing organisational needs are (or should be) reconciled with pre-existing technological solutions. The demand is for a clearer and richer understanding of the processes whereby organisations come to acquire new technology (Clark 1987, Leonard-Barton 1991).

A new focus on the social dynamics of technology acquisition has high-lighted the varied ways in which innovations are assimilated into organisations' existing technological 'portfolios' (Seaton and Hayes 1993). There is also consideration of factors that enhance or inhibit organisations' capacities to be effective acquirers and users of technology (Mansfield 1992, Radnor 1992, Bessant 1993). In the light of these issues, some have recast the acquisition and introduction of new technologies as an interaction or negoti-ation requiring organisational change as well as the development of new technical skills (Senker 1988, Senker 1992).

A central issue in the new acquisition literature is whether the adoption of tech-nology can be understood as a response to a clear set of pre-existing needs. Policy and commercial interests express a strong concern to identify 'user needs' in the technological market, but this often rests on an inadequate conception of 'need' (Webster 1994) and an undifferentiated account which portrays whole organisa-tions as 'users'. Some analysts (e.g. Walsh 1993) have questioned the sense in which such needs *can* be identified, especially in new technological fields.

A similar concern with the complexities of technology acquisition is now voiced in management studies. This is, in part, a reflection of the growing ana-lytical sophistication of the field as it has been enriched by insights from a range of approaches as diverse as gender studies and post-structuralism. New perspectives on organisations and technology are part of a fundamental reap-praisal of the assumptions and categories that informed earlier analyses of management. Previous perspectives that represented technological change as a driver of organisational change are now heavily critiqued, as are the technol-ogy-led management practices that gave birth to them (Jackson 1997). Innovation is recast as contingent, local, unpredictable and as taking place over an extended period of time. This demands a greater emphasis on the part played by managers in enacting technological change. Analyses strive, for example, to identify the key 'change agents' (Buchanan and Storey 1997) who sponsor new technology within organisations. Writers such as Clark (1995) highlight the role of managers in developing strategies to create and control direction. While Clark's and others' accounts assume an environmental reality that managers react to and master, some such as Walsham (1993b) go further, pointing to the ways in which managers rhetorically construct environments in order to appear to be 'strategic' and visibly in control.

Recent work sheds new light on the factors that influence the direction of technological and organisational change. Liff and Scarborough, for example, discuss the part played by what they term 'discourses of innovation':

> To put it simply, different discourses promote different trajectories of development, such that organisations beginning from an apparently similar constellation of goals and interests can end up with radically divergent solutions.
>
> (1994: 208)

This kind of argument should be located in a broader rethink of the nature of management and policy decision-making. Reviewing recent work, Rappert (in preparation) notes that 'decision-making processes are recognised as complex, iterative, and rarely structured into easily specifiable beginnings or ends'. As part of a wider analysis of organisational innovation, Whitley (1992) suggests that managers follow 'business recipes'. Business recipes do not, however, predetermine the course of change; instead they develop as it continues, with the construction of the nature, outcome and benefits of innovation an on-going process. As Mansell similarly explains: 'the sources and determinants of change are understood to involve processes whereby rules and resources are recursively negotiated through time' (1994a: 338).

New analyses of the acquisition and management of new technology have, therefore, moved quite some distance from any simplistic notion of the 'impact' of IT on organisations. It is worth reiterating again that this emphasis on the messy and localised nature of change is not just about technology but part of a broader reappraisal of management and organisational dynamics. In this respect Walsham, in his study of information systems in organisations, acknowledges his debt to Pettigrew's work on change in ICI:

> It is important to see organizational change as linked to both intraorganizational and broader contexts, and not to try to understand projects as episodes divorced from the historical, organizational or economic circumstances from which they emerge. The management of organizational change is not seen as a straightforward, rational process but as a jointly analytical, educational and political process. Power, chance and opportunism are influential in shaping outcomes as are design, negotiated agreements and master plans.
>
> (Walsham 1993b: 53)

Bringing in the users

The implications of this new turn in the analysis of management, organisation and technology acquisition are far-reaching but arguably yet to be explored fully. While current analyses raise awkward questions about how 'rational' or clearly 'needs-driven' management decision-making is, there has been little attempt to develop a critical examination of how notions of 'need' or 'rationality' are developed and used by managers. As Orlikowski has indicated:

> The presumption is still made that once technology is designed to embody the 'appropriate' (optimizing or informating) objectives and once managers are committed to this 'appropriate' strategy, more rewarding workplaces, more fluid organizations, a new division of labor, and better performances will result.
>
> (1992: 401)

Orlikowski proposes an alternative analysis based on a 'recursive notion of technology' that understands that 'technology is created and changed by human action, yet is also used by humans to accomplish some action' (ibid.: 405). For this to be achieved, we would argue, a broader conception of 'the social dimension' is required than much of the management and policy literature currently accepts. Despite many insights, much work remains unwilling to expand the focus of analysis beyond strategic management to explore the role of others within the organisation in shaping technological change. This theme has been opened up in Fleck's work discussing 'innofusion':

> Implementation essentially involves the mutual adaptation of technology and organisation in order that available resources may be effectively combined together to provide an overall working system (or configuration).
>
> (1994: 178)

If this 'adaptation' continues after the technology has arrived in the workplace, it follows that ordinary users of new technology, not just strategic managers, are active participants in innovation. They are involved in the adaptation of the technology to the organisational setting, integrating it into the everyday life of the organisation and, in doing so, making it usable. This focus on end-users also leads us away from the tendency in management literature to equate 'the user' with a whole, undifferentiated organisation and, instead, to be sensitive to the variety of user groups implicated in change.

The part played by users in technological change is a central concern of our book – one of the ways in which we seek to advance the discussions outlined in this section. In concentrating on users we also return to the issue of needs flagged up earlier. Organisational needs should not be viewed as fixed, stable precursors and drivers of acquisition. Instead we would argue that:

- talk of 'organisational needs' hides the variety of different needs voiced by individuals and groups within the organisation;
- needs are formed and reformed over time as an integral part of the process of innovation.

Thus, in our terms, the expression, negotiation and clash of needs voiced by different groups within the organisation, and related attempts then to construct and articulate coherent 'organisational needs', are at the heart of technology acquisition. Far from being the starting point of acquisition, the value of a new technology in an organisational setting is often uncertain, unstable and contested. End-users are implicated in the process of debating and developing needs as well as uses, usability and usefulness – the 'valuing technology' of our book title.

Of course the argument that a variety of different group and individual needs is articulated during technology acquisition and contributes to it does not imply that all needs have an equal chance of being met. Similarly, our recognition of end-users' part in the development and application of new technology is not to suggest that all participants in the process begin or end in equal or equivalent positions. Rather, it is to suggest that the inequalities of this process should be the object of study rather than starting assumptions. If we treat organisational needs as fixed and unproblematic and assume that the 'success' or 'failure' of a new technology lies solely in the hands of strategic management, we collude with those in authority who, after the event, delete the contribution of subordinates (Star 1992, Law 1994).

To sum up this section, we have highlighted the requirement for new ways of understanding the technology–organisation relation. We contend that it is inadequate to portray new technology as uniformly impacting on organisations (as the prophetic literature suggests) or else to understand technology acquisition as being about matching technology to organisational need (as an earlier generation of management literature assumed). Instead we seek insight into the messy, long-drawn-out embedding of technology into the specifics of organisations. As our case studies will illustrate, neither technology, organisation nor user remains the same during this process. Hence the book's focus on the part of end-users in what we term techno-organisational change.

So far, most of our attention has been devoted to the technology side of the technology–organisation relation. Grasping the nature, significance and outcome of technology acquisition, however, also requires an appreciation of the dynamics of the organisational setting, and it is to these that we now turn.

Organising uncertainty

There are dangers in over-generalising about 'the organisation' – even a cursory examination of our three research sites, for example, shows how organisations vary in their contexts, structures, cultures and power relations. Important differences relate to the scale and physical dispersal of organisations. It should also be noted that there are differences in the extent of rigidity/flexibility and fixity/plasticity of organisations that mirror differences between technological systems. Despite all these variations and more, there are some things we can say about organisations and organising in general that inform our discussion of techno-organisational change.

One difficulty we face when discussing 'change', technological or otherwise, in organisations is that, in one sense, organisations are changing all the time. Behind the appearance of stability, they are in a constant state of flux. One illustration of this is the staffing of organisations: people are forever moving in and between them. Thus to understand organisations as static, finished frameworks is merely to repeat the useful fictions of the organisers. The conditions in which organisations operate mean that the pursuit of stability or certainty is a continuing endeavour without hope of ultimate completion or total success (Law 1994). Developments that appear outside the organisation are a major source of instability and uncertainty. Equally, inside the organisation there are everyday contingencies that can never be entirely erased. Attempts to manage uncertainty are in continuing struggle with indeterminacy and the stubbornness of the particular and the local. In addition, different interests are at play, across an often diverse and dispersed organisational space, which contest and confound management objectives.

Despite or perhaps because of the complexity of large organisations and the chronic uncertainty and instability that threaten to engulf them, certainty is ascribed high value in organisations. While some commentators may ruminate on a new kind of 'postmodern' organisation that embraces ambiguity, contradiction and flexibility, the pursuit of certainty remains central to management. Organisational hierarchies and divisions of labour, surveillance and planning, rules and procedures – all seek control, standardisation and predictability.

In one sense, the people in organisations are a source of uncertainty: their particular backgrounds, personalities and interests may make them hard to control, standardise or predict. On the other hand, managerial strategies for certainty often coincide with and can be aided by the requirement of individuals to develop their own certainties. One element of this is people's pursuit of economic security via membership of the organisation. More broadly, people in organisations seek what the sociologist Anthony Giddens terms 'ontological security' – a stable, grounded sense of social reality and how they fit into that reality (Giddens 1990, 1991, Casey 1995). This is sustained in everyday organisational life (as it is in other arenas) via taken-for-granted continuities of hierarchy, language, routine and habit. People's own project of ontological security, within and beyond their organisational lives, will therefore be challenged by change, and their response to that change is likely to be influenced by an overriding desire for coherence and certainty.

Given the continuing struggle to contain uncertainty, the moments when organisations are deemed to be 'changing', particularly if that change is considered strategic (Scarborough 1997), are important and difficult. New technologies such as MIS may be seen by managers as routes to certainty, but their introduction will initially itself promote further uncertainty. Intentionally or unintentionally, the relationships, habits and assumptions that underpin life within the organisation are problematised. This adds a new twist to the story of techno-organisational change. As the previous section implied, new technologies do not enter organisations fully formed: their role, use and value are developed as they travel through the organisation. This construction of certainty around the technology must, additionally, be understood alongside and in relation to a parallel process of reconstructing organisational certainties.

Organising and regulating

Recognition of the on-going pursuit of certainty leads us to look at organising – the ways organisations stay organised. In this book we focus on two related but distinct aspects of organising: practices and narratives. At moments of change these are both more important and more problematic.

Organising practices structure members' actions through rules, routines and hierarchies. Practices are embodied not only in relations between people but in physical artefacts and systems – think of the written rules of the organisation or the layout of its buildings. Computer-based MIS like those studied in this book are part of the development of organising practices of standardisation, monitoring and measurement.

Organising narratives are, at their most fundamental, accounts of 'how the organisation should operate' or 'what we do' or 'what sort of organisation we are'. They have a resonance and integrating role through an organisation. They also mediate the possible interpretations available to make sense of changing conditions, such as the arrival of new technology.

In reality it is hard to find examples of practices and narratives operating in isolation from each other. This is striking when we consider the role of IT in organising, since information and communication technologies embody practices and also have a 'direct involvement in the realm of knowledge, culture and meaning' (Coombs *et al.* 1992: 52). How do organising practices and narratives fit into the story of technological change? The answer is two-fold and paradoxical. On the one hand, the introduction of new technology involves (and is often part of strategies for) changing ways of organising. On the other hand, the acquisition and assimilation of technology is often organised via existing practices and narratives. The potential tension between these two elements will be a theme in our case studies.

Organising must be discussed in conjunction with attempts at regulation – forms of control that constrain and enable organisational life. *Management regulation* seeks to govern through the use of both organising practices and narratives. The link between management regulation and technological change is strong. For some analysts, heightened control of staff and their work is always the underlying motivation behind technological change in organisations. Labour process theory, for example, views techno-organisational innovation exclusively in terms of the deskilling of workers (Braverman 1974, Wood 1982). While this over-simplifies the range and complexity of both managerial strategies and technological options, clearly one key reason why management introduce new IT is to enhance the means by which they attempt to regulate the organisation.

As our case studies will illustrate, management also seek to regulate the actual process of IT acquisition and implementation. It would be a mistake, however, to understand organising practices and narratives or, indeed, the processes of technological change as simply the outcome of managerial control.

Internal managerial strategies and tactics are only part of the story of regulation. These strategies and tactics are always developed and applied with reference to wider social relations and meanings. People's organisational roles and identities form within broader patterns of power, inequality and identity. A striking illustration of this is the extent to which organisations continue to have a gendered division of labour (Walby 1997). Clearly we cannot understand, for example, the distinctive and largely subordinate position that women have within a particular organisational setting without reference to dominant notions of masculinity and femininity, or to generalised inequalities in the labour market and the home. Thus our discussion of management regulation is complemented by consideration of *subjective regulation* – the broader conditions that constrain and enable people's ability to express identity and interest within the organisation. Why focus on subjectivity? Perhaps the simplest way to justify this is to state the – perhaps obvious – point that people's behaviour at work is not simply the product of management regulation. A fuller explanation of that behaviour might include 'subjective' factors as diverse as assumptions concerning the value of work and the development of self, notions of duty and honesty, the aspiration towards financial success, and the desire for social status.

In what sense can we associate subjectivity with regulation? As our earlier portrayal of the end-user as participant in techno-organisational change and the discussion of ontological security suggest, we do not view people in organisations as mere ciphers or dupes. On the contrary, central to our analysis is an understanding of people in organisations as active creators of their own lives, meanings and settings. Their agency and creativity are, however, bounded by existing conditions and available meanings that are regulating in their exclusion of some interpretations and the promotion of others. One aspect of this is the way that what Knights and Murray term the quest for a 'sense of material and symbolic security in the world' (1994: 29) can lead people to develop identities that are ultimately conforming or accommodating. Collinson (1992), for example, in a case study of a factory reorganisation following a company takeover, examines how feelings of uncertainty prompted by the introduction of new working practices led shopfloor workers to place greater emphasis on their masculinity. In the face of change, they dismissed new managers as not 'real men' and celebrated hard, physical labour as 'real work'. On one level, this could be viewed as resistant, but ultimately the workers' conservative and exclusive account of identity precluded the possibility of renegotiating their work role or forming alliances with other groups in the organisation. Hence, for all their oppositional and macho talk, the men were left powerless to influence the direction of change.

In the example cited above the subjective response of employees was not simply the direct result of explicit managerial strategies. There are, however, other cases where there is a clearer link between managerial and subjective regulation. Attempts to police and channel the subjectivity of workers have taken on an increasing significance; Nikolas Rose (1989) terms this 'the management of the productive subject'. A series of studies have described the development of new types of employee who are 'self-disciplining' (Garsten and Grey 1997) or engage in 'self-surveillance' (Deetz 1998). While the factors contributing to this are varied, the result is a workforce that identify with and internalise managerial goals.

Organisational cultures, group identities and technology acquisition

> Culture is one of the two or three most complicated words in the English language.
>
> (Williams 1983: 87)

As the quotation above from Raymond Williams suggests, the concept of culture is as ambiguous as it is important. Our usage of the term fits broadly with the social anthropological approach that discusses culture in terms of shared beliefs, assumptions and ways of life. A theme developed across the book is that an appreciation of a particular organisational setting as cultural is crucial to the analysis of technology acquisition.

That organisations have 'cultures' has become a truism in both academia and management. There is, however, considerable disagreement about the nature and significance of 'organisational culture'. Brunsson's (1985) work is an example where organisational culture is viewed primarily as a management resource. What Brunsson refers to as 'organisational ideologies' – 'people's values and beliefs about the organisation and its situation' (1985: 178) – increase the commitment among members towards acting in ways that serve collective organisational goals. This version of organisation culture reduces it to little more than a corporate culture designed and manipulated by higher management. Martin (1992) identifies a number of inadequacies with this 'functionalist' approach. Crucially, there are dangers in seeing culture as something mouldable to particular interests; instead, argues Martin, while culture can be integrative, it can also be differentiated and fragmented across the organisation.

Thus, any consideration of attempts to manage via the promotion of a corporate culture must be tempered by recognition of the fluidity of cultural norms and the propensity of different groups within an organisation to develop and interpret meaning quite differently. A theme of many of the later chapters will be the different ways in which people in organisations come together as distinct groups, and how those groups secure their sense of identity and through this identity play a part in technological change. The types of grouping we focus on emerge:

- within organisational routines and relationships (such as shared job role or location);
- within cross-organisational relations (such as bonds of professionalism);
- through claims to knowledge and skill (such as shared training);
- within technological practices (such as common levels of system access);
- within wider social inequalities and identities (such as those of gender);

In the light of this, rather than talk of an organisation *having* its own particular culture, we should think of organisations *as* cultures. These dynamics are as much about the interplay of cross-cutting group identities as they are about the sharing of a common culture.

Awareness of the existence of multiple groupings and varied cultural understandings in organisations has important implications for the analysis of techno-organisational change and for our attempt to 'bring in the users'. The relations and differences between groupings cannot be reduced to 'competition' (Coombs *et al.* 1992). Nevertheless, differently placed groupings do jostle for status, for resources and for their cultural frameworks to be accepted by others, to take on the quality of integrative norms across the organisation. A new technology, introduced with both explicit and implicit possibilities of change, brings fresh impetus to such interpretative battles. Where more than one grouping exists, the technology is likely to be informed by and give expression to more than one interpretation. No single grouping can be said to be in control of the acquisition of technology or determine its final assimilation into the organisation. Technology becomes the object of struggle but also has the power to disturb existing group identities and relations.

This section has set out some of the key elements of our analysis of organisational life and raised a series of issues that will be addressed later in the book. It has attempted to locate discussion of technology acquisition in an account of the inequalities, complexities and uncertainties of organisational life. In doing so, it has also emphasised the significance of the cultural setting in mediating processes of techno-organisational change. By arguing, however, that management regulation must be understood in conjunction with subjective regulation, and highlighting the complexity of the cultural dynamics within a particular organisational setting, it suggests an approach that is at once about less and more than the organisation. On the one hand, rather than generate a singular account of organisational life, the emphasis shifts to the varied perspectives of differently situated organisational actors – a recurring theme of our analysis. On the other, we must also explore how these perspectives are constituted and shared in part beyond the workplace. In later chapters we will develop this argument primarily through discussion of professionalism and gender identity. In the next section we will consider the key cultural assumptions that provide a common context in particular technology acquisitions.

Cultural contexts: valuing the technical and the instrumental

As the discussion above suggests, there are many voices and meanings at play within organisations (Boje 1995, Keenoy *et al.* 1997). Each organisation will have its own particular cultural dynamics. None the less, any discussion of techno-organisational change must also recognise an overarching set of beliefs and assumptions about technology that informs the processes of adoption and adaptation. Much of the analysis in the remainder of the book concerns how technologies come to be seen as having value in particular, localised settings. A backdrop to these processes is, however, a generalised valuing of technology. As IT enters an organisation it is already attributed with properties and powers that help guide its path.

Technological values

Amongst the range of strategies open to managers, technological innovation has a special place: technology has an aura of neutrality, universality and inevitability. This aura allows supporters to portray the technical as incontestable: the course of technological development appears 'autonomous' and relentless (Winner 1977). Technological change in organisations is seen to be, or rather is represented as being, driven by imperatives beyond the boundaries or control of the organisation. The necessity to 'keep up with' technological progress is promoted by hi-tech evangelists inside and outside the organisation; this is particularly striking in relation to IT (Kling and Iacono 1985).

Although this is often masked, 'the technical' is a powerful set of *cultural* assumptions and practices that privileges certain actors, groupings and 'solutions' over others. Much work is put into consigning people, skills, artefacts and problems to the realm of the technical or else excluding them from that realm. This enables a 'protected central space for the actors behind the technology, a protection against the critiques and challenges of others' (Rachel and Woolgar 1995: 259).

Technological culture, and its embodiment in machinery and procedures, has the potential to displace both politics and management into a neutral language of technical capability and constraint. Technical language or discourse privileges certain ways of speaking and acting and forecloses discussion and participation. For example, in her analysis of defence studies intellectuals, Carol Cohn (1987) considers the significance of their 'technostrategic' language. This language, with its own terminology and logic, helps to establish boundaries and authority:

> Part of the appeal [of learning the language] was the thrill of being able to manipulate an arcane language, the power of entering the secret kingdom, being someone in the know . . . A more subtle, but perhaps more

important, element of learning the language is that when you speak it, you feel in control.

(ibid.: 704)

Thus the language provides a sense of 'cognitive mastery' but in doing so 'does not allow certain questions to be asked or certain values to be expressed' (ibid.: 708).

Instrumental rationality

If technology has a generalised cultural value then it is, in part, through its close association with another set of defining assumptions relating to instrumental rationality. Like technology, instrumental rationality makes claims to neutrality and universality, and offers the promise of control. According to instrumental criteria, means take precedence over ends; 'efficiency', rules and formal measures are valued for their own sake. The assumptions of instrumental rationality are so powerful and ubiquitous as to take on the quality of natural laws rather than cultural beliefs. As such, they naturalise certain social categories, relationships and practices and exclude others as 'irrational'. Within organisations, articulations of instrumental rationality both underpin management strategy and make it appear legitimate, non-contestable and achievable.

Instrumentality is usually understood, or represented, as flowing from a neat, unquestionable and general logic that necessitates the on-going pursuit of efficiency. A growing body of historical and ethnographic studies has, however, explored 'the social construction of rationality from inside of organisations and organisational fields' (Dobbin 1994: 128). Reviewing these studies, Dobbin concludes that 'rationality is highly indeterminate and variable across space and time' and that 'economic laws permit a wide range of different organisational practices and strategies' (ibid.: 135). Instrumental rationality should, therefore, be viewed as a generalised set of assumptions that are enacted and exploited quite differently in particular local settings.

Enacting the technical and the instrumental: the formal representation of organisational life

The connections between the valuing of technology and the influence of instrumental rationality are evident in claims that IT, particularly MIS like those studied in this book, through their indicators, calculations and reports, can formally represent organisational life. It is these claims that make information systems particularly attractive to management as an aid to regulation. Berg argues that those behind such systems assert that 'well-designed formal systems have superior decision-making, controlling, surveying, securing, streamlining capabilities compared to us humans, whose rationality is indefinitively bounded' (1997: 405). This promise, according to Bloomfield *et al.*, contributes to the 'seductive' quality of IT systems:

> One of the principal seductions of IT lies in the belief that the technology allows abstract concepts such as efficiency or cost to be established in the concrete instances of organisational practice, that the reality of organisational life can be made transparent, opening up the possibility for rewarding and punishing adherence and deviations from the accepted norms derived from these concepts.
>
> (1994: 147)

IT is, therefore, enlisted in the pursuit of organisational certainty discussed earlier:

> the arguments, decisions, uncertainties and processual nature of decision-making are hidden away inside a piece of technology or in a complex representation. Thus values, opinions, and rhetoric are frozen into codes, electronic thresholds and computer applications.
>
> (Bowker and Star 1994: 187)

Star (1995a) argues that the belief that IT systems provide a measurable, standardised, predictable vision of the organisation is 'naïve formalism'. It assumes a world that can be neatly measured and categorised and involves 'cleaning up' the messiness of the socio-political world of organisations to produce a standardised account of reality. While the formalism of system designers envisions a cleaner, purer rendition of the reality of the organisation, what they are in fact involved in, in the words of Star (1989), is the production of a 'chain of re-representations'.

It follows that there will be tensions around the codification and standardisation of information. A MIS may come to represent (and to an extent eventually define) organisational reality, but users must be convinced of and enlisted into the logic and language of that system. Powerful cultural beliefs about the potential of technology and the logic of instrumental rationality are at play in the process but do not determine it – rather they are utilised by actors and groupings within the organisation. One aspect of this is that what is understood as technical, as the property of 'the technology', can reflect the different interpretative worlds of variously placed groups. Some groups are, of course, better placed in these interpretative struggles than others. Here we are thinking not only about occupational and professional identities but also about gender identities. As later chapters will show, the association of rationality and technology with masculinity has a highly significant role in the process (Wajcman 1993).

Changes in economic, policy and technological contexts

Within organisations the question 'why change?' is often answered by reference to apparently obvious, unchallengeable imperatives such as the requirement to be competitive or to be efficient or to keep up with technological progress. However, our earlier discussions of technology acquisition, organisational development and the discursive context all suggest a requirement to go beyond an account of change that is predetermined and externally driven. Instead the emphasis is on the on-going, localised construction of the organisation, culture and technology. Accounts that portray techno-organisational change as being driven by external imperatives have a number of fundamental limitations:

- They wrongly represent the course of change as inevitable and pre-set.
- They are over-generalised, presenting change as affecting all organisations and organisational actors in the same way.
- Organisations and users are represented as passive – at best responding to outside pressures in an appropriate predetermined fashion.
- Innovation is valued for its own sake and the refusal to innovate becomes seen as evidence of poor management.
- The boundary between the organisation and the external environment is too firmly drawn.

The failings of such accounts are summarised by McLoughlin and Harris:

> the idea of an unyielding technological and commercial imperative has increasingly been viewed as problematic, in particular, since it tends to evaluate the role of such things as management and worker attitudes, existing organizational structures and cultures, industrial relations and so on, in relation to their propensity to either facilitate or impede innovation.
>
> (1997a: 6)

We do not, however, have to lapse into a simplistic determinism to acknowledge that any organisation is part of wider technological, economic, cultural and policy environments. These contexts, and their interpretation by organisational actors, are an important influence on techno-organisational change. Following Knights and Murray, we would rather not talk of external 'imperatives' but instead understand these wider contexts as providing 'conditions of possibility' that 'make certain courses of action feasible while constraining or ruling out others' (1994: 39). Thus while 'conditions of possibility', such as 'the market', frame organisational behaviour, organisational members construct at the local level the 'external forces' that they then respond to:

> a market exists only in so much as people believe that it exists and act accordingly. Similarly, a technological opportunity or constraint exists only in so much as people believe it to exist.
>
> (ibid.: 41)

This implies that more than one interpretation of the context is likely to be present in the organisation and also that knowledge of 'the outside' is a resource to be used in organisational struggles.

Our anxiety to move beyond a deterministic account of technology acquisition should not, however, be read as a denial of the significance of wider contexts beyond the organisation. Returning to Knights and Murray's discussion of the market, we can accept their emphasis on localised constructions while also acknowledging that the 'conditions of possibility' offered by capitalism enable and constrain organisational activity in many highly significant ways. Thus, techno-organisational change must be situated within broader developments without reducing it to a simple expression of those developments. Technology acquisition is, in one sense, about how the organisation is defined in relation to shifting and multiple local understandings of the wider environment.

In discussing the relationship between the organisation and its wider context, we must also recognise that many networks criss-cross organisational boundaries. Staff and technologies, for example, both regularly move between companies within and sometimes beyond a particular sector. People within organisations are part of and are influenced by para-organisational membership groups and reference groups. Techno-organisational changes are influenced by and themselves influence extra-organisational relationships including those with competitors. Nevertheless, however constructed, temporal or local, the boundaries perceived between organisations and between the organisation and the rest of the world are crucial. Their importance is seen in the labour used to maintain them materially, legally, procedurally and discursively. The ways that organisational actors talk of having to respond to developments 'out there' by changing the organisation is itself testimony to the power of such constructions.

The innovation that takes place within a particular organisation is only one element of a multi-layered process of technological development. The question of how organisations become 'locked into' particular common innovation routes is important. This locking in relies not only on the types of internal dynamics discussed above, as wider social influences also become part of the story. This is, however, as much about the spread of 'organising conventions' as it is about 'imperatives' (Dobbin 1994: 128). Managers may believe in the optimal form of efficient organisation but their pursuit of that form involves following fashion:

> The process is driven by a widespread belief in the law-like principles of social efficiency, to be sure; however, the history of management thought and practice suggests that consecrated organizational practices change ... following the pattern of fashion whims – rather than moving ineluctably and in a singular progression toward some ultimately efficient ideal.
>
> (ibid.: 137)

Sectoral contexts

The significance of the wider environment in which techno-organisational change takes place can be further illustrated by examining the three sectors from which our case studies are drawn – retailing, healthcare and higher education. A range of factors, including heightened competition, changing government policy on the public sector and new philosophies of 'service' and staff management, provide the conditions of possibility for techno-organisational change. Some of these are shared across the case studies but there are also important variations between sectors in terms of:

- technological developments and applications;
- economic pressures;
- policy frameworks;
- understandings of 'efficiency';
- occupational mix and relations.

Retail

Retailing has been a fast-growing and highly profitable element of the UK economy. A largely laissez-faire planning and policy environment has cemented the dominant position of large store chains in the sector. Within these chains, the sector is viewed as very competitive, with profitability under constant threat from competitor innovation.

New management strategies have transformed retailing in the 1990s. The pursuit of profitability has rested on a particular understanding of efficiency with two distinct and, at times contradictory, dimensions – cost-cutting and 'customer service'. Cost-cutting is primarily sought through control of labour costs, more effective use of stock holding and cutting of supplier prices. Customer service is seen by a wide range of store chains as the solution to the influx of cut-price retailers (such as Kwik Save and Aldi in food sales). Widening and overhauling the range of goods on offer, repositioning staff as customer helpers, cutting time waiting at tills, and the introduction of customer loyalty cards all seek to compete on grounds of service rather than price-cutting. Retail marketing experts argue, for example, that such policies have enabled Tesco to take over the position of number one food retailer in the UK.

IT has played an increasingly important role in the development of the retail sector. Within the networks of retail companies, software suppliers and designers, and expert commentators there is a strong push to find technological solutions to business problems. Market leaders both in food retailing (Sainsbury and Tesco) and department stores (Marks and Spencer) have made use of IT to reform all levels of their operations. Trade journals and marketing magazines describe the development of increasingly sophisticated EPOS (electronic point of sale) systems and computerised till points. These till points sit at the centre of a network of computer systems and software that monitor trading patterns and stock levels. Retailers like Tesco use such systems to enable automatic stock replenishment. Such companies are investing in a future where data is sent out from tills to networks of computerised systems, computerised forklift vehicles in computerised central distribution depots and computer-monitored fleets of lorries (IGD 1998: 6). The use of depots, just-in-time stock ordering, or – the latest retail management buzzwords – QR (quick response) or ECR (efficient consumer response) mean that the size of store stock rooms can be reduced and the amount of floor space for trading increased. As part of this, the lead-time from stock being delivered by suppliers to depots and onto the shelf is being cut dramatically (ibid.: 11).

Large retailers often now insist that suppliers deal with them through computerised networks known as EDI (electronic data interchange). Some commentators have suggested that this is one reason why small wholesalers and producers have been forced out of the market (Bowlby and Foord 1995). Others argue that hi-tech solutions encourage greater 'cooperation' between suppliers, distributors and retailers (Fiorito *et al.* 1995). At the opposite end of the distribution network, electronic data on till transactions and from loyalty card use is increasingly being utilised to monitor, predict and mould consumer patterns.

Despite the rapid developments of recent years, the marked gender divisions in the retail workforce remain largely unchanged. Census material from 1991 indicates that 83 per cent of sales assistants were female (Walby 1997: 58). At the same time management in both stores and head offices remain predominantly male. The growing numbers of women working in retailing are an example of how the expansion of women's employment has been primarily in the service industries in jobs which are often part-time, low-paid and considered low-skilled. Therefore, wider gender relations, established identities of shop workers and changing employment patterns should be included in the conditions of possibility of the retail sector.

Healthcare

Since the early 1980s the UK's NHS has been subject to a number of organisational changes put in place by government initiatives that have sought to redefine how healthcare is provided in the UK. The NHS restructuring has brought both organisational and technological changes and begun to change the terms on which healthcare is both delivered and consumed.

The sector has been marked by a new emphasis on managerialism – transferring the practices of commercial management into the public sector in the pursuit of greater efficiency. The growth of the managerialist rhetoric can be traced back to the reforms outlined in 1983 by Roy Griffiths's report on NHS management (Griffiths 1983). Griffiths (interestingly a senior manager brought in from the retail sector) argued that the problems within the NHS came from a number of sources:

- Managers had insufficient influence over professionals.
- Managers were mainly administrators who *reacted* to problems.
- Priority was given to established ways of doing things.
- The NHS was producer rather than consumer oriented.

A new pursuit of 'efficiency' was related mainly to effective use of resources, responsiveness to local needs and interests, and living within tight budgetary constraints. Throughout the period of the Conservative government market discipline was heralded as a panacea for all problems and failures of healthcare delivery. Strategies such as the 'internal market' that included a split between the purchaser and the provider were presented as solutions to all clinical areas and all areas of healthcare. These strategies led to the creation of hospital trusts which are individually managed and which bid to Health Authorities (the purchasers) to be their providers of healthcare. Within this context the national structure of the PHLS – the main focus of our study – underwent managerial changes which reflected these wider shifts in organisational practices and narratives within the NHS: for example, since 1994 the PHLS has contracted its services to hospital trusts as part of the internal market.

Since the general election in 1997 the suitability of performance management solutions for all areas of healthcare, has, within the new Labour government, been under question. However, when our analysis of the Public Health Laboratories at Finlay Hospital was undertaken, the contract culture and performance management still prevailed and were highly significant conditions of possibility framing change.

The managerialist ethos instigated during the Conservative governments of the 1980s and 1990s had a major influence over the scale and direction of technological change in the NHS. In particular the quest for performance management and greater efficiencies meant that MIS that allowed greater auditing of performance were given the highest priority (NHS Executive 1998). A number of strategies were developed at a national level to integrate MIS into the operations of the NHS. One of the most high-profile of these was the development of a nation-wide IT infrastructure – sponsored by the Information Management Group (IMG) of the NHS Executive (NHS Executive 1995).[1] A variety of IT-based projects – many contentious and fraught with problems – were pursued to achieve these objectives: one of the more notable was the Electronic Patient Record (EPR) which the IMG developed to encourage both hospitals and primary care providers to switch from paper to electronic records capable of being integrated across the whole NHS environment.

The distinctive professional groupings and hierarchies that exist within the NHS are important to an understanding of the direction of any change. Certainly one source of dispute concerning the greater use of IT in the NHS was (and continues to be) professional challenges to the value of both IT and the new managerialism in the NHS. Doctors in particular suggested that too strong an emphasis has been given to providing information systems to produce management information, rather than systems that could produce clinically useful data. Therefore, as the Finlay laboratories we studied went about purchasing and introducing their system there was, amongst doctors and other health professionals, widespread support for greater use of IT in the clinical setting, but at the same time significant debate about the exact role that it should play.

Higher education

The higher education sector in the UK has changed considerably since the early 1980s. Many of these changes have echoed the managerial shifts taking place within the NHS. Since the 1970s, the 'bureaucratic' functions of universities have assumed increasing importance, shifting from a facilitative role that allowed 'decisions to be taken at the right time, by the right people, and on the basis of the proper information' (Moodie and Eustace 1974: 161) to a professionalisation of university administrators and greater importance being given to central planning as part of university strategies (ibid.). Central administrative departments have accordingly become more prominent, establishing new responsibilities for themselves, and taking on some responsibilities that would previously have been carried out in academic departments.

Changes in the higher education sector in the 1980s precipitated this situation. Universities began to face a wide range of challenges such as a contraction of funding, a comparative loss of institutional autonomy to outside agencies, greater uncertainty, and changing markets for teaching, research and consultancy (Lockwood and Davies 1985: 19). This continued into the 1990s, with government policy dictating a rapid expansion of student numbers, cuts in funding per student and stricter external monitoring of the quality of teaching and research. In addition there has been, and continues to be, pressure to commercialise research and to make research more relevant to non-academic constituencies (Rappert in preparation).

When the MAC Initiative – our focus in the Bancroft case study – was initiated in the late 1980s, the university sector was made up of about sixty institutions organised, for the most part, by means of committees founded on collegiate principles. Even at this stage, the sector included a range of institutions highly differentiated in both size and organisational structure.

One of the key shifts in the overall structure of higher education within the UK has been the transformation of polytechnics into universities. At the same time both 'old' and 'new' universities have become increasingly geared towards managerial concerns with 'efficiency' and cost savings (Allen and Wilson 1996); there are clear parallels here with the changes already described in the NHS. This shift has been particularly striking in the older universities, the focus of the MAC Initiative, as prior to the 1990s managerialism held far less sway there than in the former polytechnics. Consequently, Allen and Wilson identify among the old universities a general move away from collegiality and autonomy, towards centralisation and strategic planning (ibid.: 243).

Alongside the rise of managerialism and cost consciousness is a growing sense of having to become 'more competitive' as more institutions acquire university status and struggle for students and external funds. Courses have shifted, in both old and new universities, towards modularisation and semesterisation. Entrepreneurialism has become important as a source of extra income, for example from residential courses and conferences outside the teaching year, whilst partnerships are forged in numerous ways between academic departments and private industry. Each of these imposes greater requirements on a university's information management. Increasingly, external bodies, most notably the Higher Education Statistics Agency (HESA), also expect more and more closely prescribed information from universities.

As part of the managerial changes there has been an increased concern with computerisation at all levels of university life – teaching, libraries, infrastructure and management (Gardner *et al.* 1993; Breaks 1991). From the early 1980s onwards, a range of successive initiatives was launched to promote the use of IT to support teaching, learning and research, framed, in many institutions, within the context of a broader 'information strategy' (Allen and Wilson 1996, Anderson 1992). The MAC Initiative is just one element of this changing technological and organisational face of university computing.

The occupational mix and relations of the university sector are dominated by divisions between professionally oriented academics, academic secretarial and technical support staff, and non-academic central management, services and support staff. The period of managerial and organisational change at Bancroft that was taking place as MAC was formed and implemented saw some of the institutionalised power of academic staff challenged by the new management structures and philosophies coming into academia. As with doctors in the NHS, the professional status and power of this group became a factor in negotiating and shaping the conditions of possibility in the sector as a whole and in individual universities such as Bancroft.

Conclusions

There are many common features that have emerged out of discussions of the contexts of our three case studies; not least of these is the sense of rapid change that runs through each of the sectors. Each is also characterised by increased and innovative forms of management regulation. They share too a striking level of confidence and investment in technological solutions to organisational problems.

Despite the commonalities, we can see in each sector a distinct technological, policy, economic and occupational environment that constitutes the particular 'conditions of possibility' for each of the three examples of techno-organisational change we analyse in the remainder of the book. These conditions frame and influence the cases we discuss but they do not determine them. As earlier sections of this chapter have argued, the acquisition and adoption of new technology is a messy, localised process.

Acknowledgement of the contingency and open-endedness of technology acquisition is an antidote to the tidy stories that are told of the planned management of technological change. This acknowledgement encourages a degree of reflexivity about the validity and use of the notions of 'rationality', 'imperative' and 'technology fix' that so often feature in such stories. As we have already suggested in this chapter, it also implies a very different account of organising and organisational life – one that is as much about complexity and uncertainty as it is about order and control. Crucial to our approach to techno-organisational change is a view of the organisation as an arena containing many differently (and often unequally) placed actors and interests. Some sort of accommodation has to be reached between new technology and these actors and interests.

By reframing technology acquisition as a long-running process by which technology is embedded into the local setting of the organisation, we have raised a number of questions about the end-users. If the need for, use of, usability of and usefulness of a technology is not predetermined but rather developed over time, in setting, then how are we to understand this development? What factors facilitate or regulate users' participation in this? In the next chapter we explore two analytical approaches – social studies of technology and the sociology of consumption – which, we argue, have the potential to shed light on these questions.

Note

1 The Labour government in power from 1997 has marked its shift away from previous IT policy in the NHS by announcing its decision to dissolve the IMG and replace it with the NHS Information Authority.

2 The construction and consumption of sociotechnology

A recurring theme of literature reviewed in the last chapter was the requirement for a more sophisticated understanding of the processes involved when organisations acquire new technology. Analyses in this area had until recently rested on three dubious starting assumptions:

- *Assumption 1*: The course of technological development and diffusion is relatively unproblematic and has its own internal logic.
- *Assumption 2*: Technologies enter organisations fully formed and their 'acquisition' is a one-off moment of capture.
- *Assumption 3*: Decisions and evaluations within organisations concerning technology are, or should be, rooted in abstract criteria of instrumental rationality and economic benefit.

We do not wish to caricature existing work in this area or to set it up as an Aunt Sally to be knocked down ritualistically. On the contrary, as we suggested in Chapter 1, there is a growing recognition of the limitations of these assumptions and a desire to transcend them and develop alternative conceptions of technology acquisition. As the last chapter suggested, the three assumptions above can be challenged by three alternative propositions:

- *Proposition 1*: Technological development is a messy process whose contingencies make it hard to predict or direct.
- *Proposition 2*: The embedding of technology into an organisation requires considerable work and involves end-users.
- *Proposition 3*: Although powerful, notions of instrumental rationality, economic imperative and technological constraint are constructed and contested in particular local settings.

How can we explore the implications of these propositions? We will argue in this chapter that analysis of techno-organisational change has much to learn from the developing field of Social Studies of Technology (SST) and its focus on the construction of *sociotechnologies*. In addition, we will develop the theme of 'bringing in the users' established in Chapter 1. To explore this fully we propose

to borrow from a field that at first glance might seem a long way from organisations and MIS – the study of domestic consumption. Once again it is
important to be clear what we are not claiming in doing this. We are not arguing that there is a simple equivalence between the position and experience of
the domestic consumer and that of an organisational actor living through technological change (although the parallels are interesting). Rather, analytical
tools developed to understand domestic consumption can be adapted to make
sense of two important and related aspects of techno-organisational change:

- the ways in which users construct needs and utilities around new technologies – i.e. how technologies are valued and become usable and useful;
- the ways in which users incorporate technologies into their own group and
  personal projects.

The chapter is divided into three sections. It begins with an extended discussion of SST that introduces a series of insights and concepts that can be
applied to understanding techno-organisational change. It then offers a general
discussion of the sociology of consumption before considering how perspectives
from this area might be applied to organisations. The final section of the
chapter acts as a bridge between the first part of the book, which has been
largely general and conceptual, and the detailed analyses of our case studies in
Part II. This section discusses the acquisition and implementation of the computer systems in our case studies prior to when they 'went live' (i.e. when users
began to use the systems). By telling the story of the three sociotechnologies
up to this point we wish to reiterate an argument that runs through much of
this chapter – that the development of systems is far from finished when they
enter organisational space.

The social and the technological

Many of the questions regarding technological change raised in Chapter 1 have
been addressed in recent years by sociologists and historians working in what
is loosely termed social studies of technology (SST). The theme that unites
work in SST is that no neat distinction can be drawn between the social and
technical aspects of change, hence the concept of *sociotechnical change*. Within
this broad interest in 'sociotechnologies', the field includes a variety of different approaches. Bijker, Hughes and Pinch (1987: 4–5) divide these into three
categories:

- *Social constructivism*, an offshoot of the sociology of science, is concerned
  with how social factors are built into the design and content of technologies. Constructivist studies have covered a range of artefacts including
  Pinch and Bijker's work on bicycles (1987) and Bijker's other work on the
  development of Bakelite (1987) and on the redefinition of the fluorescent
  lamp during the mid-twentieth century (1992). This approach has been

drawn on less systematically in studies of a variety of other artefacts, such as ultracentrifuges (Elzen 1986), missiles (MacKenzie 1990), steel (Misa 1992) and medical technology (Blume 1992, 1997).

- *Systems* approaches explore how large technological systems involve a variety of different artefacts and institutions. Hughes' (1983) historical work on the role of the great system-builders (notably Thomas Edison) in the development of electricity networks in the USA and Europe stands as the exemplar of this.

- *Actor-network* approaches look at the interactions of human and technological 'actants' within networks. Examples such as Callon's account of attempts to develop an electric car (1986b), Latour's tracing of a new light rail project (1996) and Law and Callon's account of the development of a military aircraft (1992) focus on the problems and processes of building networks of artefacts and humans.

This bald categorisation hides some fundamental differences of perspective concerning epistemology and methodology between and, sometimes, within the three groupings (see Pickering 1992). Debates have frequently raged in SST, over issues such as reflexivity (Woolgar 1991a), relativism (Winner 1993), representation (Callon and Latour 1992, Collins and Yearley 1992), policy relevance (Wynne 1988, Webster 1994, Rip *et al.* 1995) and politics (MacKenzie and Wajcman 1985, Cockburn and Fürst-Dilić 1994, Sclove 1995, Winner 1986).

Leaving these divisions aside, SST has generated a rich repertoire of insights and concepts. In particular, the notion of *interpretative flexibility*, borrowed by Pinch and Bijker (1987) from the sociology of scientific knowledge, is useful. It helps us understand how, on the one hand, an emerging technology can mean different things to different people but, on the other hand, the range of possible meanings is framed by the qualities and features designed into the technology. To cite the classic case study in the social construction of technology (SCOT) perspective, 'the bicycle' in the 1870s was a high-wheeled machine that meant either daring and excitement or danger and foolhardiness, depending on one's perspective. As new designs proliferated and the dominant shape of a bicycle began to shift towards smaller wheels, the meaning of 'the bicycle' changed also (Pinch and Bijker 1987, Bijker 1995). As this *closure* of meaning and *stabilisation* of design become more entrenched, an artefact such as the bicycle then acquires a degree of *obduracy*; that is, it becomes less easy to change and less open to reinterpretation (Bijker 1995, Bijker and Law 1992a, Rosen forthcoming, see also Orlikowski 1992). Nevertheless, writers in SST stress the contingency of sociotechnical change, and the possibility that is always present that obduracy might be reversed (Bijker 1995).

Actor-network theorists view this process through a different lens, focusing on the powerful actors who try to construct *networks* that bring together a range of human and non-human *actants*. For them, stabilisation and obduracy are an outcome of the successful and enduring *enrolment* of actants into the network (Callon 1986a, 1986b). Callon (1986b) tells the story of how in the 1970s Electricité de France (EDF), the French electricity utility, tried to build an actor-network to develop an electric vehicle. EDF did this, first, by defining a scenario in which electric vehicles would be necessary – where the internal combustion engine would no longer be acceptable to consumers increasingly motivated by environmental concerns. By presenting this scenario as a crucial problem for a variety of different actors, EDF set about trying to *enrol* them to its project. These actors included consumers themselves; the General Electric Company, to develop motors and batteries; Renault, to assemble the chassis of the new vehicles; and various government ministries to put in place a favourable regulatory regime. Most crucially, EDF needed to enrol the new and difficult technologies of fuel cells and accumulators, without which electric vehicles could not be built. This actor-network depended on EDF successfully engaging these other actors or actants within the project, by *translating* their identities, interests and roles into those defined for them by EDF. They were all essential to the success of the network; as Callon writes, '[i]n the absence of one ingredient the whole case would break down' (1986b: 23). This is in fact what did eventually happen: Renault spoke out against the electric vehicle project and the fuel cell technology proved extremely difficult to get 'right'. Building an actor-network is thus a difficult task, needing constant maintenance work to ensure that other actors remain enrolled in the project. To lose the support of one actor can result in the collapse of the entire network (Callon 1986a, 1986b).

As the discussion above has already implied, all SST perspectives share a conception of technology not as something distinct from social relations, culture, politics, economics or science, but as part of a 'seamless web' (Hughes 1986). This web links all these elements together in ways that make it less convincing to talk about any one element in isolation from others. The apparent boundaries between the technical and the social components of an artefact or a system or a network become on closer inspection far less clear cut. As Hughes writes, delving deeply into the activities of engineers leads to the discovery that they do not think, as sociologists and historians often do, in discrete, discipline-bound ways (ibid.: 287). Rather, system- or network-building engineers (Thomas Edison is a fine example of this) will try to achieve their goals using whichever available methods – scientific, technical, financial, legislative – seem appropriate. They act, in other words, as 'heterogeneous engineers' (Law 1987), bringing together in the construction of their technologies a range of elements that might be natural, technical or social.

A theme of Chapter 1 was the limitations of technological determinism – the view that the development of new technologies dictates the direction of social and organisational change – as an account of techno-organisational change. Some earlier work in SST reacted against this perspective by proposing a form of social determinism, understanding technologies as mere expressions of social relations (see MacKenzie and Wajcman 1985). As we have seen already, however, more recent work moves beyond this, instead regarding the social and the technological as mutually constitutive. Bijker and Law (1992a) express this idea through the notion of *sociotechnical ensembles* that are simultaneously social and technical. Thus it is important when considering a bicycle, an aircraft, a power station or, indeed, a computer system not to see just the physical object itself but to be conscious of the simultaneous shaping of technology and building of society that have been involved in its development.

What is the relevance of these arguments to our study? From this introduction to SST, we can already see a number of concepts and themes that can be applied or adapted to the study of techno-organisational change. In particular:

- The notion of sociotechnology suggests ways in which our analysis of change can transcend any simplistic distinction between technology on the one hand and the organisation on the other.
- It also provides the means to understand how technology comes to embody particular decisions and assumptions about the organisation and organising.
- The analysis of stabilisation and obduracy allows us to consider the degree of interpretative flexibility that exists around new organisational technologies and how that flexibility might diminish over time.

Opening up the black box of technology

Studies that view technology and society as a seamless web highlight the ways in which the construction of sociotechnologies, and the ensembles that emerge out of that process, are a site of social struggles for status and control. The technical and the social are, therefore, blurred in the real work of technology construction. At the same time, however, we can often see practitioners striving to maintain a technology–society distinction. Other boundaries are also created in the process, including those between:

- artefacts that are seen as 'working' or not 'working', or as more or less 'valuable' or 'appropriate' in specific contexts;
- discrete points in the 'product lifecycle', from conception, design and production on the one hand to distribution, consumption and use on the other;
- people who are to be involved or enrolled in the development of a *sociotechnical ensemble* and those who are to be excluded.

A key metaphor used in SST to understand the development and power of these boundaries is that of the *black box* of technology. This notion of the black box has become common currency within SST, having been borrowed from engineering and from the economics of innovation (Rosenberg 1982, Pinch and Bijker 1987, Winner 1993). The black box refers to how the technical aspects of technology are closed off – hidden within the box – and hence left unquestioned (Pinch and Bijker 1987: 22, citing Layton). Once technologies move beyond their engineering origins, the black box comes to represent something that can be of value despite the fact that its origins and workings are not understood (Winner 1993: 431). In SST, getting 'inside the black box' has come to refer to the ways in which sociologists and historians of technology attempt to uncover the usually hidden social origins and workings of technology.

Examples of this pursuit of the social within the technical can be found in all the different SST perspectives we have outlined. In Hughes's work, a key problem in expanding electricity supply in the early twentieth century is shown to be as much about the development of consumer demand (in competition with gas) and the management of economic resources as it was about technical capacity (Hughes 1983, 1986). MacKenzie (1990), Law and Callon (1992) and Mack (1990) all demonstrate in different ways how the technical properties of large-scale national projects – missiles, military aircraft and satellites – emerge out of negotiations and disputes among political, military, scientific and technical actors. Cockburn and Ormrod (1993) show how the design, marketing and prescribed uses of microwave ovens have not simply followed the technical logic of microwaving, but involved a (gendered) shift from being classed as a 'brown good' sold alongside cameras and hi-fi equipment to a 'white good' sold with fridges and cookers. In each of these cases, opening the black box involves investigation of how the social – for which read also political, economic and cultural – and the technical interweave in the construction of a *sociotechnical ensemble*.

Once a technology has been successfully blackboxed it is inscribed with particular meanings, uses and assumptions that constrain and, to some extent, shape the user (Akrich 1992). So, female cyclists often find themselves having to cope with riding bicycles which were designed with male physical dimensions in mind, because bicycle designers routinely neglect the differences between male and female bodily proportions (Rosen 1995). In a more deliberate example, a bus driver wishing to reach Jones Beach in New York would find herself unable to pass beneath the low-hanging overpasses that cross the entry roads. This is because the architect Robert Moses wished to exclude from his showcase development poor people and minorities, who relied on public transport (Winner 1986). In each case, certain assumptions about users and society were built into the technology and these assumptions have created constraints on the ways in which users can engage both with the technology and with society.

So far, we have discussed how analysts 'open the black box'. But always implicit and sometimes explicit in SST discussion of construction and obduracy is a concern with when and by what means technologies are blackboxed in the first place. This involves questions about how debates around the technology are closed off and how the messiness of the process of development is eventually hidden. New social and political circumstances can open up the black box of technology again. Thus the opening and closing of the black box is itself an important area of study and one which has particular relevance to the analysis in this book. In our discussion of techno-organisational change not only are we opening the black box *as analysts* of technology but we also consider *how users open the black box of technology*. We will be developing the notion of 'blackboxing' in the following directions:

- Our contention is that when a technology enters an organisation, its black box, to a greater or lesser extent, is reopened, prompting questions about its social origins and debates about its use and value.
- We consider how, why and to what extent technologies are blackboxed again within particular organisational settings.
- As this implies, our emphasis is on the contingent nature of blackboxing – technologies may be open to a whole series of constructions and reconstructions.

Inclusion, exclusion and sociotechnical development

The analyses outlined above prompt discussion about power and inequality in the processes of sociotechnical development. Langdon Winner's classic discussion of the Jones Beach design cited above was used to show, in Winner's phrase, that 'artefacts have politics' (1986). The *constructivist* and *actor-network* approaches are however sometimes accused of presenting sociotechnical change in ways that ignore the issue of who is best placed to bring about change or to benefit from it, and how such change usually has differentiated impacts on different groups of people (Russell 1986, Winner 1993).[1] As Russell points out, there is a danger that relativism adopted in order to pay equal attention to competing claims about technology can easily slide into a refusal to take any position in political debate (1986, Kling 1992). Another criticism has been the relative lack of attention paid to labour relations in the production of technology and a minimal engagement with the issues raised by 'labour process theory' (Russell 1986, Mort 1995, Mort and Michael 1998). This is, in part, a consequence of a tendency in SST to focus narrowly on the processes of conception and design, stopping short of production or even bypassing it by moving straight on to the uses of finished products (Rosen forthcoming).

There are difficult questions to be answered as to which actors in the process of sociotechnical change are given a voice in SST accounts. As Winner writes regarding the *relevant social groups* that form the focus of Pinch and Bijker's analysis:

> Who says what are 'relevant' social groups and social interests? What about groups which have no voice but which nevertheless will be affected by the results of technological change? What of groups which have been suppressed or deliberately excluded? How does one account for potentially important choices that never surface as matters for debate and choice?
>
> (1993: 440)

These questions can also be asked of actor-network theorists such as Callon, Latour and Law. Actor-network theory is explicitly concerned with the problem of representation, specifically how to represent the non-human 'missing masses' (Latour 1992) that are commonly left out of social theory. Consequently, actor-network accounts include the non-human elements, such as artefacts, texts or natural entities, within the networks they describe. This representation is problematic, though, in the same way as are the decisions made by Pinch and Bijker as to which social groups are deemed relevant – in both cases, the analyst chooses whom to give voice to and what that voice is allowed to say (Collins and Yearley 1992).

Star and others seek to address issues of exclusion and inclusion by complementing talk of networks with consideration of *social worlds* (Star 1991, Clarke and Montini 1993). Star (1991) is especially concerned with a troubling aspect of the stabilisation of technologies and actor-networks, that securing stability for some can actually close off access to the network for others. An example she gives which might at first appear trivial is her own allergy to onions. She discusses the effects of her resulting exclusion – along with others such as coronary patients, orthodox Jews, vegetarians, those who are too poor to eat out, or those who prefer to support small businesses – from the standardised products of fast food chains such as McDonald's. By not being able to consume the product, Star is marked as 'other', as outside the network.

Star is thus concerned about whose perspectives Social Studies of Technology (and science) tend to represent. She advocates an approach that highlights our multiple membership of different social worlds, thus addressing 'the deep heterogeneities that occur in any juxtaposition, any network' (1991: 34). This allows ways of accounting both for the active exclusion, or *disenrolment* (Mort and Michael 1998) of some actors from a network, and for the *ambivalence* of other actors who are partially reluctant to be enrolled by network-builders (Singleton and Michael 1993). Different groups of actors can thus be distinguished as being insiders or outsiders in relation to particular processes of sociotechnical change (Law and Bijker 1992a), whether through their own choice or that of more powerful actors.

Gender and technology

Arguably, it is in the feminist work done under the umbrella of SST that discussions of power, difference and technology are most developed. Analyses of technology in the workplace and in the home, of military and reproductive technologies, and so on, have highlighted how gender is a crucial component of the 'social' side of sociotechnology (Cockburn and Fürst-Dilíc 1994, Cowan 1989, Rothschild 1983, Wajcman 1991).

Early writing by feminists on technology often portrayed technologies as inherently masculine (Griffin 1978) and/or considered the ways in which women have been denied access to technologies and technological skills (Cockburn 1983, Witz 1986). Such approaches have been criticised for an overly static and determined account of gender difference. More recent work has, in response, treated gender identities and technologies as co-constructions (Grint and Gill 1995, Terry and Calvert 1997, Webster 1993).

Now those working within SST challenge the notion that any technology is inherently masculine or feminine. Rather, some feminist studies of technology analyse the ways in which gender becomes 'inscribed in' technology at different points in its development, production and consumption. They consider, for example, the ways in which designers assume certain gender norms in their construction of technology (Cockburn and Ormrod 1993). Writers as disparate as Wajcman (1993) and Grint and Woolgar (1995) argue that we should focus on the ways in which technology becomes interpreted as masculine or feminine:

> To ask whether, for example, an artefact is (that is physically embodies the properties of) male or female or neutral is to miss the point; not only are these properties themselves socially constructed and therefore flexible, but the important question is how certain artefacts come to be *interpreted* (and this may well be disputed) as neutral or male or female.
>
> (Grint and Woolgar 1995: 54, emphasis original)

For Wajcman the answer to Grint and Woolgar's question (an answer which incidentally they would strongly contest) lies in the social and cultural construction of *a* form of masculinity as equating to being technically skilled and dominant over nature. This form of masculinity is secured in the equally constructed bond made between femininity and all things non-technical and natural.

In the light of these accounts of gender and technology, our study seeks to develop discussion of inclusion in and exclusion from sociotechnical development in the following directions:

- in our concern with the gendering of techno-organisational change and, more specifically, the gender identities of participants in that change;
- in a widening of focus to include people normally excluded from accounts of innovation;
- in our wish to explore the relationship between local inclusions in and exclusions from the development of sociotechnology *and* broader patterns of inequality.

Social studies of technology and 'the users'

As Chapter 1 argued, the call for a richer understanding of 'the users' is now frequently heard within innovation studies. From economic or managerialist perspectives, however, 'the users' remain undifferentiated and under-theorised – often little more than a shorthand for the organisation or its managers. If, however, acquisition is reframed as a long-running process and we appreciate the difficulty of embedding technology into organisational life, then end-users become central (but under-researched) characters in the story. What can SST tell us about 'the users'?

As the examples we have cited suggest, SST's dominant preoccupation has been with other phases of technological development and decision-making prior to the meeting of technology and end-user (Orlikowski 1992, Mort and Michael 1998). As such, SST most often considers 'the users' through the eyes of designers. Studies show how the developers of technologies 'construct' (Pinch and Bijker 1987), represent (Akrich 1995), identify with (Chabaud-Rychter 1994) and test (Chabaud-Rychter 1994, Pinch 1993) the real or imaginary users of their products throughout the design process. This continues as design modifications follow user feedback once a technology is in production (Cockburn and Ormrod 1993).

The specific theoretical and methodological orientations of different writers in SST can result in significantly different outlooks on the agency of users. The near-universal commitment within SST to 'following the actor' (Latour 1987) can have highly variable results depending on which actor is deemed worth following (Singleton and Michael 1993). To follow the *designers* of technology means that users will be seen primarily from the designer's point of view, and users' needs understood as a construct of designers. Woolgar takes this kind of analysis further, seeing users as 'configured' by designers in the same process by which the technology itself has been configured. As well as testing how well the technology works, usability trials also serve as a means of testing users' ability to operate the technology correctly (Woolgar 1991b). A similar configuring takes place in the gendering of users by designers, marketers and retailers (Cockburn and Ormrod 1993, Chabaud-Rychter 1994). Cockburn and Ormrod describe how safety is constructed both technically and discursively in the design of microwave ovens and in their users' manuals; users are consequently controlled in order to prevent unauthorised kinds of use.

Analyses of 'users' in SST also vary according to how 'the user' is conceptualised. The users of a technology might be a single organisation or group of organisations, such as the combined military, government and civilian agencies that commissioned and negotiated over the designs of the TSR.2 aircraft described by Law and Callon (1992) or of the land satellite described by Mack (1990). Within such organisations there will then be a variety of different groups of 'end-users' often with conflicting needs. Alternatively the designers of a new artefact such as a domestic appliance might work with a conception of larger numbers of users, whose needs are represented in the design process in a variety of ways: through the construction of knowledge about users through market research; through designers identifying themselves with users on the assumption that they have shared interests and needs; through engaging colleagues to take on the role of the user; or through the usability trials discussed above (Akrich 1995, Chabaud-Rychter 1995, Cockburn and Ormrod 1993, Woolgar 1991b, Pinch 1993).

Thus SST has much to say about how 'the users' are understood by constructors of technology and the ways in which design can constrain and enable the uses and users of technology. It does not, though, take much account of the active role that users might actually play in developing uses for the technologies; nor does it pay attention to the ways in which users disregard the configurations set by designers both for users and for technologies. Akrich (1992) describes how artefacts can be 'scripted' during the design process to support certain activities – and even certain users – but not others, even where this is not the deliberate intention of the designers. She shows how, nevertheless, users can subvert the technical constraints built into technology – in other words, where uses have been 'scripted' into an artefact, they can also be 'descripted' (ibid.).

Following users rather than designers results, then, in a different understanding of users' role in shaping technology. This is an explicit objective in the SCOT approach of Bijker, Pinch and others, where users are treated equally with designers as *relevant social groups* that can affect the direction of sociotechnical change (Pinch and Bijker 1987). Cowan extends this emphasis on the importance of users by making a more explicitly methodological point. She argues for a research strategy in the sociology of technology that centres on 'the consumption junction'; in other words, that takes the perspective of consumers as its starting point, and moves outwards from there into other dimensions such as production and distribution (1987). This position takes us back to the question of who counts as a user. For Cowan, one strength of her proposed strategy is that all technologies have consumers, whether individual or organisational (ibid.: 263). Researching the consumption junction thus provides a common focus for studying technologies of different scales, and with different *kinds* of user. At the same time, by focusing on 'the interface where technological diffusion occurs . . . where technologies begin to reorganise social structures' (ibid.), this approach gets to what is, for Cowan, the heart of technological change.

Strengths and limitations of social studies of technology

SST offers a variety of analytical tools that can aid understanding of technological change within the kinds of setting we will be discussing in this book: concepts such as *stabilisation*, *obduracy*, *blackboxing* and *enrolment* will all feature in later chapters. To us, SST's value lies, ultimately, in the very concept of sociotechnology and the particular understanding of change that flows from that concept. Despite variations in outlook and approach within the field, there is a shared assumption that change is heterogeneous, messy, contingent and emergent, and that technologies are born out of conflict, difference, or resistance (Law and Bijker 1992). In the construction of technological artefacts and systems, struggles between different groups and actors, and technological and environmental constraints, work together in ways that are hard to anticipate entirely but then become 'built' into the eventual outcome. Technology thus gains a solidity that in turn limits further options for change.

From an SST perspective the boundaries between the 'development', diffusion' and 'implementation' of a technology blur. It is debatable, however, whether SST has fully come to terms with this insight. Focus on the construction of generic technologies rather than their enactment in particular settings misses an important element of the story. To put it another way, much SST considers *delocalisation* – the ways in which the activities of specific groups of technologists are turned into generally accepted and used artefacts. We must also consider, however, accompanying processes of *relocalisation*: the form and purpose of technology are, to a greater or lesser extent, renegotiated locally as it is integrated into organisational life. Technological change involves multi-layered social constructions: the introduction of an innovation into an organisation inevitably prompts the generic 'black box' of a technology to be reopened locally.

As we have already suggested, studying users provides new insight into sociotechnical change and encompasses groups often excluded from SST accounts. It is no coincidence that feminist studies have pioneered this focus on the user, highlighting the role women can have in reconstructing the technology which they use (Martin 1991). As Webster has explained:

> seeing technological change as a process, rather than concentrating on the finished artefact, restores an awareness of the centrality of women in technology; they are no longer passive recipients of technologies, as users, but important actors in the process of development.
>
> (1996: 6)

What interests us, therefore, is the part played by end-users in the embedding of a technology into an organisational setting. While our approach derives in many ways from SST, in putting end-users at the centre of our analysis, we are extending the implications and reach of SST rather than simply applying its insights. What we offer is our own localised reworking of SST. In addition we seek other means to understand the position of users in techno-organisational change; for these we turn to the study of consumption.

The consumption of new technology

Social Studies of Technology provides us with a range of concepts and tools that can be adapted to understand the role of the user in techno-organisational change. In addition, to shed further light on this, we wish to draw on insights taken from the sociology and anthropology of consumption and adapt them to organisational settings. These insights help us explore two interrelated issues:

- how technologies are embedded into the fabric of organisations and incorporated into the projects of organisational actors;
- how, over time, within particular settings, and to particular groups, technologies come to have value.

The processes of consumption

There is a fast-growing but disparate collection of social science literature on consumption (for summaries see Miller 1995b, Slater 1997). Much of this work is of little relevance to our discussion since it is generalised theorising about the social significance of consumption. There is, however, a growing body of work that studies consumers and consumption using ethnographic approaches, and shares a preoccupation with *the processes of consumption*. This work has its roots in social anthropology but now spans the disciplines of sociology, geography, media studies and social psychology.

Crucial to the ethnographically informed work on consumption is an understanding of consumers as active creators of meaning. Consumption is studied as a process involving the acquisition, use and evaluation of goods. This process involves building on existing collections of goods, experiences and competencies. Neither the vision of 'economic man' making rational choices on the basis of product and market information nor the 'dupe' of cultural critiques of consumerism does justice to the problems people face in consuming or the sophistication with which they confront those problems.

Once a mass-produced good enters our lives – through purchase or some other means – creativity is required to turn it into a personal or domestic object. Daniel Miller uses the idea of 'reappropriation' to understand this process: consumers engage in 'creative strategies of consumption to appropriate that which they have not created' (Miller 1990: 53). After being acquired from the commercial world, the status of a good is gradually altered:

> This is the start of a long and complex process by which the consumer works upon the object purchased and recontextualizes it, until it is no longer recognisable as having any relation to the world of the abstract and becomes its very negation, something which could be neither bought nor given.
>
> (Miller 1987: 190)

The various attempts to describe these processes share a view of consumption as a dynamic process of meaning transfer (McCracken 1988). Silverstone, Hirsch and Morley's study (1992) of the consumption of media messages and technology developed a highly influential approach that considers how goods are 'domesticated' into the 'moral economy of the household'. They identify four (not entirely distinct) stages in this process:

- appropriation – the route to possession of the good;
- objectification – goods are added to existing systems of objects and meanings via arrangement and display;
- incorporation – as goods become part of the everyday routines and politics of the household they become invisible as commodities;
- conversion – goods become implicated in relationships within the household and between the household and the outside world.

It should be noted that, within this typology, many goods are never fully incorporated into the household and that the incorporation of any good is provisional as, given the instability of the wider cultural context, it may lose its place within the household's moral economy due to changed circumstances.

Silverstone *et al.* have themselves been influenced by anthropological work that views consumption as 'eminently social, relational and active rather than private, atomic or passive' (Appadurai 1986: 31). Miller develops the concept of 'objectification' to take discussion of the social role of goods further. By objectification he means:

> the use of goods and services in which the object or activity become simultaneously a practice in the world and form in which we construct our understandings of ourselves in the world.
>
> (Miller 1995a: 30)

Social anthropology looks at goods as cultural resources – as carriers of meaning and mediators of social relationships (Douglas and Isherwood 1980, Sahlins 1976, McCracken 1988). Seen in this light the processes of consumption are therefore about the *incorporation* of goods into individual and group projects. The aspect of this most frequently discussed is social demarcation – the use of goods as markers of status competition and group identity (Bourdieu 1984). But this is only one of a series of projects that goods are implicated in. Domestic consumption and home decoration, for example, can be as much about the representation of self, family history and links to the past as they are an other-directed expression of taste (Czikszentmihalyi and Rochberg-Holton 1981, Gullestad 1984). In his most recent work Miller (1998) discusses how the shopping behaviour of a group of North London households is best understood as part of a 'moral project' of loving and caring for others. Silverstone (1994) links the consumption of media to the quest for ontological security already discussed in Chapter 1: consumers use information and communications technology to wrestle with the requirement for a clear sense of who they are and how they fit into the world. A range of writers has also highlighted the ways that goods feature in our daydreams and fantasy life (see for example Campbell 1987).

The multi-faceted character of consumption behaviour is well summed up in one review of the area:

> consumption processes are driven by performative processes directed at impressing others, processes directed at reassuring oneself, and also processes forming links and bonds with significant others.
>
> (Longhurst and Savage 1996: 296)

Expressed in these terms, it is easier to understand the link between viewing goods as cultural resources and discussing consumption in terms of process. For goods to be incorporated into any of the projects described by Longhurst and Savage can require considerable effort and ingenuity on the part of consumers.

If goods are understood as cultural resources then their value is neither pre-given nor inherent; demand for goods and the utilities they provide are not absolutes that drive the consumption process but instead emerge out of that process (Sahlins 1976, Bourdieu 1984, Appadurai 1986). The development of value is therefore central to consumption. As Silverstone *et al.*'s four-stage model suggests, goods come to have value to people as they integrate them into their everyday lives. This is, of course, bounded by a wider context (i.e. goods enter our lives already loaded with meanings), but the need for, uses of and value of goods are developed and redeveloped in particular social settings. It is striking that the term *interpretative flexibility* crops up here just as it did in SST accounts of the stabilisation of technology. This flexibility actually varies considerably between goods *and* settings. One of the authors of this book's study of home computing (already briefly outlined in the Introduction), for example, argued that, initially, the home computer was a novel good without a clearly defined role and function; this presented early consumers with special problems and opportunities regarding incorporation (Skinner 1992).

Consuming technologies in organisations

We are not alone in understanding organisational actors as consumers (Du Gay 1996, Noble and Lupton 1998). In adapting approaches taken from the study of domestic consumption to the study of techno-organisational change, however, we are not claiming a simple equivalence between private consumption and organisational practice. There are obvious differences between the circumstances of people when they consume new technology in an organisational, and in a private, setting. The distinctive features of consumption in organisations we will consider in later chapters include the following:

- Most consumers of new technology in organisations have little direct influence over its initial selection.
- Consumption in organisations is more clearly and closely regulated than consumption in the private realm. Thus private consumers will often make sense of their experience in terms of 'choice' while organisational consumers do so in terms of 'constraint'.
- Although consumption in organisations is differentiated – we do not talk of organisations 'consuming technology' but rather see organisational actors as consumers – it is strongly mediated by shared identities (such as those based on occupation) and a sense of membership of the organisation

Having recognised these distinctions, we should be careful not to exaggerate them. There are limitations to the common-sense model of private consumption based on the notion of an autonomous individual making personal purchasing decisions:

- Often the space to make choices about private consumption is highly bounded – think, for example, of the consumption of state housing or healthcare or, in a different way, of that jumper you have to wear when you visit relatives because it was a Christmas gift! Private consumers feel a whole range of material and cultural constraints on their consumption.
- While *management regulation* is not a factor in the same way as it is with organisational consumption, we can talk of the *subjective regulation* of private consumers.
- Private consumption is mediated by membership of social groupings: social classes (Bourdieu 1984) and youth subcultures (Hebdige 1979), for example, are both constituted through shared patterns of taste.

With this discussion of the similarities and differences between consumption in private and organisational settings in mind, we shall now outline a series of benefits of using consumption approaches in conjunction with SST to understand techno-organisational change.

The role of end-users in innovation

Consumption approaches allow us to explore the position of the end-users of technology who – like private consumers – are active creators of value but whose position is qualitatively different from those directly involved in production.

> To be a 'consumer' as opposed to being a producer implies that we only have a secondary relationship to goods. This secondary relationship occurs when people have to live with and through services and goods that they themselves did not create.
>
> (Miller 1995a: 17)

By recasting users as active participants in innovation we consider how users are involved in embedding (and hence redeveloping) technology in organisational settings. We are also, following Miller, exploring how they live with technologies not of their making and, in his term, 'recontextualise' them. This is not to assume that all processes of consumption or all consumers are the same. As Silverstone writes in a discussion of Miller's notion of recontextualisation:

> The point here is that there is an indeterminacy at the heart of the process of consumption . . . because of the different kinds of potential for recontextualisation available in different commodities. And it is also indeterminant because individuals and groups within society have different economic and cultural resources at their disposal with which to undertake the work of recontextualisation.
>
> (1994: 119)

The valuing of technology

As Chapter 1 argued, old-style management models of technology acquisition rested on some highly questionable assumptions about usability and usefulness as fixed, inherent qualities of technology. Factors taken as starting points for the analysis, such as the need for, use of and utility of a particular technology, are actually nebulous, often contested and changing. Studying acquisition in terms of consumption processes allows us to analyse how technologies are 'valued' over time in particular settings by particular users.

Stabilisation and incorporation

In the discussion of SST earlier in this chapter, we considered the issue of how technologies are embedded into local settings primarily in terms of the *restabilisation* of sociotechnology. A consumption approach complements this with consideration of how people in organisations develop value as they *incorporate* the technology into personal, professional and group projects. The extent to which those values come to be shared across the organisation (and the inequalities inherent in that process) is open to question. In Silverstone *et al.*'s notion of *conversion* we also have a means of exploring when, how and why technologies come to mediate the position of users within organisational relations.

Interrogating economism and instrumental rationality

As Chapter 1 suggested, notions of efficiency and economic constraint play an important role in technology acquisition. They are not, however, absolutes that drive techno-organisational change. How then can we explore the construction and deployment of these notions during technology acquisition? Here again work on consumption may provide part of the answer.

There are parallels between our interest in economism and instrumental rationality and attempts within consumption studies to transcend the dominant neo-classical model of consumption behaviour. As we have already suggested, the thrust of much of the best work on the practice of consumption has been to challenge the view of the consumer as a utility-maximising individual and the portrayal of consumption as utilitarian needs satisfaction (Fine 1995). Some analysts move beyond this to examine the ideological power of economic rationality as a system of representation (reviewed in Miller 1995a). The roots of this analysis go back to the anthropological critique of 'practical reason' as an explanation of social behaviour (Sahlins 1976). It is only in recent years, however, that this critique is beginning to develop as part of what Miller terms an 'ethnography of capitalism' (1997).

A growing body of work considers the influence of the utilitarian framework – exploring how consumers seek to be rational, think of themselves as sovereign individuals and struggle to stay in control of their consumption (see for example Lunt and Livingstone 1992). It also considers how consumption involves translations between different spheres (notably the market and the household) each with its own very different rationality (Silverstone *et al.* 1992, Miller 1998). These arguments are particularly evocative for us since so much of our analysis is about the ways in which processes of consumption and the accompanying constructions of value are differentiated across organisations. In making sense of their consumption, people in organisations will deploy and wrestle with abstract notions of a generalised rationality. So much of their behaviour and, indeed, technology acquisition is, however, about translations and disjunctions between different localised values.

Continuing the construction of sociotechnologies, beginning the consumption process

As this chapter and Chapter 1 have set out, the distinctiveness of our approach lies in the focus on sociotechnical construction *after* technologies enter organisational space. As a prelude to discussion of how new technology is consumed in our three research sites, however, we will describe the development of the computer systems in question as sociotechnologies *prior* to the moment when they first confronted the users. The phase we are describing can be seen as both:

- a part of the on-going development of the MIS in question as sociotechnologies, as through their specification, selection and modification they are adapted to the specifics of the organisation;
- the beginning of the processes whereby these sociotechnologies are consumed in organisations.

Each of the accounts below is divided into, firstly, a bare-bones description of the system, secondly, a discussion of the specification and selection of the system, and, thirdly, some indication of how the system was implemented by management.

Brodies and the Staff Organiser

The system

The system we call the Staff Organiser is a staff planner that was introduced into all 1200 Brodies stores. While the Organiser is a particularly sophisticated example, this type of staff management system is now the norm amongst the major high street retailers. The Staff Organiser uses till transaction data collected from the store EPOS system to produce plans that allocate staff to tasks throughout the store day. At the busiest times, the Organiser concentrates staffing on so-called 'priority tasks' such as operating cash points and providing 'customer service'. Priorities are set centrally in the system and cannot be altered by stores. The system also has built-in, standardised criteria for determining how long tasks should take – how long to serve a customer, how long to tidy shelves, and so on – that cannot be changed by stores.

The Staff Organiser both holds and generates information about store operations. The 'store model' is the template that details the departments and work teams throughout a store. It also includes information about the opening hours of the store and, significantly, a structure for when different store activities such as deliveries or shelf-stacking should take place. Data is also entered about staff, including the hours and days they work. Supervisors provide details about the skills of each member of staff and rank their proficiency at each skill using categories included in the system. From this the Staff Organiser generates a 'skills matrix' and a profile of staff for each department that can be used to identify areas of weakness where training is required.

There are various indicators of and targets for 'effective' use of staff built into the workings of the Staff Organiser. The most critical are measures of 'scheduling success' – a percentage that indicates how much of priority activity is unstaffed. These 'priority shortages' are then used in stores and by Brodies area managers as signs of departmental and store efficiency.

The system uses local and central data to produce detailed staff plans for each department in the store. Each shopfloor member of staff is listed on the plans, alongside a grid of codes and symbols that map her or his day in fifteen-minute segments. This includes which activities they should be doing and when their breaks are. The plans also indicate where shortages appear and where staff can do 'concurrent tasks' (undertaking more than one task at the same time).

Specification and selection

The Organiser was an adaptation of a system 'bought in' from an outside company. The purchase, modification and piloting of the Organiser took two years. The Operations Improvement Department (OID) in Brodies' Head Office was responsible for the introduction of the Organiser. However, various other departments took part in specification and purchase. Training and Implementation designed the process of roll out and piloting. Store Systems were the in-house IT specialists in charge of modifications to the Staff Organiser. The politics among these departments and competing implementation priorities were important contributors to the eventual shape of the system and the experiences of stores.

The decision to go ahead with the purchase was taken at an executive level. Various departments bid for their purchase plans to go forward on the basis of cost-benefit analysis of what productivity and efficiency gains could be expected from a new piece of technology or an alteration in operational practices. Head Office managers represented this as based on principles of efficient and rational change management. However, their combined accounts of the design and implementation of the Staff Organiser and other software and hardware going into stores revealed a more complex, *ad hoc* and contingent process. In addition, while the approval process was designed to prioritise business benefits, those behind the Staff Organiser and the new infrastructure acknowledged that 'technical' questions were driving many of their decisions, with business benefits being constructed to match the technological solutions available. One of the Head Office managers in charge of the implementation of the system commented on how business benefits were developed over time: 'it is a bit subjective, but it is a way to bolt onto it a tangible benefit'.

Our interviews with Head Office managers also suggested that, during development and implementation, the system was envisaged as having a number of different roles and benefits. The Staff Organiser was presented as a tool to aid store supervisors, a means for more efficient management of labour resources, and a source of information to enable monitoring of store performance. While these different accounts of the Organiser were far from mutually exclusive, they do point to a degree of flexibility around the primary uses and utility of the system that was to persist during its introduction and later evaluation.

The purchase of the Organiser was presented to us as a carefully managed and rational process. The project manager in OID in charge of the purchase explained:

> It was quite a precise process. We identified what we required in functional terms, in output terms, basically it had to be easy to use and easy to maintain. We then took that specification out with us and did a trawl of the market, of software houses. We decided to go for off the shelf rather than bespoke, for reasons of speed . . . Then we bench tested two finalists and chose the software package we wanted.

The same manager admitted, however, that the software purchased 'was pretty useless in terms of what we wanted'. At first the suppliers were asked to make alterations to this but later the source code for the software was purchased and Store Systems at Head Office were put in charge of customising the Organiser. Here, as at other points in the acquisition, the politics between Store Systems and OID were a factor. People in Store Systems had always argued that they should have designed the Organiser in-house and there were constant tensions over what changes could and should be made to the system. The manager in charge of customisation in Store Systems believed that the system would never be fully customised because 'I think the OID department, the business in general, need educating in terms of, if you buy a package it is a package, it is a black box.'

Implementation

The process of rolling the system out to stores took a further two years. Every store, regardless of size and product range, received the same system. In the end, the decision was taken to implement the Staff Organiser before many of the changes OID wanted were made to the software or the projected hardware infrastructure was available. According to the manager in Store Systems this was a business decision made because OID felt that 'they could get huge benefits from implementation of [the Staff Organiser] whatever platform it was on. However we could get it out, the business was happy to accept that.'

The introduction of the Staff Organiser was further complicated by the fact that it was not the only implementation occurring in stores. As well as the software discussed here, and other associated systems, new management strategies were being introduced which radically altered the workings of stores. Speaking with managers in Head Office responsible for the different implementations, it was clear that tensions did exist within the contrasting and sometimes conflicting priorities of the different projects. Training and Implementation had bid to be in charge of both the implementation of the Staff Organiser and the management changes. However, this had been rejected and the territorial struggles over ownership of the different implementations continued.

Prior to the Organiser arriving in stores, store managers, their management team and (in small stores) supervisors were briefed about the new system at area meetings. These meetings served the dual purpose of introducing the stores to the system and also explaining to management the preparations they needed to begin in order to get their stores ready for the implementation. The content and structure of the briefing process changed considerably over the two years of roll-out. The manager in charge of the briefings argued that they had made the mistake in the early days of focusing on the functionality of the system – what it did and how it did it. What he felt they had not done was 'sell' the system by explaining its business benefits. The OID manager in overall charge of the Organiser echoed this sentiment:

> it is effective change management. It is absolutely stupid to introduce a major technological change into stores without . . . pre-selling of the benefits. It is primarily a marketing exercise. If I was to balance the importance of marketing, to the importance of it working, marketing is far more important.

The implementation of the Staff Organiser in each store took four to six weeks. During this period all the cabling and hardware were installed: the only part of the process completed by outside contractors. While the equipment was being installed, the store manager, management team and supervisors were given training on using the Staff Organiser. The training – a combination of multimedia and face-to-face sessions – varied according to job category, with store managers being given the most training. Sales assistants were not given any training. It was left up to supervisors how much they informed these staff about what was happening. Most did give their staff briefings and produced charts that explained the codes and symbols used in the new plans. Six weeks after implementation the implementer would return to the store and check to see if any problems had emerged.

A key aspect of implementation was the production of the 'store model' and 'skills matrix'. Managers and other key members of the management team worked with the implementer to develop a model of store operations and a profile of staff in the system. This can be seen as the latest stage in a process whereby, as the Staff Organiser went live, a set of standardising and centralising assumptions and priorities was already built into the system.

Finlay Hospital and the Patient-Based System

The system

We have called the IT system at Finlay the 'Patient-Based System' (PBS). Compared to the Staff Organiser at Brodies, the acquisition of a new IT system at Finlay Hospital was less explicitly related to the direct management of staff time. While the new system had the capacity to be used to measure staff efficiency and overall labour costs, it was primarily concerned with a more effective management of clinical tests undertaken by the hospital laboratories.

PBS is a modular system, each module reflecting a different aspect of hospital activity and patient administration: Patient Care Enquiry, Admissions, Microbiology, Pathology, Theatre Management, and so on. For the laboratories we studied, PBS is also a *patient-based* – as opposed to the previous sample-based – record system of all tests carried out in Microbiology and Pathology laboratories. This allows management information data to be collected and bills for contractually agreed work to be produced.

The new system requires all samples to be registered to patients before tests are conducted, whereas previously it was possible to bypass registration, as a paper-based test request form went with the specimen into the laboratory. Once registered, a bar code is produced and placed on the sample: by scanning the bar code the laboratory staff can access the patient's file and enter details about the tests being carried out and the results found. The system also sets protocols for tests – outlining procedures to be followed and the appropriate responses to results. Because the system is Pathology-wide, laboratory staff can also access information on tests on a patient's samples being conducted in other laboratories. It was anticipated that a year after going live PBS would be linked to the hospital information system support (HISS) and this would avoid the need to re-record patient information already entered. The HISS link would also mean that staff on wards could order tests before sending samples to the laboratories and use the system to find out results without having to wait for notification from the laboratories.

Access to the PBS is tightly controlled through the use of passwords. Project Team members have access to alter fields, codes and the look of different windows. Doctors and other senior medical staff have access to validate test results before they are sent out to the hospital wards and GPs. Other laboratory staff have access to read information and enter test results and patient information.

Specification and selection

PBS is the first system at Finlay purchased for *common* use in all the different laboratories. Previously, each laboratory had its own system, some paper, some computer-based and some a mix of the two. In Microbiology the previous computer system had been developed specifically for the PHLS nationally and was used in all UK PHLS laboratories. This system was, however, considered out of date and difficult to support. The decision by senior management in the Microbiology laboratory to become part of the PBS purchase meant that the laboratories at Finlay would be operating a different system from other PHLS laboratories in the region, many of which also decided to purchase new systems around the same time. The decision reflected as well a desire to bring the laboratories at Finlay together and to move from sample-based systems to a single patient-based system which could integrate clinical data on patient tests across all laboratories. In addition, the arrival of the internal market and the contractual relationships the laboratories had with each other and with the hospital necessitated the introduction of common and standard data across the laboratories.

The decision to go for a single system was taken jointly by PHLS senior management and the Pathology Executive Committee – with Pathology agreeing to pay half the costs. A Project Team was then formed, made up of a senior management figure from each laboratory, a representative of hospital administration, and one consultant. The process was guided by procedures laid down by the European Commission and the NHS for major acquisitions of IT. This required the production of a tender document made up of the operational requirements for each laboratory and a business needs case specifying the cost savings made possible by the new system. From a shortlist of bids and after site visits in the UK and the US, the Project Team chose PBS – an American system – from six possible alternatives. PBS itself had previously been rejected by the hospital as its wider information management system (HISS) because it was too expensive. PBS is usually purchased as a whole-hospital system, and Finlay is the only UK hospital using it specifically as a laboratory system. As we shall see shortly, this was to cause some problems during the first stages of implementation.

The purchase of PBS involved a series of compromises and negotiations. Before the purchase, two of the laboratories had unsuccessfully argued that the other six should adopt the system they had recently acquired and reshaped to their needs – for them, the acquisition of PBS would mean much of this work would have been wasted. The laboratories' separate 'wish lists' were modified as the 'collective wish list' of a single unit: as one of the project team remarked, ' they had to lay aside their departmental hats'. At the same time, this process of stabilising around a common set of operating requirements reflected the differential power of different laboratories in the hospital organisation. The most dominant laboratories – such as Cytopathology and Haematology – could ensure that the specification was more likely to meet their central requirements than the minor laboratories, such as Molecular Genetics. In addition, because the system was seen as expensive, the hospital administration (not the laboratories) pruned the contract specification down to 'what they could afford', and in doing so, excised some important facilities the laboratories assumed would be provided.

Since the system was designed as an administrative system for US hospitals, its core structure – based on repeat billing of fee-based patient tests – meant that a patient's specimens could be distributed across multiple account numbers (for payment of tests in the US). This caused possible errors and misunderstanding during the implementation phase. PBS's US heritage also meant that the system was designed to register results electronically, displacing paper-based records; the Project Team did not, however, anticipate that the introduction of PBS would mean the abandoning of paper altogether. Moreover, PBS's US pedigree meant that it did not arrive with the capacity to follow up patients, a legal requirement in some of the laboratories, such as Cytology and Clinical Genetics, where patients may need repeat examinations.

As part of the purchase contract, the suppliers agreed to modify some of the modules and to construct some new ones for the smaller Pathology laboratories. This capacity was to be configured into the system during the implementation phase and could not be properly tested until after going live.

Implementation

Members of the Project Team responsible for purchasing PBS became deeply involved in modifying the system to fit with laboratory requirements. The exact structure and content of the laboratory and patient administration modules within PBS had to be finalised on site. The Team members received little or no help from the hospital's IT department, which was struggling to cope with the implementation of the HISS at the time.

While cabling, hardware and software were installed, members of the Project Team were trained by the PBS suppliers and then expected to customise the system. The Project Team were given access to fix programming problems, and supported via on-line assistance and maintenance from the supplier in the US. Project Team members were, therefore, primarily responsible for redesigning the look and content of the windows to be used by laboratory staff. They also put in place various protocols on access to PBS and regarding laboratory activity. In many respects, therefore, the laboratories had bought the skeleton of a system that they had to flesh out to meet their requirements. The extent of necessary and possible modifications surprised some in the Project Team. The representative from Haematology explained:

> With [PBS], it is so flexible, you can custom so much of it, that was almost a disadvantage, because it meant so much work to do it. Every single person in the laboratory had exactly their own screen designed, exactly their own colours designed, on their screen. Every single doctor in this hospital could have had their own report format if they wished, and it just went on and on and on. We actually had to draw the line and say that we only do this and that.

This power to 'draw the line' to achieve a stable system gave the Project Team interpretative power to define information needs in each laboratory. The collective culture of the smaller laboratories was maintained by inclusive consultation during the customisation. In the larger laboratories, however, management took the lead in defining 'needs' to be met by the system.

The Project Team felt they should secure the support of laboratory staff for the new system during the first few months after purchase before 'going live'. Here the wish to 'consult' the potential users of the system had to be set against a desire to keep control of the development of the system and, indeed, the implementation process. The Team also had to balance the benefits of involving some staff in the development of modules against a requirement to maintain the credibility of the system by underplaying its uncertain and unfinished form.

A room in the basement of the laboratory building was set up with terminals and here the Project Team trained their staff to access the system, find information and enter data. In all, the acquisition process up to the point of 'going live' took eighteen months. All the laboratories – except for one – went live on the same day.

Bancroft University and the MAC system

The system

The acquisition of a new IT system at Bancroft University is distinctive among our case studies since it was the product of *inter*-organisational as well as *intra*-organisational decision-making. The development of a university management and administration system was the result of a national university sector decision rather than of Bancroft's management alone. Consequently, there was less of a clear sense here of why the system was bought or what objectives it was intended to meet than the systems in Brodies or Finlay. This was compounded by the diffuseness of organisational authority at Bancroft and meant that the rationales for the system offered by the various interested groups within the university were not totally coherent across the organisation as a whole.

The new MIS at Bancroft is called the MAC (Management and Administrative Computing) system.[2] This system is, like PBS at Finlay, modular, comprising six components: Student Records, Finance, Physical Resources, Payroll and Personnel, Research and Consultancy, and Management

Information. Each module has a project manager who oversees the running of that module, and a module support officer who solves problems with the module and maintains the data held in it. We will mainly discuss the Student Records and Finance modules.

Student Records is used to maintain data concerning all students registered at the university. Information is transferred into MAC electronically from UCAS (the national university applications agency), and then completed within the university – partly in the Registrar's Department and partly within the academic department where a student is based. The information that academic secretaries must input into MAC includes students' course options, personal tutor and registration for examinations. The system can then be used for searching individual records or for running reports, both centrally and locally.

MAC Finance is used to post all financial transactions that take place in the university – purchases of supplies, sales of goods, student fees and accommodation payments, and so on. The financial elements of other modules also come through Finance, notably the costing and coding of stores items and of research projects. Consequently, there are two kinds of use of this module, as there are with Student Records: inputting and extracting data. With Finance, though, individual users tend to be responsible for just one or other of these uses rather than both. So clerical staff in the Finance Department and the secretaries of laboratory managers in academic departments *input* data into the system regarding research projects, invoices or payments; whilst laboratory managers, heads of department, and central officers such as management accountants *extract* data for organisational and management purposes.

As indicated above, MAC did not enter Bancroft attached to a clear set of organisational objectives, and was seen by many as a step backwards from existing information systems in the university, which consisted of a mixture of paper and computerised systems in the case of Student Records, and a simpler Finance system which we have called KOREA. Nevertheless, there were a number of purposes that management and departmental staff identified MAC as serving. These were, most notably, the role of Student Records in meeting external monitoring and validation requirements, but also the general benefits that were expected to derive from the greater capacity for planning organisational activity that might be achieved with management information. This was something that was seen as a necessary capability in the ever-changing and uncertain university environment.

Specification and selection

The MAC Initiative was established in 1988 by what was then the University Grants Committee (UGC) (this eventually became the Higher Education Funding Councils for England, Wales and Scotland). The objective of this initiative was to encourage universities to co-operate in developing common information systems. The funding councils provided a total of £11.2 million over several years in order to facilitate this. The UGC commissioned consultants to produce a 'Blueprint Document' of university information needs, which was completed in 1989 (University Grants Committee 1989). The 'Blueprint' identified the six areas for which management information was needed, and individual institutions were required to produce a *migration strategy* identifying their own information needs from this 'Blueprint'. On the basis of this process, universities were grouped into *families*, according to common sets of needs that had been identified. Each family then proceeded to define its individual requirements, and commissioned software accordingly. The approaches taken by families varied, from the setting up of a limited company through to the shared development of existing in-house systems (see Goddard and Gayward 1994, Gilmore *et al.* 1994).

Nationally, there is debate over the overall success of the MAC Initiative, since each different family has experienced numerous problems both in the development and design of software and in its implementation (Goddard and Gayward 1994, Gilmore *et al.* 1994, Williams 1995, Mason *et al.* 1998). A key problem has been the unfortunate timing of MAC within the context of the broader changes in the higher education sector that we highlighted in Chapter 1. MAC's system architectures, coding and data structures were overtaken by a number of factors that could not have been anticipated in 1988/9 as MAC was being established, including the progression to university status of the former polytechnics, the general shift to semester-based, modular courses, and the broader move away from the use of terminals linked to mainframe computers towards Windows-based desktop PCs supported by central servers.

Problems of this kind were then replicated and compounded as systems began to be developed within the MAC families. At least two families suffered setbacks at the design and testing stages, resulting partly from the extent to which this was a new experience for both universities and software houses. In the words of one group of participants, 'unwittingly the universities had become forerunners of the new approach of "evolutionary development", with design changes being made during the early stages of implementation' (Gilmore *et al.* 1994: 13).

The family that Bancroft joined was constituted around a shared desire for an integrated, modular system, a specific hardware platform, affordability and early delivery. The family commissioned a software house to produce the system (although in fact two modules were subcontracted out), based on specifications derived partly from the family members' migration strategies, and partly from the closer involvement of a few lead universities from within the family. This was a later source of dissatisfaction for Bancroft staff, who saw the system as compromised by the need to accommodate too many different requirements, when the 'Blueprint' had only envisaged MAC systems providing 85 per cent of any individual university's information needs. Nevertheless, Bancroft itself only took a marginal role in defining the system's specifications – one or two senior staff took part in early discussions, but soon dropped out of the process. Bancroft thus lost the opportunity of shaping at an early stage the system they would then adopt, missing, for example, the possibility of developing its own in-house systems for the whole family. Instead, along with other family members, Bancroft contracted with the software house to purchase the system's modules, which were then supplied over two or three years during the mid-1990s.

Implementation

Of our case studies, MAC was the one that took the longest time between conception and implementation – eight years from the UGC's commissioning of the 'Blueprint' until the Finance module went live at Bancroft.[3] The implementation of MAC within Bancroft was staggered over three years, module by module. The order of implementation was determined partly by the availability of the modules from the supplier, and partly by internal factors, notably how badly a new system was needed in any particular area. Hence Student Records was implemented first because the information systems in the Registrar's Department were in urgent need of updating, whilst Finance was delayed since a new Finance system had been purchased only a few years before MAC. This rationale was later regarded as a mistake by many, who saw Finance as the pivot around which the other modules needed to be placed – hence it was commonly believed that many of the problems with MAC derived from not implementing Finance first.

The implementation of Student Records was staggered, with the progressive addition of new intake years of undergraduates, and then postgraduates. During the two years that followed this initial implementation, an organisational management and support structure for the system was established – partly following dissatisfaction with the existing management of the system and partly as a result of a general review of the university's information systems. The university's IT Steering Group oversaw the system under the leadership of a new, Pro-Vice Chancellor (PVC). He brought in an overall system manager, module leaders for each of the modules being implemented, and module support officers who were responsible for the integrity of the data and for helping and encouraging end-users. Technical support was provided by the Management Information Systems Department, which was merged with Computer Services as part of the IT review. It was this department that met up periodically with users at other universities to discuss problems and solutions, and which implemented the upgrades which came once or twice a year from the suppliers. A monthly Consultation Forum for users of Student Records was also instituted at this point.

The second module to be implemented was Physical Resources, which unlike Student Records was contained mostly within one department, Estates, and hence proved less problematic. Then Finance went live, two years after Student Records, along with Research and Consultancy and the financial components of other systems. The Personnel module was the only one not to have gone live during the time of our research, although this was in process by our last visit.

Problems to do with producing reports from MAC, in both Student Records and Finance, were addressed with the implementation of the 'Data Warehouse' alongside MAC. This was produced in-house by the MIS Department, following consultation with other organisations where data warehousing had been developed. Phase One of Data Warehouse went live in the summer of 1996, involving the downloading each night of all data on MAC as flat files. Any user with access could then upload this data the following morning and import it into a spreadsheet or database, bearing in mind that they would be working with slightly out-of-date information. Phase Two of Data Warehouse, which went live in spring 1997, kept the downloaded MAC data on-line, eliminating the need for users to upload it themselves. Further phases were planned, with the aim, for example, of allowing images as well as text to be stored – this would make it feasible for the Data Warehouse to replace completely the paper student files held in academic departments, including student photographs.

Conclusions

In each of our case studies the acquisition of a new management information system required a major investment of resources. Strategic managers saw new technology as a route to the modernisation of the organisation. We can also see from the outlines above that the initial acquisition and implementation of the systems was difficult, messy and drawn out. In each case the technology acquisition had been rigorously costed and planned; nevertheless, the exact role and benefits of the system remained open to clarification or renegotiation.

In each case a system was 'bought in' from outside the organisation and then unblackboxed and developed further as a sociotechnology by managers and IT professionals. This further development was shaped by a complex range of factors and interests and was influenced by assumptions about the organisation and 'the users'. During the process of further development, actors wrestled with ambiguities around, firstly, to what extent the system was able to be customised and, secondly, when the system could be said to be finished and ready to be passed on to end-users. These were not neatly resolved when any of the systems went live.

We can also see in each case a perception amongst implementers of 'the users' as a potential problem, and of the requirement to sell them the benefits of the system and enlist them in the implementation. Here as well there is a potential conflict between the promotion of a finished system, control of implementation and the requirement to continue modifying systems once they enter users' lives. Instabilities and uncertainties remained relating to the role and future of the system. This is most striking at Bancroft University, where discussions about replacing the MAC system were well under way before the existing system had been fully implemented. Much remained to be resolved as the systems entered the lives of end-users.

The chapters in the next section will explore in detail the engagement between the Staff Organiser, PBS and MAC and their end-users. As earlier parts of this chapter and Chapter 1 have argued, these systems encompassed much more than technical features – they are best understood as *sociotechnologies*. The shape and role of these sociotechnologies already exhibited a degree of obduracy by the time they reached the user; this was formed in the context of wider conditions of possibility and further shaped during the stages of specification, selection and implementation outlined above. But these sociotechnologies were to be further developed – de- and re-stabilised – as they were integrated into local organisational settings. Users had to be enrolled into the system. As they incorporated it into their organisational lives and individual and group projects, they also contributed to the construction of its usability and utility. Hence in each of our three cases, going live was only the start of a complex set of processes that changed the technologies, the organisations and the users.

Notes

1   This critique of SST is also applicable to the sociology of scientific knowledge (SSK) from which, as stated above, many SSTers derive (see Ashmore and Richards 1996).
2   MAC is the only one of our three systems for which we have not given a pseudonym. The familiarity of our audience with university systems, and the need to contextualise the Bancroft MAC story within the national setting of the MAC Initiative, would make it difficult to anonymise the system convincingly. At the same time, the large number of organisations which acquired MAC means there is little risk of the system's identity compromising the anonymity of our actual research site.
3   The timeframe for implementation has varied considerably across the university sector as a whole – some universities had MAC installed far earlier than Bancroft, whilst others failed to complete implementation. Many have even abandoned their MAC systems altogether, although this is not the place to evaluate the MAC Initiative as a whole (for this, see Mason *et al.* 1998).

Part II

Case studies in techno-organisational change

3 Closing and reopening the black box

This first empirical chapter is concerned with the MAC system at Bancroft University. It examines how, following the implementation of the system, the organisation and the technology at Bancroft were shaped and reshaped together in what was – as we have indicated in Chapters 1 and 2 – a very messy process of techno-organisational change. This process involved taking a generic, delocalised, sector-wide system and then localising it within a particular setting. It also involved struggles among different organisational groupings over the control and direction of change.

In order to understand this process, we will focus here on three interrelated issues. Firstly, we will draw on the *black box* metaphor that was used in Chapter 2, looking at how the system was blackboxed, unblackboxed and reblackboxed several times as it became embedded within the organisation. Secondly, we will look more closely at another issue discussed in Part I of the book; that is, the tension between *delocalisation and centralisation* of technology and authority on the one hand, and *localisation and autonomy* on the other. This was played out at Bancroft in relation especially to the differences between the assumptions about organisational authority that were built into MAC, and those held by certain groups of staff. Thirdly, we will be addressing the ways in which both the blackboxing of MAC and the central–local tensions that emerged with its implementation highlight the importance of *enrolling users* in the organisational adoption of technology. We will explore how the managers of the MAC implementation found ways of bringing on board certain – but by no means all – groups of users. Across these three issues, then, there is a further tension in our account of techno-organisational change between the desire of managers to seek and impose centralised standards, and their need to negotiate change with users.

These negotiations place different organisational groupings in a variety of roles and positions as participants of change, some finding themselves more able to act than others. In Chapters 4, 5 and 6 we explore this differentiation in terms of professionalism, organisational cultures and gender identities. In this chapter, though, we focus on the structural dimensions of techno-organisational change, notably the different positions of staff within university authority structures. Linked to this are how closely individuals' roles in the organisation relate to its 'core business', in this case teaching and research, and also the meaning attached to their geographical and spatial location within the organisation – although what feels like a great distance from the centre at one organisation may be no distance at all, in a literal sense, at another. We will show, then, how this complexity of location, space and authority at Bancroft resulted in different staff having widely contrasting relationships to, and abilities to influence, change.

The chapter is structured as follows. In the next section, we will examine how the black box of MAC was constructed, deconstructed and reconstructed as it was passed from national to local contexts, focusing in particular on assumptions about centralisation and standardisation that were built into the system at an early stage. We will then look at the very different organising narrative of local autonomy that underpinned academic life at Bancroft, notably the understandings that academic and related staff held about their role within the university. We will examine how the tension between standardisation and centralisation on the one hand, and autonomy and localisation on the other, was played out, focusing on two modules of MAC and their users. Comparing the different experiences of these groups throws some light on the question of why certain users have more capacity than others to influence the direction of techno-organisational change – in other words, why some can open up the black box of technology and reconfigure what is inside, whilst others have no choice but to accept the black box as it is.

The black box of the MAC system

Central to our analysis in this chapter are the ways in which organisational technology solidifies around certain assumptions, and how challenges to these assumptions can lead to a reconfiguring of the technology, of the organisation and of the groups within it. This draws particularly on the notion that certain aspects of technology can become blackboxed and taken for granted. Assumptions about the nature of a technology, about the setting in which it will be placed, or about its users within that setting can be 'built' into the system and thus shape or constrain how it is then used. In Akrich's terms, certain meanings, uses and values will have been *inscribed* into technology in the design process (Akrich 1992). Once this is done, the technology can be regarded as a blackboxed amalgamation of the material artefact with pre-scribed rules for its use and assumed properties of its users (Woolgar 1991b). If this blackboxing together of the material and the social is left unchallenged, a kind of technological momentum develops, as an infrastructure is formed around it that both reinforces and reproduces that taken-for-granted state, making it appear fixed, 'obdurate', and less open to reversal. Nevertheless, black boxes *are* frequently reopened, although little has been said in the sociology of technology about what happens when the obduracy of technology is reversed (Rosen 1998, Hommels 1998). This is what we will explore at Bancroft, as the opening, closing and reopening of the MAC system was carried out several times by a variety of different groupings, with differentiated effects for different groups of users.

Openings and closings of the MAC black box

The story of the MAC Initiative in British universities involved a multi-layered set of social constructions of the technology at a number of organisational and political levels. At each stage in the life of MAC it was blackboxed at one level within the higher education sector, only to need reconstructing and re-embedding at the next. It was by no means the case that the system was entirely transformed at any one of these points, since many aspects of the system remained continuous throughout. Nevertheless, each stage of this process affected subsequent reshapings of the system, so that it had been closed and then reopened again a number of times prior to its final implementation within universities. At the point of implementation, too, it was necessary to open up the black box again in order to localise it – and once more, whilst much remained constant from the generic version, MAC as a whole was transformed as it was established as a localised system.

The history of the MAC Initiative – detailed in Chapter 2– indicates how drawn out and complex the process of blackboxing and reblackboxing the system was, involving a progressive shift from the more abstract to the more concrete, and from the more universal to the more local. MAC began life on paper, as a proposal put together and discussed by government agencies. This policy document was then opened up for scrutiny by consultants and universities themselves, and reconstructed in the form of design specifications for a generic system, the MAC 'Blueprint Document' (University Grants Committee 1989). Already, then, what was at this stage little more than a broadly conceived plan had gone through two different constructions. Following this, MAC's form and meaning became less uniform, as different versions of it were developed separately. Universities were grouped into four 'families', each family extracting from the 'Blueprint' whichever features it felt it required in order then to build its own MAC system. This entailed deciding, for example, how integrated the six modules of MAC should be, which software language to write it in, and which hardware platform to run it on, as well as how much of a university's information needs were required to be met by this one system. Each family then followed its own paths towards developing a finished system, for example by first commissioning software engineers to produce a system to their specifications, and then testing it until it was possible to sign it off as acceptable.

The design and specification of the four different versions of MAC up until the point of local implementation within specific universities were, then, the work of a range of actors – the family management teams that oversaw the process; lead universities that took on a role in first helping to shape the product and then testing it; the software engineers commissioned to write the systems and respond to lead universities' feedback; and the various management and IT consultants who helped the whole process along (Goddard and Gayward 1994, Gilmore *et al.* 1994).

What these actors were constructing, in a collective way, was a *delocalised* system, designed to suit perhaps as many as twenty disparate institutions. Once MAC had passed from a family to individual universities, though, each institution underwent a very different kind of implementation (besides our own account of Bancroft, we know of two other, not entirely dissimilar, accounts of local implementations, in Pollock 1998 and Sillince and Mouakket 1998). The systems had to be *localised*, tailored to the particular needs, assumptions and practices of that university. In effect, what had begun as a single artefact at the level of the University Grants Committee had diversified by the time of local implementations into a variety of heterogeneous systems, each peculiar to its own organisation – something that does not appear to have been fully appreciated or anticipated by either the UGC in commissioning MAC, or the MAC Managing Team that they appointed (Mason *et al.* 1998).

What are the implications of this process for local implementation? How did the progressive blackboxing of MAC – first by the UGC, then in the 'Blueprint', and finally by the families and their software consultants – then impact on the ability of users within a university to make the system part of their everyday environment? We focus in this chapter on one particular dimension of this, the standardisation of information and centralisation of control that MAC required. The blackboxing process that took place as MAC progressed from a national to a family product always involved a degree of centralisation and standardisation. Standardisation of information across the whole university sector was a crucial motivating force behind the concept of MAC. Nevertheless, whilst the resulting management infomation system were intended to meet standard requirements at the broad sectoral level, the grouping of universities into families provided a mediating position between the central and the local, allowing for some variation among the four families. As the specification and design of family products became more firm, there was, though, a further fixing within these individual versions of MAC of standards that had been set centrally at either the family or 'Blueprint' level. Each individual university was subsequently faced with a system whose design had taken account of its needs at two different points during the process (during the consultations that preceded firstly the 'Blueprint' and secondly the formation of the families), but which was now an amalgamation of the needs of up to twenty universities, and thus wholly acceptable to none of them (Goddard and Gayward 1994, Gilmore *et al.* 1994, Sillince and Mouakket 1998).

On acquiring MAC, then, Bancroft found itself in possession of a system that made certain assumptions about university organisation and structure which only partially matched assumptions held about organisational life by university members. Most significantly, the system embodied assumptions about the centralisation of control and the standardisation of information at universities which clashed with a narrative of local departmental autonomy that had, as we will show, a traditionally privileged status within academic life.

We will turn now to a discussion of centralisation and standardisation in technology before examining in more detail the narrative of academic autonomy.

Centralisation and standardisation

As suggested in Chapter 1, centralisation and standardisation underpin the very concept of a management information system, since generating information that will facilitate the analysis and further planning of organisational activities requires both the practices of inputting data, and the data itself, to be standardised to a significant degree (Ewart 1985). It is understandable, then, that assumptions about the form of university information, and about who should be in control of it, were built into the MAC system, both before MAC arrived at Bancroft and then in the way it was then set up within the university. This led, however, to a number of tensions in the local implementation process. The dynamic of localisation and delocalisation was in fact played out in the MAC story at two parallel levels. Firstly, the MAC Initiative as a sector-wide development can be seen as an attempt by national actors to impose standardisation and central control on individual universities; secondly, there were tensions *within* Bancroft as the university's administrative centre was seen to be trying to impose central control and standardisation on non-central departments, including some service departments as well as the academic departments we focus on here.

These two interlinked dynamics were evident – often at the same time – in many ways as MAC was deployed at Bancroft. For example, the particular data fields available on a student's record in MAC reflected national needs for student information that had been defined through the 'Blueprint Document' and then through family-derived specifications. They did not necessarily match the needs of any individual university, and then within Bancroft they did not reflect the needs of local users in academic departments; the latter might require information about the student which was of no relevance for central administrators in supporting funding or statistical objectives. Another example, from the Finance module, was the fact that MAC assumed there was only one central store for stationery or scientific equipment for the whole institution, whereas Bancroft actually had both central stores and local departmental stores. Because of such disjunctions between different contexts – national or local, central or departmental – acquiring a new management information system is likely, by its nature, to require a reorganisation of information to meet standards which have been 'built' into the technology.

Discussion of standardisation within SST studies shows that this concept can apply not just to information and information tools such as MAC, but also to a wide range of scientific and technological knowledge, equipment and practices. Schmidt and Werle (1998) discuss how standards have emerged through negotiations among technical, political and commercial actors in the railways, electricity, telephony and their main case study of telecommunications. Mallard (1998) examines the different dimensions involved in the standardisation of scientific measurement, which requires being able to ensure consistency both among different scientists all using their own instruments, and of identical instruments used in different settings. This science of measurement, metrology, aims at 'stabilizing measurements in time and space, ensuring that instruments give stable and uniform results in different places and at different moments' (ibid.: 594). Timmermans and Berg show how the establishment of protocols in medical practice aims to make actions 'comparable over time and space' (1997: 273), ensuring that the same procedures will be followed in all appropriate situations.

These authors all show how protocols and standards emerge contingently out of negotiations among a variety of actors and interests. This often brings together actors at different local, national and even international levels, highlighting the economic, social and political dimensions of what at first glance might seem purely technical decisions (Schmidt and Werle 1998). Other important aspects of standardisation include meeting legal requirements and maintaining credibility for the standards (Mallard 1998). As Mallard points out, the objective of standards setters such as metrologists is 'to specify, purify and stabilize the relations between an instrument and its environment' (ibid.: 593, Star 1989).

Stabilising standards is not, though, a straightforward accomplishment. The promoters of a particular standard must enrol others to their cause and then ensure that the standard is maintained and adhered to. Timmermans and Berg argue that a crucial aspect of this is the relationship between a new standard, or protocol, and the pre-existing infrastructures, procedures and practices which will be changed or replaced. For them, it is crucial that rather than attempt to displace preceding methods entirely, new protocols need 'to incorporate and extend those routines' (1997: 274). Timmermans and Berg show how the oncology and resuscitation protocols they studied involved a 'process of grafting [the protocols] on to a strongly pre-configured world' (ibid.: 283), building on and developing existing theories and techniques. Standards which defy such traditions are likely to face severe opposition, and perhaps fail to achieve their goal of standardised practices.

The authors we have discussed here tend to see standardisation as a collective project, perhaps led by particular actors and involving some struggle over definitions, but achieved only through a common acceptance and valuing of particular standards. From a slightly different viewpoint, though, standardisation can be seen as a means by which particular actors or groups of actors achieve *control*, often at a distance. Telecommunications committees, medical experts, and legislative bodies responsible for measurement all use standards as a means of controlling the activities of others, who are often far removed from themselves in space or time. Law terms this phenomenon 'long-distance control' (1986a), and argues that this is achieved by means of a combination of documents and instruments that contain distilled knowledge and experience, and the embodied skills of the people who represent the 'centre' at its peripheries. These 'drilled persons' ensure that standards are maintained, however distant they are from the source of standardisation. Despite Law's focus on how central control is achieved, then, his argument is consistent with that of Timmermans and Berg, that central objectives are accomplished locally. The notion of regulation introduced in Chapter 1 also helps to understand this accomplishment, since drilled persons are both regulated by the centre they represent, and must also, in a local setting which might be some distance from that centre, internalise and reinterpret standards subjectively if they are to enrol others to the central cause. Centralisation and standardisation are, then, intertwined, as shown in the way that Law's case study of medieval navigation (1986) depended not just on precision in documentation and instrumentation, but also on both the external and subjective aspects of control.

With the MAC system, standardisation and centralisation were together built into its design at the universal (national) level, but these were then reinforced locally as those implementing the system at Bancroft continued to prioritise its centralising and standardising elements. However, as the system was distributed across the university, another dimension of universal–local relations came into play, between the university's administrative centre and its academic departments. Central (and national) assumptions came into conflict with competing departmental assumptions based on an organising narrative of autonomy that underpinned university life for many staff. We will outline this narrative before going on to explore how the black box of MAC was opened up in attempts to resolve this tension between different assumptions.

Narratives of authority and autonomy in university life

As indicated in Chapter 1, British universities have traditionally been diffuse organisations, with a high degree of autonomy over their own internal affairs which was matched within their organisational structure by the autonomy of individual departments. The authority structures of universities are complex, and until recently there has been relatively little scope for any one section of a university to dictate the actions of any other. As Moodie and Eustace write (discussing the situation in the 1960s and 1970s), universities are characterised by:

> an untidy diffusion of responsibility and a proliferation of centres of initiative and decision-making which are related to one another in ways which are not neatly bureaucratic. There is no direct and comprehensive chain of command, and the notion of an order being issued from one person to another is generally felt to be alien to the way in which British universities should govern their affairs.
>
> (1974: 21)

Within this context, Moodie and Eustace consider academic departments to be the basic unit of a university, a situation which has emerged since the nineteenth century. They regard departments as the locus firstly of autonomous academic decision-making, and secondly of academic staff's primary identification within the organisation. Departments are centres of administration and governance, organising the labour and time of their staff, providing and monitoring equipment, and allocating funding for teaching and research. Departments are also the basic unit of representation in wider university governance structures (ibid.: 60-1). The autonomy of departments, they argue, 'makes of every university a "federal" structure rather than a strongly centralized system' (ibid.: 61).

Nevertheless, there is more to a university than just its academic departments. The increasing pressures on universities outlined in Chapter 1 have underlined a growing uncertainty within the sector. Consequently, some writers have identified 'management' as an increasingly important component of university life (Lockwood and Davies 1985), with a greater role, therefore, for non-academic managers. Nevertheless, universities have remained complex organisations whose authority structures continue to allow for only 'limited manageability' (ibid.: 40), with a tendency towards organisational conservatism that is maintained by features such as the complicated committee structures that any new decision has to pass through. Of central importance also is the independence of academic departments, whose strength continues to provide 'clear limits to effective institutional authority and management (and thus to "top-down" innovation), unless that authority is merely the transmission into the university of external requirements' (ibid.: 36).

This account of universities continues to apply in the 1990s, even in an institution such as Bancroft, where governance structures were being reviewing during the period of our research. Universities have a comparatively lax form of management regulation, and the sharp contrast to our other case studies, in particular Brodies, is very striking. Despite the rise of managerialism and the dramatic changes in the higher education sector of the 1990s, MAC was introduced into a setting at Bancroft in which the tradition of departmental autonomy still held sway among academic staff as an organising narrative. Those working in central administration had different experiences, being used to a tradition not of autonomy but of meeting objectives set by central managers and external bodies. Whilst central managers could compel their own staff to comply with their requirements, they lacked the same ability to compel academic and related staff. They therefore had to find ways to give MAC meaning for these users if they wished to enrol them into this techno-organisational process.

Central–local tensions over MAC

Establishing and maintaining standards

As indicated above, in order to use MAC effectively, there was a requirement to rethink significantly how the university ordered its information – ranging from the coding of items held in laboratory stores to the titles of teaching modules. The adoption of MAC therefore resulted in a vast amount of labour being expended in firstly developing standards for data entry, and secondly ensuring adherence to these standards.

Two episodes in the acquisition and implementation process illustrate this point, and demonstrate how departmental staff helped in the process of standardisation. One example pertains to the Finance module, the other to Student Records. Although Bancroft is a single organisation, those responsible for MAC had to manage information across a diverse range of users; consequently, it was necessary in the first place to bring these groups together in order to establish common features of MAC such as coding standards, notably within the Finance module relating both to stores items and to research project codes. In particular, the laboratory manager from one science department worked with the central supplies officer to establish a common set of codes across the major university stores. Despite the many hours of work this entailed, MAC coding structures were still found later to be highly problematic in a number of ways. As we have already mentioned, the sub-system in MAC for stores was found to assume the university had one central store rather than a number of local stores, and it also lacked any easy method for coding non-stock purchases. Codes themselves were found to be overlong and cumbersome, and several staff in both academic departments and central administrative offices criticised the haphazard and analytically inadequate way in which the coding structure had been set up. There were also complaints that data entry in the system was vulnerable to error. Despite the effort that went into establishing standards, then, these still proved highly problematic, satisfying neither central nor local actors. We will return to these kinds of issue in our examination of usability and utility in Chapter 7.

As Timmermans and Berg make clear (1997), at least as important as the establishment of standards is the work that must be done over a long period of time in order to *maintain* them. Standardisation is not brought into effect simply by identifying codes, but requires a great deal of on-going maintenance work to regulate adherence to the standards. This was clearly evident in the Student Registry, where part of the relationship with academic departments centred on this need for constant reiteration of the organising practices around information required by the centre. MAC's Student Records module posed problems for standardising academic-related information, not at the detailed technical level of coding structures but at the more basic level of needing to ensure across all departments that the same categories of data were being entered into the same system in the same way. However, secretaries in academic departments initially prioritised their own local systems over MAC because of the difficulties they experienced using the new system. This caused problems for Registry staff, who therefore sought ways to change secretaries' working practices. A turning point came in the academic year prior to our first visits to Bancroft, when the examinations officer had begun to use the data in MAC for setting up examination halls. With MAC, courses had been allocated centralised numbers that indicated which method of assessment was to be used, whilst individual students' records in the database identified which modules they were to be examined in. It was thus theoretically possible to pull from MAC a list of all students taking any particular exam, and set up the hall appropriately. However, as several people told us, some twenty or thirty students turned up for exams to find they were not expected. The reason for this, according to the support officer for the Student Records module:

> lay . . . in departments maintaining their own database, because what was happening, the examinations officer and his assistant would be over at [the examinations] hall and they would phone up the department concerned and say, he's on my database, but he wasn't on MAC. So they were maintaining their own database but not MAC.

The solution to this problem was a strongly worded letter to all academic secretaries from the PVC who headed the university's IT Steering Group, resulting apparently in 100 per cent accuracy the following year.

What these two cases highlight is the need for constant policing of standards and of coding structures if these are to be adhered to, and the work that consequently goes into maintaining standardisation beyond the point at which those standards were set. The diffuse authority structures at Bancroft meant that whilst management regulation could be brought to bear on staff to a certain degree, in stressing the need to use the system properly, it was more effective for management to invoke the subjective regulation of secretaries themselves through making them aware of the negative effects on their students of chaos during exams. Subjective regulation is not, though, always so easy to invoke as in the above incident. In the following sections, we will examine other ways in which local users came to some kind of accommodation with MAC, either through benefits that were provided by the centre, or through their own need to ensure the integrity of MAC's data.

Local autonomy and central control

Standardisation is facilitated by centralised management of data – by a central body that can dedicate itself to ensuring that standards are maintained, even if, referring back to Law (1986), that is carried out by local agents. In the case of Bancroft, the role of the centre in managing MAC was perceived in academic departments as a means less of facilitating standardisation than of controlling and trying to change local practices. For departmental staff, standardisation was felt to mean for the most part a threat to their autonomy, which then raised questions over whose needs the new system was designed to meet.

MAC's introduction in many universities – including Bancroft – was accompanied by a relatively small investment in the extra staffing that new IT systems usually require (Mason *et al.* 1998). Consequently, whilst administrative managers endorsed the centralisation of control that was blackboxed into the system, at the same time they sought to overcome the extra work involved in running a new integrated database by decentralising the work needed to maintain MAC's data. Managers in the Student Registry required academic secretaries in departments to input some of the data that they needed in order to produce reports for HESA, whilst in the Finance Department it was planned that financial reports that had previously been produced each month for departmental laboratory managers would no longer be made available centrally – instead, laboratory managers would be taught how to produce these for themselves.

The result of these changes was a high degree of reflection about the organisational distribution of responsibilities. Staff in academic departments mostly continued to adhere to the narrative of autonomy we have discussed, focusing on their freedom to act in whichever ways they felt best suited their local priorities and responsibilities, especially in relation to teaching and research. Against this, it was felt that the MAC system represented an increasing centralisation of control over information in the university that prioritised the needs of the centre over those of academic departments, whilst at the same time placing onto departmental staff much more of the responsibility for maintaining that data. This was resented among academic-related staff, not only as an imposition of external control but also as a strain on resources and time, since departments – just like the centre – were rarely able to take on additional staff to cope with the increased workload. For these staff, then, MAC represented a reduction of the control they had over their own information and over their work, and this constituted a direct challenge to the autonomy that was for them a key feature of the organisation.

Perhaps a little ironically, the narrative of local autonomy did hold some sway at the centre too. Senior administrative staff were proud to identify departmental autonomy as a unique feature of how Bancroft implemented MAC compared to other members of the same MAC family. One central actor told us that that the allocation of new responsibilities to academic secretaries had been seen as an attempt to '[bring] the users in . . . to [move] the responsibility and the ownership out to the users' (MIS officer). Another aspect of this was a feeling that 'in the past [departments have] been spoon-fed enough to survive on, really we want to expand on their own information that's available to them, and enable them to be more autonomous really in their own decisions'. There was also at the centre a view that control of finances should be distinguished from the freedom to make policy decisions:

> I think departments have a lot of freedom, although interestingly enough, that freedom is not necessarily measured in the amount of money that they're given from the centre. They have a lot of freedom I suspect because they are able to pursue and develop policies and then come to the centre and ask for funding – and they will, by and large, providing it is a good idea, get it.

The Finance officer who said this was quite happy for academic departments to make decisions about how to conduct their activities, but wanted to retain for the centre ultimate control of finances, including, 'it has to be said, the opportunity to exercise more control if it wants it' (ibid.).

In contrast to this central view, for departmental staff the new responsibilities for information that came with MAC embodied the standardising, and more importantly the centralising, assumptions that underpinned the MAC system. Crucial to this perception was the feeling that whilst responsibilities for data entry had been dispersed, decisions about the method and timing of data entry were still being handed down from the centre with no space for discussion.

This struggle indicates an ambivalence among central managers and MAC support staff at the centre between centralisation and localisation. As rhetoric, the narrative of autonomy had some resonance at the centre. However, in relation to day-to-day organising practices, it was far more important for central actors to uphold the integrity of centrally required data than that of the narrative of departmental autonomy:

> When we started off one of the things that was emphasised, I got huge groups of people together and said look, this is an integrated system, you may not want this data but you're responsible for putting it into the system, somebody downstream has got to use it, you've got to make sure it's clean.
>
> (Senior Finance officer)

In this context, standardisation was felt to be crucial, and this then entailed centralised control, even if that required overriding local autonomy. As one of the key implementers of MAC told us in response to being asked whether departments felt they owned the system: 'they have a responsibility to maintain the data'. Supporting central needs was seen as more important, then, than having a sense of local ownership, and ownership of the system was felt in academic departments to lie more with the centre than locally.

Within the centre, it was those staff with the most direct responsibility for MAC who tended to be the ones most closely aligned with the MAC assumption of centralisation, since it was these staff whose work was most dependent on the data entered into the system. The role of the Student Registry, especially, in cajoling academic secretaries to use MAC as prescribed gave the Registry a key role in trying to regulate departmental organising practices. This role reflected the varying importance MAC held in the work of different groups of staff. Those staff whose work depended more on MAC were seen by departmental actors as getting the most benefit from it. In contrast to academic secretaries, the Registry was highly dependent on MAC data for its twice-yearly 'HESA snapshots'. These provided data on student registrations that fed directly into the annual funding allocated to Bancroft by HEFCE (the Higher Education Funding Council for England). We were told by the person in the Registry responsible for compiling the HESA snapshots that 'if we don't get our statistical information in then it's a £1,000 a day fine after a certain date'. This made it essential for the Registry to ensure this data was completely accurate. From their point of view, academic secretaries had to 'get rid of this attitude, [central administration] and departments, we're all in it together'. Of course, from academic departments' point of view, that 'togetherness' was constructed around central rather than local conceptions of need. It was also underpinned by a different set of imperatives to those which shaped departmental information use; that is, requirements that were external to the organisation but which had explicit financial implications – although departmental staff *were* sensitive to this need at the centre to meet external requirements.

Academic departments, central administration and the IT Steering Group

Academic departments form only a part of Bancroft's organisational structure, although they account for the majority of staff, and the relationship of academic and related staff to the centre is just one dimension of a complex set of intra-organisational relationships. It is important therefore to consider a number of questions: why was the issue of autonomy and centralisation so prominent generally in the accounts we were given about the acquisition of MAC – by both departmental and administrative respondents? Why did the problems with MAC of staff located outside academic departments not attract as much central concern as those of academic-related staff, especially academic secretaries? And why did the concerns of non-academic staff play a far less significant role in the local reshaping of the system?

A key component in the answer to these questions lies in the power relations and organisational hierarchies of the university. Academic-related staff enjoy a privileged position regarding organisational narratives about the university's 'core business' of teaching and research. However, the playing out of techno-organisational change involves a far more complex interaction of organisation and technology than simply translating existing power structures onto a new information system. This will be brought out by our examination of how different groups even *within* academic departments had significantly different experiences in the degree to which they felt their information needs were met. Of MAC's six modules, we will be concentrating here on just two – Student Records and Finance. Each of these was problematic for many of the staff using it, despite quite contrasting programmes of implementation. We will trace the very different ways in which problems were dealt with for the two modules, in order to highlight how the shaping and reshaping of this technology were intertwined with the shaping and reshaping of organisational authority structures.

Staff in an organisation can hold a variety of different identities based on different organisational and extra-organisational groupings. Particular groups of staff respond to techno-organisational change in different ways. Our concern here is with identities based on structural location within the organisation, and the status that can be afforded by certain associations among different occupational groupings – in this case, by the way non-academic staff in academic departments nevertheless adopt identities associated with the academic narrative of autonomy. The story at Bancroft shows that this appeal to status by association is not sufficient in itself to allow a group to achieve its objectives, and the achievement of such objectives can be more, or less, successful for different occupational groupings. Nevertheless, when accompanied by an important strategic role in the upkeep of information on a system, an association with the organisation's 'core business' can provide a crucial boost to a group's demands for benefits.

Academic secretaries and student records

There is a strong consensus across all staff in Bancroft that it is teaching and research that are the primary role – the 'core business' – of the university. The work of academic secretaries clearly underpins this 'core business', and it was significant that secretaries understood their role within the university, through their close association with academics, in terms of the narrative of autonomy. Since the university's structure, as we have discussed, prevented central actors from being able absolutely to compel secretaries to use MAC in the ways that the centre required, it was important for the IT Steering Group to take seriously the criticisms made by secretaries over the implementation and subsequent working of MAC. Since the centre was dependent on the data it required secretaries to input, to ignore their concerns could be damaging not just to the core business of teaching and research but also to the integrity of MAC data, for outputs such as the HESA snapshots. These concerns consequently fed into the eventual reshaping of MAC such that the system came to suit secretaries' perceived information needs and workloads better. Other staff were not so lucky, though. We will look shortly at two groups of staff whose concerns were far less effective in bringing about change. Here, though, we will examine the way MAC highlighted the relationship between secretaries and the centre, in terms of the tension between autonomy and centralised control.

Academic and related staff, along with some central administrators, generally believed that prior to the introduction of MAC academic departments had enjoyed a high degree of autonomy from the centre. It is interesting to unpick quite what this autonomy entailed. Prior to MAC, far less departmental information had been required centrally. The administration of teaching and research in academic departments had been seen as autonomous, with academic secretaries responsible for supporting teaching staff and students, and to a lesser extent research staff. Central requirements did not impinge on this except for the periodic filling in of forms. In particular, the centre did not constrain the activities of departmental staff in terms of what they did beyond filling in these forms, nor how they organised their own information. The introduction of MAC changed this, reshaping the university's conception of its information needs, constructing needs at the centre that did not exist beforehand and new ways in which these 'needs' were to be met locally. Secretaries were now required to enter certain data fields onto MAC, often constrained in terms of when and how this could be done. This led to a high degree of recalcitrance and even resistance which we will examine below.

Secretaries' sense of departmental autonomy in the face of these new requirements was expressed in a number of different ways and embodied several issues around organisational relations and authority structures. To begin with, there was a strong sense of resistance to any kind of central interference – as indicated in the examinations story above. MAC was seen very much as an attempt by the centre to interfere locally. Hence there was a reluctance firstly to switch over to new, centralised information systems, and secondly to share information and the responsibility for it with the centre. As two academic secretaries put it:

> One of the problems is that all the departments in the university are very autonomous, and are not inclined to share their knowledge or their information or their systems, unless they're absolutely forced to. Had we been a university which had perhaps a central computing system that everybody used to start with, it would have been much more easy to introduce. It's a whole new culture we've had to learn.

> [Bancroft] is interesting because departments have been terribly autonomous . . . and the plus for the administration in the past has always been that they have been very supportive and departments have taken decisions and the administration has to some extent tried to provide what sort of support they need. A lot of departments have found this [new system] incredibly intrusive, that the administration needs to know these things and they [the departments] don't.

These two quotations indicate some of the complexity of Bancroft's organisational relations, and show how the introduction of MAC came up against an already-existing organising narrative that underpinned local conceptions of the relationship between central administrative offices and other parts of the university. Since this narrative was founded on notions of local autonomy, decentralisation and separation of academic from administrative work, the problem for those implementing MAC was one of trying at the same time to do two things: firstly, as Timmermans and Berg stressed (1997), to embed the new system within existing organisational structures in order to ensure a smooth implementation, and secondly, to alter the organisation and its narratives in order to accommodate aspects of MAC that did not sit well with autonomy. This endeavour was hindered by a combination of technological and organisational constraints.

Student Records had initially been 'sold' to academic secretaries as an improvement on their existing systems, and many embraced it at that point with enthusiasm. A secretary in a social science department told us:

> when it was announced that there was going to be this database I thought great, that's exactly what I've wanted, I've been sitting around for years thinking I really ought to get my own database going, and then thinking no I can't be bothered, I haven't got the time, I don't really know about this. So when they said they were going to do this I thought, great.

However, up to three years after the initial implementation, academic secretaries generally felt they were only just beginning – with the introduction of the Data Warehouse – to see any benefit from MAC. Overall, MAC was perceived to be an imposition from the centre which allowed the latter to produce information needed for its reports to HESA in a way that minimised the need to invest further staffing resources at the centre.

One important issue for secretaries was their time, and the constraints set on it by the new system – an issue that was identified as important in all our research sites, especially by the staff with most status. Academic secretaries did not have especially high status in Bancroft, except by associating themselves with the narrative of academic autonomy. They thus prioritised their responsibilities to the academic community over the requirements of central administrators. MAC challenged this prioritisation, since the Student Registry required secretaries to take on a number of quite time-consuming data input tasks on the system, whilst constraining them in terms of when they were allowed to do this work. For example, secretaries were required to enter students' module choices into the system, but it was important for the Registry not to do this until the current academic year was completed in the system. Consequently, it was originally only possible for secretaries to enter the following year's module choices quite late in the summer – a time when they were generally either on holiday or dealing with the new year's intake. This was, then, a job that was frequently left undone until it became more convenient. The compulsion from the centre that this kind of job had to be done was one of the factors that meant MAC was resented by academic secretaries, who felt that central administrators were ignoring their claim to autonomy, and undercutting legitimate lines of departmental authority. As one secretary put it:

> they are requiring us to do things at certain times, whereas I consider my line manager as my head of department. They're not asking him if they can ask me to do something, they're coming straight to me and saying you've got to do something.

The implementation of MAC was felt to have overridden the interests of academic departments and their secretaries, whilst providing no benefits to balance against that: 'after a couple of years . . . we haven't got anywhere with it . . . we were putting all this information into [it] and getting absolutely nothing out of it at all'. During the period of our research, this particular problem was solved with the introduction of a new 'preference screen' on the system that allowed academic secretaries to enter the data at any time they chose during the summer term. The Student Records support officer would then transfer the data from this preference screen into the main system, once the system had progressed into the new academic year. It took a long time, though, for the legacy of such problems to disappear – something we only just began to see as our research visits were ending.

Whilst secretaries were unhappy with their new centrally derived responsibilities under MAC, this example shows that the centre did try to find ways of making it less problematic for them. At the same time, the secretaries recognised the *external* obligations being placed on the centre: in one secretary's words, 'if they say they need it, they need it, I'm not arguing with that'. So, whilst they resisted to a great extent the *assumptions* of standardisation and centralisation that were built into MAC, and were hence reluctant to incorporate it into their daily practices, this did not represent an outright rejection of the Registry's need for MAC data.

However, the secretaries' actions with regard to MAC did constitute a clear statement that it provided no benefit to them, and at the same time demonstrated their continued adherence to the narrative of departmental autonomy. Having found early on that MAC did not live up to their expectations for it, academic secretaries chose to maintain their local databases – whether paper or electronic – as a priority. They updated MAC only once they had completed what they saw as more important work, or as a result of direct coercion from the Registry. Academic secretaries' initial 'resistance' to MAC thus took the form not of any explicit refusal to work with it but simply of an indifference to it that left MAC student data insufficiently accurate from the point of view of the Student Registry. On being presented with the black box of the MAC system, academic secretaries thus took a look inside it but then dismissed it as being of no value to them. Those at the centre – notably the Registry and MAC support staff – were faced with a need to construct value for secretaries in order to prevent them from simply closing the black box up again, and ignoring it.

Responding to this challenge was what central MAC support staff had done in introducing preference screens, which were just one example of a range of efforts made to enrol secretaries into using MAC. These included, firstly, improving communications around MAC, for example by including a secretary on the IT Steering Group and setting up a new Consultation Forum for them; secondly, the MIS Department established the Data Warehouse. As we outlined in Chapter 2, this was developed in-house as a means of solving a particular problem with MAC – that it could be very slow in generating reports. Academic secretaries told us stories of having to wait several hours to download data from MAC, which might mean that they no longer needed that information by the time it was ready. In many cases, reports had to be left to run overnight. What happened with the Data Warehouse was that all the data in MAC was downloaded each night so it would be ready for importing on the following day into a standard database, spreadsheet or word processor package in order to produce reports. This meant that one would always be working with yesterday's rather than today's data, but it was available immediately rather than after a long wait.

Although they had not yet had much experience of it whilst we were interviewing them, Data Warehouse was already seen by academic secretaries as a great enhancement of MAC, promising some long-awaited benefits that were expected to make up for the problems they had encountered with MAC itself. Whilst the Data Warehouse itself was not expected to be a perfect solution, it was seen as a very positive development:

> we all feel that at last we're getting something we want out of it. It has this term made my job a lot easier, in just the few ways I've used it.

The Data Warehouse was expected, at the least, to bring the information held on MAC up to the level of reliability that secretaries felt they had with their local systems. With time, it in fact emerged that some secretaries felt they got a great deal of benefit from Data Warehouse, in particular in terms of its speed against MAC. Other secretaries had less use for it – one told us she would probably only need to use it once a term to compile course details. Nevertheless, the introduction of the Data Warehouse, even more so than the other ways in which secretaries were brought on board, was seen by them as evidence that the centre was beginning to take their concerns seriously. As one secretary told us:

> I think they've realised that, and departments, they're being asked to use it, the departments have got to be able to get something out of it. I think that's why the Data Warehouse has been developed. On looking at it it seems to be the answer to all the department's problems.

The effect of the Data Warehouse in helping to enrol academic secretaries clearly involves some ironies. Many secretaries did not actually expect to use it very much, it did not solve the usability problems with MAC itself which were commonly identified as most pressing, and, as we found in our later interviews, some secretaries had failed to find time to attend training courses even a year after it was first introduced. Whilst the Data Warehouse was, then, seen as an effective solution to some of the problems with MAC, its introduction was, more importantly, highly effective in signalling to secretaries a more constructive engagement with their concerns by the university's centre – it indicated the importance to the centre of finding ways of bringing on board this particular group of users. In the next two sections we will discuss other users whose complaints did not receive the same degree of attention, a difference we will try to account for in the conclusion of the chapter.

Laboratory managers and the finance module

Despite sharing with academic secretaries a close identity with the teaching and research-based 'core business' of the university, laboratory managers in science departments had a very different experience with MAC. They were far more exercised by problems of how 'usable' MAC was, because MAC played a much bigger role in their day-to-day work. This is something we will examine in more depth in Chapter 7 in relation to all three of our sites. Laboratory managers also had a more acute sense that whilst they were meeting central needs, the centre was not meeting theirs. In fact, for laboratory managers, certain forms of support that they found crucial to the meeting of their needs prior to MAC were withdrawn during the early implementation period of the Finance module. This resulted in serious grievances against the centre that laboratory managers felt were not being taken seriously.

On a day-to-day level, laboratory managers had very different information needs from academic secretaries. Unlike secretaries, they were concerned about the reliability of MAC data because of the implications this could have for their own departmental information. Their work included overseeing all purchases and stores requisitions within their department, as well as externally funded research projects. Consequently MAC Finance was not just an occasional irritation for them as Student Records was for academic secretaries, since both laboratory managers and their secretaries had to use MAC on a regular day-to-day basis instead of just at occasional set times during the academic year. Like academic secretaries they found the system cumbersome and difficult to use. The secretary of a laboratory manager might have to enter into the MAC Finance module substantial numbers of purchase orders each day, but this was found to be a far more time-consuming and laborious process than it had been under the KOREA system that had preceded MAC, because the structure and organisation of data in MAC were perceived as less intuitive and less easily navigable.

A feature of MAC that became important in how useful it was felt to be by laboratory managers especially was the distinction outlined earlier between entering and extracting data. This was described to us by the Head of MIS as follows:

> There are two phases in place with data of this type. One is what I call enquiry data, and the other one is transaction processed data, and really one is a method of putting data in and the other one is a method of pulling data out. The MAC system was designed for a transaction processing system, convenient screens to put data into the system, so that there are more convenient paths. But we still have the users who require to extract data, operational data, and require management information.

Whilst many of our respondents would have disputed the claim here that trans-action screens in MAC were convenient, laboratory managers certainly found the extraction of data problematic. This was compounded by a decision in the Finance Department no longer to provide them with monthly financial reports, on the grounds primarily that it took up a lot of staff time to produce, separate and then distribute them. Instead, Finance wanted departments to access the data themselves through MAC. This related back to the partial support we have already highlighted that some central actors expressed for the narrative of auton-omy, whilst at the same time actively promoting a centralised system.

MAC Finance went live around the same time as we began our interviews at Bancroft. Consequently, whereas with Student Records we were observing developments some time after the system was initially implemented, with Finance we observed the first year of the system in real time. During that period, central and departmental users wrestled with technical and organisa-tional problems in their endeavours to make the system usable and useful. We also observed the coming on-line of Data Warehouse for Finance, which lagged a little behind the Student Records Data Warehouse.

Problems with the implementation of MAC Finance and the Finance Data Warehouse meant that the switching of responsibility from the centre to depart-ments did not in fact happen as planned. Laboratory managers went for several months without any overall reports at all from Finance – not, it turned out, because of the policy decision, but because of technical difficulties both with MAC Finance and with the Data Warehouse. During that period, laboratory managers were forced to generate their own reports as best they could from the Data Warehouse, or go without the financial information they needed. By the time we spoke to the laboratory manager in our core group of respondents a year after MAC Finance went live, the reporting issue was no longer so central to his dissatisfaction with MAC as were problems over data entry. In a sense, the aim of devolving responsibility for reporting had succeeded by accident, and had also been incorporated into the narrative of departmental autonomy as a case of self-reliance and survival in the face of poor central support:

> I have not had a confirmatory report from the University for at least five months, so whether my accounts tie up with their accounts I have no idea.

> Using the Data Warehouse, any reports you want off it we generate our-selves and I generated mine months ago.
>
> (Laboratory Manager)

Consequently, from the Finance Department's point of view, this change in organising practices from a central to a departmental basis represented a MAC 'success'. The capacity of departments to generate their own information inter-nally had been an underlying objective in the implementation strategy for the Finance module, irrespective of the reasons why this actually came about. This points to a paradox inherent in MAC that we identified earlier, that whilst it centralised both data and control over organising practices, it also had – from the centre's perspective – the potential to enhance the autonomy of departments, by giving them greater access to and control over their own information. For the centre, then, it was not the case that reduced central support diminished departmental autonomy, and by our final visit to Bancroft, a sense was beginning to emerge that MAC might eventually provide some utility for laboratory managers.

Laboratory managers took a longer time, though, to begin to see it like this. Like academic secretaries, they did recognise the difficulties faced at the centre as well as departmentally:

> We have argued the points as we need them, but I appreciate that they have problems as well as us and we can normally cope, although certain things like those fields that are missing on the orders we will keep pressing for as much as possible, get as nasty as possible. But we can normally cope with most things.

Nevertheless, when it came to criticism and complaints about MAC, laboratory managers were noticeably more vocal than secretaries: they were highly critical of the quality of the system, of the initial implementation process, and also of political manoeuvrings among senior staff that they believed to underpin many of the implementation problems experienced.

Laboratory managers were also more cynical than academic secretaries about the IT Steering Group's attempts to improve communications. Secretaries were certainly conscious that their co-option into the process of change management was perhaps motivated more by the need to placate them than to resolve their difficulties:

> I think that they had these MAC meetings, that they're trying, but you do get the feeling that it's 'let the girlies come and talk, but we're not actually going to take any notice of what they say'.

But on the whole, secretaries believed that the Student Registry, which hosted the monthly Consultation Fora where secretaries could air problems and complaints, was genuine in its wish to improve communications and to try to resolve the difficulties being experienced:

Interviewer: Do you go along to the Forum?

Academic Secretary: When I can, yes. In fact I set that up, that was set up for us to protest in the first place, and we got together as a group of secretaries to talk to each other about what problems we had, and then went to present them to central administration and they took that on board. They started to run that as something that was useful to them as well, which it is.

In contrast to this attempt at a two-way exchange of information between academic secretaries and the Student Registry, one of the biggest complaints by laboratory managers was their exclusion from any such process. In particular, whilst an academic secretary was co-opted onto the IT Steering Group, laboratory managers felt they had been deliberately excluded from this, because, in their view, they were likely to ask too many awkward questions:

> We've been banned. All laboratory managers have been purposely, in my opinion, excluded from MAC meetings.

Furthermore, laboratory managers did not feel the academic secretary on the Steering Group could adequately represent their views:

> she won't be entering any data on at all, she'll be entering a little bit, so she's our sole representative. They don't use purchase ordering or stores or anything like that, so she will be going along to talk about Student Records . . . she wouldn't have a clue quite frankly. All the representation from the laboratory managers was withdrawn once it was known we were going to be awkward. We would say, look this is going to cost us money, it's costing us money there's no doubt about that.

This sense of not being represented exacerbated for laboratory managers their dissatisfaction with MAC and with its management and implementation.

We showed earlier how academic secretaries resisted MAC by simply not using it until they were faced with a combination of coercion (in the form of limited management regulation), co-option into the change management process, enticement through additional functionality and a compulsion to regulate themselves in order not to harm their students. In contrast, as we have seen, laboratory managers 'resisted' the system more at the level of being extremely vocal in their complaints. Despite that, though, their dependence on the outputs of MAC for their work meant they felt they had no choice but to ensure that departmental data was entered into the system as effectively as possible, in the hope that this would result in reliable financial reports. Laboratory managers were dependent on these reports for their work and had no alternative local system to fall back on as secretaries had. They could not, then, threaten the centre in the way that academic secretaries could; it was in their own interests to try to find utility in MAC, in a way which was not the case for the secretaries. On opening up the black box of MAC, then, laboratory managers were not able, like the secretaries, to compel the centre to reshape for them what they found inside. However, clerical staff at the centre often found themselves unable even to open up the black box, as we will show in the next section.

Clerical staff in Finance and the Student Registry

As indicated by Moodie and Eustace (1974), central administrative staff in universities have never had recourse to an organising narrative of autonomy. Rather, their role has always been one of meeting the requirements of others – the committees that run a university, the external bodies that regulate the higher education sector, or senior management within the administration. Central users of MAC at Bancroft were consequently subjected far more strongly to management regulation than departmental staff, with less freedom to dissent even if they regarded the system as highly problematic in terms of usability and utility. Clerical users of the Finance module that we spoke to in the Finance Department especially felt dissatisfied with MAC, as did one of the clerical officers who used Student Records within the Student Registry. However, making claims to autonomy was not an option for these users.

Central clerical staff experienced the same kinds of problem of usability with MAC as departmental staff, but they neither expressed their dissatisfaction publicly in the way that departmental staff did, nor saw their concerns acted upon as was the case for academic secretaries. The perspective of the clerical officer within the Student Registry that we spoke to was interesting in that his experience of MAC was very similar to that of the secretaries. Like them, he told us how he and his colleagues had been 'sold' MAC as a vast improvement on their previous system, and had built up their expectations of it accordingly. Once it had been introduced, though, he found it far slower than his old system and more cumbersome in terms of keystrokes. Where he obviously differed from academic secretaries was in his acceptance of the need to use the system despite its failings. He was responsible for maintaining the data in certain parts of the Student Records module, and gave us no indication that he had ever considered refusing to use MAC.

The same was true of clerical staff in the Finance Department. These staff had previously worked with the same KOREA system as laboratory managers, which they told us they had enjoyed using. They found MAC far slower and less easy to use, with no apparent prospect that it would improve:

> I've asked about that several times but no it can't be done, in fact I don't think anything we've asked can be done, can it [to colleague]?

The drop in quality that they identified in the shift from the old system to the new one seriously affected their job satisfaction and enjoyment of their working day: 'It's spoilt the job really, it has spoilt the job.' Furthermore, again as with laboratory managers, no effort was made by MAC support staff or central managers to resolve the problems that clerical staff experienced, which they had been told was not possible:

> They say they can't do it for technical reasons. I would think they would have to pay for that, wouldn't they, they'd have to pay extra to get that changed.

The way these staff voiced their objections to MAC was not in the same public way as academic secretaries and laboratory managers did, but in expressions of mutual support within the office. This took the form not just of complaining (and listening) to each other about the system, but also in practical ways, such as helping each other to solve problems, and jointly finding routines to bypass some MAC keystrokes. They were, then, not just passively accepting an imposed system, but actively finding ways of working with it, albeit within regulated limits. Given that these finance clerks were all women in junior positions, there were clearly dynamics of gender and power at play, both in their inability to effect change and in the strategies they used to deal with problems. This gendered dynamic was not straightforward in the way it was played out across the university, though. Female central administrative clerks shared with male laboratory managers a lack of choice over whether or not to comply with a poor system; in contrast, the strategies of female academic secretaries were effective in overcoming technical and organisational obstacles. Gendered relationships to techno-organisational change thus interacted with other factors at Bancroft, notably how vulnerable a particular group was to management regulation, and the kinds of narrative that underpinned occupational identities. The identities of clerks were mediated by an administrative culture that was clearly different from that in academic departments, and the narrative of autonomy in particular held no power at the centre. Any claim to autonomy that central administrative staff might make would not be taken seriously by central managers.

Conclusion: enrolling differentiated users in techno-organisational change

We have examined in this chapter the relationship with MAC of different groups of users based on their spatial and structural location within the organisation, their position in relation to the university's 'core business' and to related organising narratives, and their occupation within the academic-administrative nexus. These factors influenced whether different groups found MAC more or less usable and more or less valuable for their own work, and their varying capacities to challenge actively aspects of the system that they found *un*usable or value*less*. These issues will be examined in more depth in Chapters 7 and 8, but we want here to consider why some groups of staff were better able than others to express their dissatisfaction with MAC, and why the concerns of some and not others were taken seriously by the IT Steering Group.

Central to the story at Bancroft are the varying outcomes of endeavours by different groups of staff to open up the MAC black box, and of the different degrees to which central managers tried to enrol these groups of users of the system. MAC was a technology which had already been opened up and changed several times before it entered this local setting. What we have shown in this chapter is a situation where three different groups of users wished again to challenge the workings of and assumptions behind the system. Only one of these groups was able, by doing this, to compel central managers and MAC support staff to reconfigure it in ways that would benefit the group.

Put another way, central managers had few sanctions they could draw on when faced with resistance by academic secretaries. In contrast, the other two groups had little choice but to use the system, whatever they felt about it. The ability of academic secretaries to maintain their distance from the centre, supported by the narrative of autonomy, made it necessary for central managers to find more proactive ways of enrolling them that were not necessary with the other groups. Enrolment can, then, take many forms, and does not necessarily result in willing compliance. Nor is enrolment a one-way process. Successful enrolment requires a mutual adjustment of needs, responsibilities and expectations among different organisational groupings, including managers, and ultimately requires not only that a group of users has become enrolled, but also that they have come to an accommodation with and *incorporated* the technology into their group 'project', an issue we will return to more fully in Chapter 8.

This discussion highlights the importance of adopting a differentiated understanding of 'users'. At the national level, MAC has tended to be seen as having single institutional users (see, for example, Mason *et al.* 1998). Looking more closely at the story of MAC within one institution shows that there are in fact many different groups of users, with differentiated conceptions of their information needs and of the purposes of the system. Through the course of our fieldwork at Bancroft, the importance of meeting the needs of users became more prominent in the comments of senior management at the centre. Nevertheless, their conception of 'users' was dominated by an image of academic secretaries rather than of other users, even though by this time the Finance module was causing a great deal of difficulty for others too.

As we have shown, there are aspects of the system that made it impossible for *everybody* in the university to feel that they could benefit from it, particularly at the point where technical constraints limited the possibility of improving the situation solely through organisational changes. Thus, whilst it was possible to invite academic secretaries to meet and discuss ways of improving the Student Records module, this was less feasible with Finance, with its complex coding structures and links among the many Finance sub-systems and across system bridges to other modules. When a senior Finance officer put it to us, then, that 'there are people who I think are net losers, they've ended up with more work and nothing out of it', it was clearly staff such as the Finance clerks to whom he was referring.

In contrast, the organisational and technological changes introduced to enrol academic secretaries meant that for this group things improved considerably as MAC became more embedded within the organisation. Whilst by the end of our research the secretaries were by no means net beneficiaries of MAC, they were hopeful of at least *finding* benefits, primarily through the Data Warehouse. The time it had taken to reach this point with Student Records – since the initial implementation – indicated that users of Finance might face a long wait before they too could feel some optimism about the system; this was especially so given the technical problems with both MAC Finance and the Finance Data Warehouse during their first year. Improvements for central clerical staff were far less likely to emerge even than for laboratory managers.

The differences in the experience of the three groups of staff we have discussed add some complexity to our understanding of the power dimension of organising narratives and structural relations within an organisation. The narrative of autonomy seems to have been a crucial element of this dynamic, but only for those staff located in parts of the university where autonomy had historical purchase. At the same time, the effectiveness of any group's claims to autonomy over the production and provision of central information depended to a great deal on how important their *local* information was to the centre, and their position within the power structures of the university.

Neither academic secretaries, laboratory managers nor administrative clerks were powerful groups within the university. Academic secretaries and laboratory managers did, though, share a location within academic departments, and thus a claim to the narrative of autonomy which was such a strong feature of academic life. In contrast, administrative clerks had no capacity to draw on such a narrative. Nevertheless, if any group could claim truly to have achieved autonomy from central administrative interference, it was the academics themselves, not the secretaries or the laboratory managers. Academics had barely any involvement in MAC at all, and whilst changes to the governance structures of Bancroft meant that their independence was far from what it had been two or three decades earlier, they were shielded from day-to-day interactions with the centre by two different groups of support staff. Of the two, academic secretaries were less vulnerable both to central sanctions – since they did not need central data as laboratory managers did – and to central management regulation – partly because of the centre's greater need for their co-operation, but also because the university's diffuse authority structure meant that they were not answerable to central managers. Combined with the fact that their membership of the IT Steering Group was 'sponsored' by an academic – the PVC who brought them into the group – they were hence better able to invoke the narrative of autonomy than laboratory managers, even when they had begun to comply with central demands.

A significant outcome of the MAC story was a dynamic shifting of intra-organisational relations, bringing about new alliances among staff. Academic secretaries, especially – but also laboratory managers – began as a result of the problems they experienced with MAC to discuss issues together and to regard themselves as a coherent group which had not existed previously. This strengthened their resolve in resisting – or at least giving a low priority to – the system. The centre was then confronted not simply with a few intransigent individuals resentful of a changing work environment, but with a co-ordinated group sending out memos to their heads of departments and boards of studies demanding that their problems be addressed. Acquiring MAC clearly involved, then, changes to the organisation and to particular organisational groupings as well as changes in technology.

Nevertheless, one of the key lessons from this case relates to the point raised by Timmermans and Berg about the importance of 'grafting' new protocols and standards onto the world that pre-exists them, rather than trying simply to erase and replace it (1997). Whilst both organisation and technology are malleable and contingent, a degree of continuity is also needed if the process of techno-organisational change is to result in an obdurate system (Bijker 1995). Attempting to override existing organisational dimensions of technology completely is likely to lead to a failed implementation. At Bancroft, the narrative of departmental autonomy was 'built' into the variety of systems that pre-existed MAC; much of the resistance to MAC at departmental level resulted from the way in which the new system then allowed no scope for autonomy. It is notable, therefore, that when a degree of autonomy was reintroduced for academic secretaries – through the reshaping of the technology and of its organisational support structure – secretaries became more willing to find benefits from the system and to comply with it. The reluctance of laboratory managers to find an accommodation with the system reflects the way that central actors did not make similar efforts to readjust the system for them.

In the next three chapters, we will look at other dimensions of techno-organisational change which complement our study of Bancroft. Our case studies of Finlay Hospital and the retailer Brodies provide other examples of how new information systems do or do not build on existing aspects of the organisation, of the ways in which users are differentiated in the process of change, and of what kinds of reshaping of technology, organisation and users take place as new systems become embedded within an organisation.

4 Professional identity in techno-organisational change

As shown in Chapter 3 the system sponsors at Bancroft had to acknowledge and enrol key social groups. This proved difficult, in part because the implementation of MAC involved attempts to standardise practices in an environment that was organised around a narrative of structural autonomy. Enrolling key users in an acquisition process also requires sensitivity to other forms of autonomy. One such example is the formation of groups around the prestige of being professional (Freidson 1988). From the perspective of system sponsors, professional groups are crucial users from whom they must gain approval, even though the technology may alter the basis on which such groups have traditionally gained power and prestige (Ackroyd 1996).

This chapter examines the notion that IT can threaten claims to autonomy based on professional identity. We present an alternative way of understanding how professional groups respond to and, in the language of consumption studies, incorporate new technology into their professional project. Our argument is that this process of incorporation helps to situate or resituate the professional group in the social world of their organisation. The chapter begins by outlining some existing ways in which professionalism has been understood in sociology. One claim is that professionalism is in decline, in part due to the influence of new standardising technologies. After questioning this perspective, we suggest alternative ways of understanding both the construction and the maintenance of professional groupings, using ideas raised in Chapter 2. In the core of the chapter, we use material drawn from Finlay Hospital to consider how different claims to professional identity and autonomy played a part in embedding PBS in the organisation. This will be done by detailing the experiences of doctors and MLSOs in the Microbiology laboratories and clinical scientists in Tissue Typing. The conclusion of the chapter is that variations in the ways the different professional groups constructed their identity and others responded to that identity played an important role in shaping both the technology and the new professional relations that emerged.

Constituting the professional

The study of the professions has a long history in sociology (Freidson 1994), one that has at times been dominated by an account of both their rise in industrial capitalism and their decline in late capitalism (Dominelli 1996). The argument runs that particular professions were born at different points in relation to the development of industrial capitalism and the modern state. Key to the emergence of professional groups such as doctors, lawyers and civil servants was the functional specialisation of tasks, expertise and knowledge in sites such as medical practice, judicial systems and state bureaucracies (MacDonald 1995). Professions have been identified as those groups that could claim certain exclusive rights over knowledge and expertise valuable to either the state or the interests of capital (Boreham 1983). Different kinds of strategy have been identified which help maintain the exclusive rights that such groups enjoy. While some analysts focus on strategies such as exclusive or controlled membership via guilds or professional certification, others have concentrated on more sociopolitical strategies which allow groups to exploit inequalities based on gender (Witz 1992) or class.

The power of professional groups is reproduced through various institutional relationships: either the profession is strong enough to regulate itself, or it depends on state or capital regulation. While some professional groupings such as doctors or solicitors are seen as extra-organisational, others are tied to various types of organisation. For those only found in a specific type of organisation, their status and power are dependent on that setting and the way they are deployed by organisations. For those enjoying an extra-organisational status, some of their power and prestige are independent of the organisation. While various different occupations are identified as professional, importantly, there is always an acknowledgement that not all professional groups enjoy the same amount of power and prestige: social workers or teachers have a much more precarious professional position than, say, doctors. Again, the changing shape of capitalism and the state has been seen as a significant factor in determining just how much power and prestige a particular professional group can obtain.

In describing the key properties that identify a group or occupation as having attained professional status, certain key aspects have developed out of these understandings:

- *indeterminate skill*: that is, practices and abilities that develop through experience that cannot be taught but are shared by those within the profession (Dent 1996);
- *determinate expertise*: the key abilities and areas of knowledge that those wishing to join a profession must obtain, usually through some form of education and certification, in order to become a member (Boreham 1983);
- *ownership over an area of knowledge*: the boundaries that through informal or formal mechanisms give a group controlled access and ability to use a particular area of knowledge (Witz 1992);
- *discretion*: the privileged right that professions have to use their own judgement (Johnson 1972);

- *authority over their own activities and the activities of others*: the ability that professionals have to regulate their own members while being able to regulate the activities of others who are seen as non-professional or of a lesser profession (Witz 1992);
- *vocational prestige*: the notion that professionals provide for the greater good of society and are therefore valued for that role (Saks 1995).

More recently, debates about the decline of professionalism have emerged. These perspectives are often linked to debates about the advent of late capitalism and post-Fordism (Aldridge 1996). It is thought that the factors which have triggered the shifts towards these new modes of capitalism and state control have less need for the forms of knowledge and skill production facilitated by professional groups and relations. For example, it has been suggested that professionals are losing in power and influence to managers as their specialisms and expertise become replaceable and dispersed across a range of new occupational groups (Reed 1996). For some, this is a democratisation of knowledge and expertise – a sharing out of the privileges which came with professional status. For others, one form of regulation – professional control – is being replaced by another – performance management – that is better suited to the shape of capitalism at this moment in time. This debate has been particularly heated in the public sector professions (May 1994, Hugman 1996). New forms of technology, linked to new management practices, are often presented as one factor in this shift away from professional power for groups such as social workers (Dominelli 1996) and clinicians (Dent 1996).

This account of the rise and apparent demise of professionalism has a number of merits to it, most notably: the connections made between the structures of capitalism and the state and the fluctuating position and shape of professional groups; the awareness that not all professional groups have the same amount of power; and finally, its focus on the more recent emergence of new working practices that pose a threat to occupational boundaries and the status of established professions. However, there is at least one major weakness with the argument: it fails to do justice to the complex processes involved in acquiring skills, knowledge and control of technology through which professional identity has been constructed in the past and the present.

Blackboxing the sources of professional identity

The phrase 'professional project' is often used in the above accounts, but what is involved in this project? It appears to be the simple appropriation of a pre-existing body of knowledge as the preserve of one group, when this appropriation is beneficial to the workings of state or capital interests. If instead we think about a professional project from the perspectives discussed in Chapter 2 we can rearticulate it in relation to the notion of the 'black box' of technology (Pinch and Bijker 1987). Reed has suggested that 'blackboxing' (1996: 583) a particular area of knowledge and expertise as the property of a professional group helps secure its occupational identity and status. Although Reed is here using the term 'blackboxing' in a different way to that suggested in Chapter 2, there are some useful parallels that can help us retell the story of professionalism. Following the metaphor of the black box of technology:

- Members of a professional group make use of various resources that they can incorporate into their professional project: for example, technology, knowledge, and skill.
- Securing status as a professional group requires members of the group 'blackboxing' these resources in such a way that it leaves the group's ownership of them unquestioned.
- For a variety of reasons the black box can be reopened, allowing questions to be raised about the activities and boundaries of the professional group.
- Resecuring professional identity involves considerable labour to blackbox new or altered sets of resources.

Thinking of the professional project in terms of professional members being involved in local processes of appropriation akin to those studied in domestic consumption makes clear that what is involved in constructing professional identity is not the simple adoption of pre-existing technology or knowledge. Instead, this process involves actors appropriating and constructing such resources as symbols of their professional identity. By focusing on a key appropriation resource – knowledge – we can make this clear.

Appropriating knowledge

Considering appropriation from a consumption perspective means that we must think about how professional actors can construct and interpret a body of knowledge which allows them (1) to claim ownership of that knowledge and (2) to identify it as useful to the context in which they operate. It also involves mapping out the ways that a group attempts to consolidate this construction through a series of practices that secure its position and authority in the world as professional. In the words of Fournier, the professional project 'entails not only an occupational group appropriating a field or discipline as its exclusive area of jurisdiction and expertise but also the making of this field as a legitimate and valid area of knowledge and intervention on the world' (1997: 3).

The first stage of mapping out how groups attempt to construct professional status is to see knowledge, in the words of Knights, as 'constructed within a context or situation – an historical, geographical, moral, political, philosophical, and social space' (1997: 5). The body of knowledge and the professional identity develop together, shaping the meaning of each other and constructing the boundaries that mark out their legitimacy and status over other forms of knowledge and expertise. Miller and Rose discuss the ways in which bodies of knowledge are constructed through 'procedures of notation, ways of collecting and presenting statistics' in such a way that they are 'rendered in a particular conceptual form and made amenable to intervention and regulation' (1990: 5). What we would add is that the conceptual form that emerges in a professional project also serves to justify its unique ownership of a body of knowledge. The form that information takes also provides the space in which the profession can exercise and perform what becomes accepted as their indeterminate skill. Ownership over the form, as well as the content, of information is therefore an important ingredient in securing and maintaining a professional group.

Several things follow from this view of the constitution of the professional via their appropriation of 'useful' and 'valuable' resources that can be black-boxed. It helps make clear that the act of becoming professional through the construction and ownership of resources such as a body of knowledge is about power. In naming and labelling knowledge in certain ways, in dictating the form information must take to enable the production of knowledge, and in the performance of indeterminate judgement, a particular view of the world is given legitimacy over others. Challenging the professional's identity can include questioning the privilege given to that view of the world. This points to the importance of enrolling others outside the group in adopting its values and outlook in order to secure its position.

IT *and clinical autonomy in healthcare*

One sector where professional identity is said to be under threat from new standardising technologies is healthcare. How does our presentation of professional projects respond to this debate and shape our analysis of the Finlay case study?

Healthcare in the UK is marked by the influence of various professional groups with different levels of power and prestige. Clinicians in particular have been significant in shaping the distinctive organisational practices of the NHS. Ever since the introduction of the NHS, the negotiations between the state and this profession have continued to guarantee an autonomy over clinical decisions that helps clinicians make claims to professional status and identity. Even so, it has been suggested that the position of professional status is under threat from the growing influence of IT in the healthcare context. In particular, IT systems which allow greater sharing of information across professional and organisational boundaries (notably HISS systems and electronic records) are seen as incommensurate with established notions of clinical and professional autonomy. Such systems require a shift away from the types of skills and knowledge practice which doctors have appropriated into their professional project, and instead place a higher priority on following standard protocols and models.

It is reasonable to suggest that the new forms of technology and new management approaches, such as clinical audit and performance management, that have emerged in the NHS have opened up the black box of professionalism in relation to various professional groups – not only clinicians – in the NHS (Elston 1991). What is less reasonable is to assume that professional groups will remain passive in the face of such a process. What becomes important is establishing:

- how professional actors in different groups in the NHS respond through constructing a new articulation of their professional project that they can enrol others in;
- how the varied levels of power and prestige that different professional groups have been able to generate within the NHS influence the ability of actors to reshape their professional project.

From our discussion of the acquisition of PBS in Finlay in Chapter 2, we can see that the new system had the potential to unsettle the existing standards of information, which served as cultural resources to support claims of clinical autonomy and status for various professional groups in the laboratories. What labour did different groups undertake to retain their position? Were all groups successful in retaining a claim to professional status? These are our questions as we turn our attention to the various clinical users in the laboratories at Finlay.

Enrolling professional projects during the purchase of PBS

In Finlay Hospital the process of acquisition and enrolment was complicated from the beginning. Crucial to this was the existence of more than one significant professional group that needed to be enrolled. If we briefly return to the purchase of PBS we can identify how existing professional groups were part of the early decisions to choose the system, and find evidence of the – at times conflicting – attempts at enrolment that had to take place. What this also indicates is the varied levels of influence and status different groups making a claim to professional identity had in the processes involved in purchasing the IT system.

Management imperatives associated with the valuing of performance and resource management were important rationales for the Finlay Project Team. These 'imperatives' helped shape the decision to purchase a system that would allow the various laboratories within Pathology and beyond to buy one system to 'fit' all their needs. During our time visiting the laboratories, rumours over the PHLS and various other laboratories being privatised or centralised within other hospitals were a continuing source of uncertainty and fear. Any such move was seen as a threat to the autonomy and professional ethos of the various laboratories. This fear and uncertainty informed the acquisition process. Those who took the decision to integrate the laboratories via a new IT system saw this in part as a defensive manoeuvre to ensure Pathology's continued autonomy from central hospital management and commercial influence. In the words of the IT specialist who took on leadership of the Project Team:

There are lots of reasons why Pathology is potentially vulnerable from the outside world. It's something that could be nicely cherry-picked, by a company that wanted to cherry-pick it. So we needed to argue to our critics who said that we were disparate, that we were separate departments and all run higgledly-piggledly. I think that was an over-simplified criticism, but we did need to attempt to get ourselves together.

A sense of protection through numbers also encouraged the smaller laboratories to join with a single system. The head of Tissue Typing explained: 'So when it comes to costing, contracting, negotiations and so on – you don't wish to negotiate as the Tissue Typing lab – you wish to negotiate as the Department of Pathology.' This meant that enrolment of the different laboratories into a unified technical solution was relatively easy. Fears over a loss of professional autonomy because of a single shared system were minimised because of the perceived bigger threat to structural autonomy in the shape of managerial and commercial standardisation.

An indication that established professional groups were taken seriously at this stage is seen in the care that was taken to ensure that certain clinical needs – identified by clinical professions in the various laboratories – were written into the operating requirements of the new system. The Project Team were careful to identify the clinical information needs of each laboratory as part of the acquisition process. This care reflected the belief that clinical staff were important users to be enrolled in the system. In particular, doctors in each of the laboratories were consulted to some degree. The level to which other professional groups – such as clinical scientists – were included at this point varied from laboratory to laboratory and was an indication of the level of power that different groups had in each laboratory. In reflecting clinical needs constructed mostly by the doctors, the priority was to include their existing information requirements in terms of form, content and depth, rather than seeking to redefine these to meet the priorities of the system. The head of the Project Team explained that they purchased PBS because it appeared to sustain clinical priorities in the type of information it would provide and the forms of knowledge capable of being obtained through its use: 'you had a system which clearly saw availability of this sort of information as one of its aims in life, you were keeping the medical staff happy'.

Professional groups were obviously playing a part in the initial acquisition process. However, various factors led to a variation in the levels of participation that the different groups were able to undertake in decisions about the new system. The first is that while the Project Team may have wished to ensure the inclusion of pre-existing clinical needs into the system, this intent does not appear to have been shared by those in Finlay's Finance Department. Their view was significant because it was Finance who negotiated the contractual details with PBS's American suppliers. After months spent developing the operating requirements to integrate the needs of the different laboratories and protect the clinical staff's interests, much of this work was undermined by the unilateral decision of Finance either to remove some of the requirements or to downgrade others to being merely options. When this was discovered, several of the laboratory heads on the Project Team were furious. A chief technologist from one of the smaller laboratories explained: 'somebody went through with a red pen and just said, take it out, take it out, take it out, with no redress at all'. Financial priorities not only appeared to have displaced clinical ones, but had also been used to determine which of the clinical needs would be given more, and which less, importance. The contracts drawn up by Finance managers clearly posed a threat to the clinicians' professional autonomy.

Attempts to reclaim autonomy began as soon as the contract changes became known. One laboratory head explained how some elements of their requirements were reintroduced after they 'yelled very loudly'. Even so, he suggested that the whole episode had left a 'sour note'. Other members of the Project Team only discovered the changes when the system was in use and they contacted PBS's designers over missing capabilities:

> I had one very embarrassing telephone conversation with our senior consultant, on a conference call to the States, complaining that they hadn't set up something that we had asked for . . . to be told that it wasn't in the contract . . . that was absolutely appalling.

Enrolling Finance, a key requirement if the purchase of PBS was to go ahead, thus compromised the attempts to enrol the professional groups in the different laboratories.

The second factor shaping the influence of professional groups in purchasing decisions was that although the groups were taken seriously by the Project Team, it was those situated in the larger laboratories who had the most say. For the smaller laboratories joining the system in order to protect themselves from commercial and centralised management practices, their requirements were regarded merely as options to be included if possible. One representative from a smaller laboratory stated:

> It was very obvious at that time that there were the core component of major labs and the minor labs and it was obvious . . . at the stage of tender, that the core labs were going to be very well catered for by available packages . . . And if anything got dropped off the end of the acquisition process, it would be the smaller labs, probably because we were going to be more expensive to customise the systems for.

Later he explained:

> Being the Cinderella of the procedure became clearer, closer and closer to the live date, and some of the issues that were still outstanding such as the interfaces with haematology analysers became more and more pressing.

Our problems and niggles became a much lower priority and a list of them is still outstanding.

Project Team members from the larger laboratories acknowledged that some priority was given to them. However, they asserted that this did not lead to the smaller laboratories having to use a system ill-fitted to their information needs. In the words of the Project Team leader:

We already had some difficulties – and I don't mean to belittle them – departments like Tissue Typing, whose workload is a tiny fraction, you couldn't afford to have them wagging the dog. But none the less, they were entitled to be there and to their thing. Ultimately, the feeling was, certainly among the larger labs, that if we couldn't find a system that sorted out the tiny people, they would have to be scratched off the end. As it happened, we ended up with a system that we felt suited everybody reasonably well.

Attempts to enrol professional groups were important to the acquisition process. However, this process was compromised by factors – including conflicting management priorities – which limited the extent to which professional values and needs could be built into decisions. These early experiences are testimony to the existence of conflicting professional groups across the different laboratories. For what we have already seen is that different professional groups can have differing values and needs. Hence where there is more than one professional group in a setting, the implementation of a system can involve negotiating between groups and identifying which ones are to be treated as the most significant users, or which are the most relevant for securing the system within the organisation. In the following sections, we will explore this in relation to two of the laboratories that acquired PBS – Bacteriology and Virology (collectively known as Microbiology). There were two professional groups working in these laboratories, yet they were unable to exploit the language and practices of their respective professional statuses to the same degree.

The doctors and the MLSOs

Microbiology included two groups of staff that identified themselves as having particular levels of professional status: doctors and MLSOs. Actors in both groups drew on resources of skills and expert knowledge in trying to secure their professional projects. Both groups also had external validation that helped support their status in the shape of university qualifications, professional accreditation and state certification. However, the external support available to the doctors in Microbiology was more substantial and organisationally secure. A significant aspect of MLSOs' training was performed and monitored in the laboratories. On completion of their local technical training they were eligible to become members of the Institute of Medical Laboratory Sciences, a national body overseeing members' interests, rights and obligations within the PHLS, as well as promoting research within the field. The MLSOs' institutional membership, qualifications and training in the laboratories had validity external to the PHLS. However, the history behind and value of the medical qualifications of doctors had validity that extended much further. The varied levels of external and organisational support were significant to the role both groups could play in shaping PBS.

Deskilling through protocol – the MLSOs

During our description of the acquisition of PBS in Chapter 2, we explained the way that various protocols were built into the system by the Project Team. These reflected how management defined the operation of their laboratories and the role of the different staff working there. In Microbiology, management constructed information needs in such a way as to provide a standardised model of good laboratory operation.

The standardised protocols mapped out testing procedures for all patient samples that entered the laboratory. Based on the information provided, PBS protocols determined what tests should be carried out and the antibiotics that should be prescribed. While PBS was to be used by all grades of staff from trainee laboratory aid to consultant, protocols affected the MLSOs the most. The principal role of MLSOs was to test individual samples of patient specimens that arrived each day at the laboratories, and PBS became an integral part of the laboratory activities involved in this area.

Prior to PBS, MLSOs would record on paper their tests and analyses over a series of days. When the tests were completed, they would enter the results into the computer system. With the introduction of PBS, samples were first registered on the system at reception before being collected by MLSOs for plating up and subsequent screening for micro-organisms. MLSOs worked on 'benches' which handled particular types of specimen. Following overnight incubation, the results of the tests were entered the next day direct to PBS.

As part of the predefined protocols constructed within PBS, doctors on wards became able to order the tests that they wished to see conducted on the samples sent to the laboratory. The MLSOs were thus removed from decisions about what happened to a sample. Instead they were interacting with a system that informed them of what test to do, and what to do within that test. It provided the pre-set fields in which to enter the results and then finally told them what was to happen as a result of the findings. This shift was further confirmed by wider working practice changes that were introduced by the Microbiology management. In comparison to the previous model where an MLSO would follow through a specimen over a number of days from arrival to result, now no individual MLSO had responsibility for handling all elements of the test procedure for a particular specimen. Instead, on a rotation basis, MLSOs would work on one element of the test procedure for all samples coming in to a particular bench.

These features of PBS alongside the altered working practices posed a challenge to MLSOs. The standardisation and fragmentation of tasks at bench level, coupled with the arrival of ward-ordered tests which the MLSOs 'knew' at times to be incorrect, meant resentment built up quite quickly among bench staff. This resentment led them to feel that their occupational status and expertise in the laboratory were under threat. As one commented, about the arrival of 'ward-ordering':

> If somebody said to me how do I think the system's deskilling, the main point I think is the ward-ordering, where the doctors and nurses on the ward are actually deciding what tests we do, rather than saying this is the specimen, this is the problem, and then letting us decide which organisms might be causing the problem, and therefore which tests we need to carry out to isolate them.

Trainee MLSOs were at a point in their career where they were working to obtain the skills and expertise that would give them status in the laboratory and a claim to professional identity. They saw PBS as taking away their opportunity to obtain the skills that would give them professional status. One trainee commented that the system had 'taken a bit of the specialism out of it. It's taken a bit of those skills away.' The claim was being made that these skills were tied not merely into particular qualifications but to a wider MLSO profession. Moreover, skills were understood as something acquired through the work one did, and the space and time one had to do it, rather than the ability to follow PBS-derived routines:

Trainee: I prefer to be trained and get my own experience and rely on my own judgement, rather than get this on the computer and it says do a gram, got this result, put it into the computer, it says do a tube – I don't want that – I want to think.

Interviewer: You want to decide for yourself?

Trainee: Yes, because otherwise you become like workers on a production line then. And there's going to be no enjoyment in that at all. You've got to be constantly making decisions, it keeps your mind working, keeps you alert, whereas if you rely on a computer you just become unskilled.

These skills and practices were important resources in helping secure the MLSOs' professional project. When the exercise of such skills is removed or denied, the outcome can be a weakened sense of professionalism. Trainee MLSOs saw the changes as a threat to the space in which they could both develop and sustain a sense that what they as MLSOs brought to the laboratory was indeterminate, vital and unique. Without the space to perform their constitutive skills and knowledge, their significance to the laboratory was reduced and their connection to the wider MLSO community minimised.

The language of the 'production line' was also used by MLSOs who had finished their training. Thus, Grade One MLSOs would describe how they felt they were being treated as 'factory workers':

> The whole reason we went to university, or bettered ourselves for want of a better word, was because we didn't want to do that factory work, and they are trying to push it back that way.

They saw themselves as being redefined as and ultimately replaced by 'relatively unskilled people doing the same thing over and over' and found this approach individually unsatisfying and 'soul destroying'.

The Grade Two MLSOs – MLSOs with greater authority and say over the activities of more junior MLSOs – also felt that they were being downgraded by the demands and limitations of working within new operating procedures, especially given their higher qualifications:

> The scientific input for us is going, you feel that you are working as a pair of hands, you are not really using the scientific qualifications that you have, that you have been trained to use . . . It's like working in a fish and chip shop, you have just to get on with the job.

Over time, as PBS became more fully integrated into the laboratory, the issue of deskilling intensified. When asked whether she felt in control of PBS six months into the study and almost a year after the system had been introduced, one MLSO replied:

MLSO: No, it's telling me what it wants done. You've got to give it the information that it needs. If it's generated a list you've got to feed it its answers. There's not an awful lot of control there, no.

Interviewer: Is that substantially different to how you were working before?

MLSO: Yes, you decided what you were doing, and in what order you were doing them in . . . we are basically working to its needs.

Like the trainee MLSOs, this Grade Two's concern was wider than simply about qualifications not being used. The format of information demanded and useful to the system – 'it' – was incompatible with the format of information MLSOs believed to be useful and valuable. Her expression is of powerlessness, an inability to do anything about this incompatibility, to decide what her information needs were. In addition, her disquiet relates to a loss of time and mental space within which to perform, and thereby secure, what MLSOs considered to be their valuable and useful act of tacit judgement:

> We are having to work very fast, we don't really have any time to do what

> I would call developmental work . . . Thinking about what we are doing, why we are doing it, how we could do it better, and maybe having half an hour here and there to try something different . . . If you are a professional person, you want to have a little bit of space to think about what you are doing.

The MLSOs regarded PBS, therefore, as posing a threat to their professional status and identity. The occupational boundaries MLSOs drew around the body of knowledge and skill that comprised their project and positioned them within the laboratory did not map onto how PBS functioned. MLSOs – of all grades – spoke of these aspects of the system as deskilling, because they stripped them of responsibilities which they believed were central not only to their role but to how they defined their professional identity. Significantly, 'deskilling' was a term volunteered by MLSOs and others at Finlay rather than proposed by us. Of all our research sites, it was in Finlay that this term was used the most by respondents to describe circumstances under the new system.

Like all claims to knowledge and judgement, MLSOs' claims were situated and malleable and could, in principle, be defended. We have suggested that the elements that make up a professional project are flexible resources that can be deployed in different ways. Therefore, it is possible that MLSOs could have developed a strategy that rearticulated those components in such a way as to regain a sense of professional status. However, what followed suggests that for the most part MLSOs were unable to execute such a reinvention. This failure requires an understanding of the organisational contexts and power relations within and between occupational groups that can restrict such attempts.

One strategy MLSOs could have used might have been to seek to incorporate new components – such as the new technology itself – into their articulation of professional identity. Instead, much of the MLSOs' activity focused on defending the existing boundaries of their expertise and areas of judgement within the laboratory. Firstly, they experimented together with different ways of arranging work practices around the system to improve their working relationship with it. One MLSO described how they had changed things:

> Because we have different sections, and everybody moves, we sat down and looked at the ways we had been told how to do it and decided we didn't like that, so we tried out different things, like you take the plates away and I'll key in the results, just different ways.

They took an active role in integrating the system into the laboratory that made it less disruptive to the established ways of doing things. Secondly, they informed managers of categories of specimen, type of specimen or result that they argued were missing from the fields for entering information and results into the system. Thirdly, vocal unhappiness over the 'production line' approach led management to find new ways for the MLSOs to work with the system in order to accommodate some of their grievances. The wound bench was one particular area of conflict where MLSOs won the right to change working practices:

> On the wound bench what they [management] suggested doing first of all was to have one person reading the plates, somebody else sitting on the computer, and somebody else doing sensitivities on those plates. We [MLSOs] decided we couldn't work like that, we couldn't have somebody just reading the plates just to tell somebody else to type it on the computer, and then passing that plate onto somebody else. So we decided that one person would do it all, they'd have their plates, they'd put their stuff on the computer, then they'd do any further work on it.

Finally, because of their complaints, the ward-ordering screens were altered to allow MLSOs access to revise or ignore ward-ordered tests where they thought alternative or additional tests were required.

In these four ways, therefore, MLSOs were able to retain some of the resources they had developed to secure their professional project. Yet these successes were accompanied by some important losses, most importantly in the way the senior Microbiology managers regarded the work of MLSOs under the PBS regime.

The managers were aware that the system required different ways of handling specimens but did not regard this as tantamount to 'deskilling' the MLSOs. They argued that the old computer system had also included a protocol for tasks which MLSOs had been expected to follow; the new system had just tightened this up. Management defined the scope, quality and significance of MLSOs' interpretative role in such a way that a reduced role in test selection was not tantamount to deskilling. They perceived the skill of MLSOs as being primarily their ability to interpret sample tests – rather than choosing tests or deciding what should be done in light of a test result. The space for negotiation over this point was therefore limited because management and MLSOs defined the body of knowledge and expertise of MLSOs differently. As the Microbiology manager said:

> I don't see the use of [PBS] as a deskilling process at all, it's a tool to use, to process the work. The thing of deskilling was I think that people felt that [PBS] was forcing them to do things in a standard way. What I'm saying is that everybody should have been doing the standard operating procedures. The whim 'I'll do this', they consider that as deskilling because now they can't do that. I don't see that.

One of the key reasons why MLSOs had such a difficult time in asserting their definition of the scope of their interpretative role is the past occupational history of Microbiology's management: the managers of Microbiology had begun their careers as MLSOs. Some of them occasionally still worked on the bench, either at weekends or when the laboratory was short-staffed. This past history meant that MLSOs could not claim that management were 'complete outsiders' who knew little about laboratory work. Instead, what they claimed was that in becoming managers these former MLSOs had lost or forgotten their previous role, in part because the identity and role of an MLSO had changed in the intervening period. As one MLSO explained when he complained about the lack of consultation that had taken place during the customisation process:

> MLSOs should have been asked what we wanted from it, because that was something we were never asked. They relied very much on people like the [MLSO manager's] experience, but he hasn't worked on the bench for ten or twenty years. Although he works Saturdays his knowledge of everyday stuff, silly little things like it would be easier if that box was there, rather than there . . .

The very types of knowledge and understanding on which the MLSOs based their claim to professional status are those which they believed management no longer had. By separating management from being 'proper' MLSOs, the MLSOs staked a claim to what constituted an MLSO and what did not. Even so this separation did not prevent management from making their own inter-pretation of what the MLSO was, and they did this in such a way that, from the perspective of MLSOs, it minimised the professional content of their role. The result was a reduction in the opportunities that MLSOs had to assert their interpretation of what gave them a professional identity.

As the chapter turns its attention to the experience and strategies of doctors under PBS, contrast the MLSOs' situation with that implied by a consultant's response to a question about skill: 'I didn't have any skills that were suscepti-ble.' What is it that enables one professional group to see itself, and to ensure that others see it, in these terms?

Controlling validation – the doctors

Consultants are the final medical authorities in the Microbiology laboratory at Finlay as elsewhere in British hospitals. One of the tasks that had to be com-pleted in Microbiology was the final authorisation or 'validation' of the test results that went out of the laboratory to GPs or to ward doctors. The doctors' principal daily task lay here in the checking and confirmation of tests. Other activities – relating to clinical research, epidemiological work, advice to external bodies, etc. – were also part of their role in the PHLS, but our respondents saw validation as central. The doctors wanted to retain control over the results that left the laboratory, over the information that was presented to them in order for them to validate a result, and over when and how they carried out validation.

Given the centrality of validation to the doctors' expression of their profes-sional identity, they might have expected PBS to be set up in such a way that their control over validation was ensured. Although a consultant was on the Project Team, which indicates some acknowledgement that the doctors' interpretation of their needs was taken seriously, we have seen that the final specification reflected a wide range of interests in the PHLS, Pathology and the hospital. Moreover, PBS is an American system, and US laboratories do not require validation via (the equivalent of) a doctor: authorisation is given by someone who is similar in status to an MLSO. In addition, PBS was developed originally to handle records and results in Haematology and Biochemistry laboratories where much of the testing and 'validation' (e.g. of blood type) is done automatically via robotics. PBS treated validation, therefore, as a matter of routine, and structured the information on tests in a non-selective, standardised, sequential way. Although some attempts were made at the customisation stage by the Project Team to build in the doctors' validation requirements, this did not satisfy the doctors.

From the Finlay doctors' perspective, the way that PBS structured validation denied them the time and space to deploy and develop both determinate and indeterminate aspects of their professional identity. Rather than the listing of results that PBS offered:

> What one wants is some kind of order for them to be presented to you, you want to look at certain types of information, clinical details, information about the patient, what the report says, and what tests we have done in the laboratory. You want the option of looking further into that, what the results were, the details of the tests.

Again, the form and content of information was an important site for the display, acceptance or denial of professionally based constructions of information requirements. The 'order' present in the system did not match the ordering priorities of the doctors, an ordering they used and constructed to cement their autonomy and authority. The most immediate problem after implementation, however, was the issue of results leaving the laboratory before a doctor had had a chance to look at them: 'The bottom line at the moment is that some reports, positive reports, are going out without us having had a look at them.'

Control over validation included control over the work of MLSOs. Doctors complained that the system interfered with their oversight of the work going on in the laboratory:

> We knew it would change our job because we would no longer be doing what we called green crossing, i.e. going and getting all the specimen forms from MLSOs and looking at what they were doing . . . We also knew, because the system essentially allowed the lab to go paper free, we wouldn't get what we called the forty-eight-hour specimens, which were the cards for specimens which were currently being worked on, so we could see what they were doing.

The validation role was such a significant element of the doctors' professional project that they could not accept the system as anything but a 'disaster', as 'horrendous'. PBS, then, posed an important challenge to their position, which the remark 'I didn't have any skills that were susceptible [to PBS]' glosses over. In fact, the doctors had to engage in a number of strategies as part of their professional project to secure their position relative to others in the laboratory. They had to labour to retain the bond between a socially accepted and unique body of knowledge, skill and judgement and their boundaries as a profession. Consumption of the technology was therefore far from a passive process for the doctors. The strategies they developed were responses to two particular types of threat that PBS posed:

- a threat to their specific body of expertise;
- a threat to their control over the pace and time at which reports were made.

Both these threats undermined the resources of indeterminate judgement and specific skills that gave them their much-prized clinical autonomy. Let us look at each of these in turn.

Firstly, PBS meant that all the information on patients, including their clinical details, was held on the system, whereas previously clinical details were recorded on paper and held in the laboratory. Moreover, PBS presented all results in a standardised format for review and validation by the doctors – it did not differentiate some results as more significant than others. All results, therefore, were listed for consideration, yet out of 200 results that a doctor might consider, perhaps forty would be seen as needing a doctor's special attention. Finally, the doctors found that the system provided a much greater range of information than they had previously sought or needed, so much so that they did not feel in control of the information contained in PBS. In these ways, PBS posed a threat to their articulation of their sense of professional identity, especially in its tendency to close off indeterminacy:

> Very often the system doesn't allow a lot for interpretation or uncertainty, which often arises: you know, you might put up a difficult organism that you want to spend a couple of days identifying, and you wonder how on earth you are going to get this onto the computer. There isn't a code for it, or there isn't a comment box that you can put it into when you're running a paperless system.

So how did they respond to this problem over the months following PBS's implementation?

The doctors' claim to tacit, indeterminate knowledge of microbiology – 'it's an art rather than a science, it's an acquired skill really, an experience, it can't be something that's just learned from a book' – was used to ensure that the system was changed such that their interpretation of anomalous results would be given priority:

I found a way of putting specimen comments on the computer records, which come up any time the [MLSO] looks at a specimen. Therefore I can flag that specimen for a patient 'if there's something interesting, *let me know about it'*.

(emphasis added)

An MLSO might recognise the anomaly, but the doctors would be the ones to interpret it. The doctors were here finding opportunities through their customisation and consumption of the system to perform their interpretative role, a role crucial not only to the 'validation' of results but also to their position and autonomy. This claim to be able to deal with particular microbiological problems was given more weight by the additional claim that, as a teaching and research hospital, Finlay handled a 'more difficult range of patients, with more sophisticated problems, so you have to be a more sophisticated microbiologist'. What is significant is that the definition of indeterminacy that doctors adopted as a way to protect and justify their professional identity was similar to that of the MLSOs. As we shall see, what differed was the acceptance by others of the doctors' definition.

Secondly, doctors were able to ensure that the PBS managers introduced new procedures into the validation process. Whereas initially the volume of results for review meant that completed tests needing action were 'lost' in the queue of all results, these could now be identified as 'overdue' and in need of urgent attention. The managers adjusted PBS to provide more selective test runs. The doctors argued that they did not want to go through all the tests and asked management whether the system might be reconfigured so that validation of non-significant (i.e. 'negative') tests could be handled by MLSOs. Some changes in this direction were made, although management argued that technical limitations meant they were limited in how far they could address any further the doctors' problems.

Rather, then, than take a blanket approach which demanded that validation return to the structure and format of information and data that preceded PBS, doctors attempted to reconstitute what they 'needed' PBS to provide. They did this so that their validation role, and their autonomy over what for them really mattered, could continue. This indicated the malleability that they adopted when faced with PBS, a malleability that allowed them to incorporate some of the functionality of PBS into their efforts to sustain their project.

Thirdly, in addition to formal adjustments to the system itself, the doctors asked MLSOs to communicate significant results to them *on paper* (as in the pre-PBS days) so they were dealt with sooner rather than later. Finally, they used PBS to strengthen their own knowledge base and the institutional 'space' they occupied. Using the link PBS had with other laboratories – such as Biochemistry and Haematology – they could gather more information on patients, and, through this, were able to play a wider role on the hospital's clinical stage. Rather than a barrier to the performance of their judgement, the system became a medium through which they could exercise it in the hospital more widely, not only for other doctors to see, but – perhaps more crucially – for hospital management to see. On a related front, PBS was eventually regarded as more useful than the previous system because of its capacity to trace information for epidemiological purposes, part of the public health researcher role the consultants played beyond their immediate responsibilities within the laboratory. Heightening the importance of this role to the constitution of their professional project again shows the malleability of the doctors' approach. It also indicates that the doctors had begun to incorporate PBS into their newly articulated professional identity.

In terms of the threat that PBS posed to the doctors' control over their time, while the system's capacity for integrating and broadening information may have allowed them to deploy their specialist expertise on a wider front, it also made new demands on their control over their working day. This is because other professional colleagues elsewhere in the hospital – the doctors on the wards – expected to be furnished with validated reports much earlier in the day, direct to their local computer terminals. The result was that lunchtime working to get reports out on time (by 3.00 p.m.) was commonplace. The checking of results in the validation 'queue' was felt to be 'mind-numbingly boring, I don't think it is an appropriate use of my time'.

During our time spent with them there appeared little that the doctors could do to re-establish their control over the timing or length of validation. This would have required either new software that would reduce the number of results for checking, yielding up more validation to MLSOs, or negotiating with ward doctors for later delivery of results.

Apart from these specific responses, the doctors used their membership of a particular professional culture as a broad resource to counter the threats posed by the system. Identification with a wider professional culture was an important medium through which their identity and status could be sustained. Not surprisingly, perhaps, new doctors recruited to the laboratory were forewarned of the problems posed by the system – 'I said to her "our computer's awful", and when she came for a look round, one of the consultants said to her the computer's fairly difficult to handle'. New recruits learnt that the system did not always support professional interests. Established doctors' links to the wider profession were also deployed as a resource. For example, the company that supplied PBS was interested in selling the system to other hospitals in the UK. Finlay doctors were prepared to use their position in the national network of clinicians to leverage more improvements: 'I'm quite happy to phone up the clinicians and say 80 per cent of it's wonderful, 20 per cent I cannot recommend it to you as it stands.'

Without a full (professional) seal of approval, the market for PBS would be very limited. The Project Team knew this too, and used the doctors' professional position as a means of extracting further improvements to the system. In so doing, they confirmed and helped to reproduce the specialist knowledge claims of the clinicians. Rather than deny the professional status of the doctors, as they did with MLSOs, the Project Team used and therefore validated them. While the doctors still signalled disquiet, management were prepared to pass on their grievances to PBS's suppliers and thus play a part in the doctors' performance of their identity. Managers' support of the doctors' professional project was seen in their withholding of 10 per cent of the final fee to the suppliers until the problems with validation were sorted out.

The difference in attitude towards the claims based on professionalism made by MLSOs and doctors are marked. Doctors used a body of knowledge, secured in legal statute and medical authority, to retain and define their privileged professional position. The ability of their professional identity to remain relatively unchallenged was based on the willingness of others to accept it as justified, valuable and useful. The professional identity which secured MLSOs' status was less firm; they were unable to get others to act upon their interpretation of their professional status and value. Doctors also had greater opportunity to be flexible in their approach, for example in the way they altered certain elements of what really mattered to them in their control, use and conception of information needs. Although the doctors were not completely happy with the system, their concerns and professional identity – and not just their reports – were validated.

The micro-organism: tissue typing

The significance of professional groupings to the shaping of PBS in Microbiology was influenced by the presence of more than one group claiming professional status. The relationship between the two groups and the varied responses to them by management was central in shaping events. What happens when only one professional group exists? How does such a group articulate its sense of professionalism during a time of change and how do management respond? To look at these questions we turn to the specialist Tissue Typing laboratory.

As indicated in the Introduction, Tissue Typing was much smaller than the Microbiology laboratories. The function of the laboratory is focused on identifying the tissue types of potential transplant patients, keeping track of the condition of patients in need of transplant operations, and doing research on and monitoring the long-term success of transplant procedures. An aspect of this work involves being on call when donor organs become available so that an attempt can be made to match the organ to one of the patients. This requires records to be accurate and up-to-date, because the preciseness of match between patient and organ is crucial to a successful transplantation. Before the introduction of PBS the laboratory ensured the accuracy of its records via a complex multiple book-based system which retained detailed logs on the condition and compatibility of patients requiring either organ or bone marrow transplants.

While PBS was being negotiated, a new head of Tissue Typing was appointed. The new head came from a laboratory that had been computerised, and he believed that becoming part of the purchase of PBS would be beneficial in a number of ways. We saw in the earlier section that he thought membership of PBS was a way to make a formal, organisational link between Tissue Typing and the larger laboratories in Pathology and the PHLS. In addition, he saw a significant change such as computerisation as a way of making his mark on the department and signalling changes in the operation and running of the laboratory. Therefore the decision for Tissue Typing to purchase a computer, and PBS in particular, was the result of a complex set of social and managerial dynamics that meant that the purchase 'made sense'. During the purchase process minority laboratories like Tissue Typing argued that they found themselves expected to use a system designed with the larger laboratories in mind. In our discussion of Tissue Typing we will consider the influence of this context to the changes introduced by PBS and the professional labour undertaken as a result. This discussion will focus on the clinical scientists, including the head.

In many ways, the clinical scientists constituted and maintained their professional identity using similar types of strategy to those of the doctors and MLSOs in Microbiology. In particular, the scientists stressed the uniqueness and value of the indeterminate judgement that they performed via their interpretation of clinical data and evidence. One clinical scientist explained that the laboratory had considered using robotics for test analysis but that this had been rejected because a computer 'is not as good as the human eye. There is a lot of interpretation in your work.' As with the doctors, and not the MLSOs, others supported the way that they constructed their indeterminate judgement in the rejection of robotic technology.

However, other elements of the professional project pursued by these actors in a smaller laboratory appeared to have been different before PBS was introduced. While clinical claims to professional autonomy in Microbiology involved a differentiation among staff, in Tissue Typing autonomy operated at a level which involved all the clinical scientists as a group. In the words of one of them: 'We all more or less do the same things, it's a very small laboratory, we all do whatever needs to be done and we are all on call.' The operation of the laboratory, and what was seen as making it distinct, was the hierarchically flat and integrated work approach, which was not fractured by competing or differently valued professional groups. The knowledge and expertise that each member brought to the laboratory were shared and developed collectively. The bonds between laboratory role, organisational role and sense of professional status within the laboratory were close in ways that did not exist in larger laboratories where there were competing professional groups.

As in Microbiology, the clinical scientists raised issues with PBS that related to the apparent incompatibility of the priorities constructed in the system with their professionally secured needs. Some of the issues that were raised echo those of the doctors and MLSOs, again suggesting some common elements in the constitution of professionalism in both sites. One of these is in the time spent using PBS. This complaint is similar in many ways to those of doctors in Microbiology. Firstly, the scientists believed that they were being forced to spend too much time on the computer: 'Initially I had anticipated it would take a lot less time than it does. That's because the system hasn't really been designed for Tissue Typing. It's been adapted to try and take our needs into account.'

Secondly, they thought that this time was wasted because it was being spent providing information of no relevance or use to the scientists. One scientist described why she preferred their old paper system:

> The strengths basically were that you . . . didn't have to fill in as much information as you do now onto the computer screen. You didn't have to fill in the consultant name at all, because that was the responsibility of the admin person.

Thirdly, having to provide this information, which often meant time on the phone chasing up information which the system (but not they) required, reduced the flexibility and autonomy which they could exercise in how they spent their time and ordered their day. As with doctors, autonomy was being challenged by set fields that both demanded information they believed to be irrelevant and dictated the moments at which that information could be provided.

The clinical scientists asserted that the specific needs of the laboratory, and by implication their needs as a professional group within it, were ill served by the system. In another echo of Microbiology, the format, scope and temporality of information requirements in the system were challenged: 'The problem for us is we deal with patients for a long time, like renal patients. We are in a way a difficult department because our patients aren't in and out and dealt with.' In the context of Tissue Typing's articulation of its specialised and unique nature, this lack of compatibility was presented as a result of being more rigorous and careful than other laboratories: 'sometimes we look up a result we have requested from another department and I think they are not as thorough regards the checking'.

This complaint that the system denied their needs allowed the clinical scientists to further their professional project via a claim about the uniqueness of the laboratory:

> Well it wasn't designed for us, if we had had a system designed for us I am sure it would have been wonderful. I don't think it's computerisation that is the problem, it's our particular program and the fact that it doesn't really fit our needs.

The minority status of the laboratory, rather than being a hindrance to the maintenance of their professional identity, became a resource and an opportunity to secure it: 'You are endlessly trying to fit in with someone else's system, which isn't terribly relevant.'

In other ways, the system became a stimulus to alter the content of professionalism in the laboratory. This occurred in two ways and led to the articulation of professional identity becoming less collective and more exclusive to particular laboratory members. The first aspect of this was that disunity appeared within the laboratory over what informational requirements should be present in PBS. This disagreement indicated competing definitions over the body of knowledge and information that was useful and valuable to the laboratory, and therefore to them as a professional group. The disagreement centred on what format of information retrieval was necessary to make useful clinical interpretations of tests in the area of organ rejections. A clinical scientist explained the disagreement:

> We entered all the screening results into a book and the strengths of the reactions were catalogued there and which panels they actually reacted against. Now we have lost that. Now we get a percentage of reactivity which basically indicates that they produce antibodies against tissue types. Before, you could have a look at which panel members they had reacted against, now you get reactivity against a percentage of the panel . . . This is one area we were worried about losing.

Significantly, the fault line lay between the new head and the existing clinical scientists: 'Our director also doesn't feel, he comes from a different system, he doesn't feel it's any loss really. I miss it, and other scientists miss it too.' As well as indicating that competing definitions of information need have emerged in the context of the system, this disagreement tells us something else about the way in which information and knowledge become useful: it indicates the situatedness of utility and value. The clinical scientists had developed a body of information that they regarded as producing valuable knowledge, which also helped secure their professional clinical status and that of the laboratory. Coming from another site with different practices, the new head could not see the utility of the information or the value of the knowledge that clinical scientists sought to protect.

The second area of disagreement that posed a challenge to existing definitions of professionalism in the laboratory focused on access to PBS. While most in the laboratory agreed that PBS was problematic because of its design, there was less agreement about how far it was genuinely incompatible. The laboratory was having difficulties in registering patients correctly, a common problem being the production of 'multiple accounts' which scattered patients' details and test results across different accounts. Potentially, this could lead to clinical error as well as meaning that accurate monitoring and billing of laboratory activity became difficult. Competing interpretations quickly emerged of where the blame for this problem lay. For some, PBS itself was the problem; others saw the problem as the result of incompetent use. The deputy head was clear that the problem was with poor use. This led her to reduce certain members' access to the system:

Things go wrong and I have had to limit some people's use of the system to the more simple tasks. Once they have that under their belt they can do, say, other things such as verification. The problem is that at a touch of a button you can get a record that is completely wrong.

The competing interpretations of where the problem lay and the decision to exclude certain scientists' use of PBS led to tensions in the laboratory. One clinical scientist said: 'Overall it [PBS] has caused more problems and caused more stress, the stress has a ripple effect. Relationships get so strained.' Those targeted for exclusion felt that they were being singled out and ill-treated rather than helped. They felt it unfair that blame was focused on them rather than on the technology:

> You can complain or you can ask, but because everybody is insecure about the system and everyone is struggling, if someone else has a problem or messes things up for everyone else the reactions are extreme. Stress levels are very high . . . It's quite aggressive.

This had various implications for the constitution of professionalism in the laboratory. Firstly, it fractured its collective basis. The clinical scientists no longer shared a singular and united interpretation of need and value. Secondly, in its place a new professionalism was emerging which was only open to certain members of the laboratory who were happy to and could use PBS. The ways in which using the technology was incorporated into the professional project resituated the project as only open to particular individuals able to display the newly valued skills. Thirdly, this meant that PBS was becoming a part of the professional project of some clinical scientists but not others. Being able to use and see as valuable the structure and format of the information held in PBS was becoming part of being a professional in the Tissue Typing laboratory. The deputy made it clear that she saw PBS as a vehicle for her exercise of professional judgement, alongside other professionals in the hospital:

> I find the patient enquiry module very good. Previously we had no way of seeing how a patient was doing ourselves, other than if we had feedback from another surgery. Now if we have someone who is transplanted with a kidney we can go into patient care enquiry and pick up the biochemical results and decide for ourselves.

The clinical scientists in Tissue Typing adopted some of the same strategies as doctors and MLSOs, but also adopted others in the different context of their smaller, 'specialised' laboratory. The result was a malleable approach that led to a reconstitution of what a professional was in the laboratory, as something that involved PBS. It also led to a reconstitution of who was a legitimate professional, and placed the technology as a crucial resource in the local strategies of key laboratory members.

Conclusion

Within both Microbiology and Tissue Typing, the arrival of PBS altered the way that tasks were done and information was handled. These changes posed a threat to the knowledge, skill and autonomy claims made by MLSOs, doctors and clinical scientists. This threat had two key implications. Firstly, the system itself was unblackboxed as different groups challenged its priorities and values. Secondly, at the same time the claims that these groups used to unblackbox the system were themselves challenged. The end result was the involvement of users in a changed system, a changed organisation, and a changed articulation of their professional identity.

There were significant differences in the way PBS affected the professional space occupied by MLSOs, doctors and clinical scientists. Doctors under PBS, as with the old system, continued to depend on MLSOs to produce results for validation, and ensured that the way the system was set up secured their authority not only over validation but also over the MLSOs. MLSOs found their professional space reduced by PBS, and even though managers believed that the interpretation of results was an extremely important professional skill, this could not be used to enhance MLSOs' position. In effect, many MLSOs felt that the introduction of PBS had not only confirmed the boundaries between them and the doctors, but through its perceived deskilling had meant new barriers were appearing. In Tissue Typing new barriers that appeared were shaped in part by variations in access to PBS that installed new hierarchies amongst the 'professionals' in the laboratory.

Each of the occupational groups discussed here was affected by and in turn had a capacity to mediate PBS in different ways. In Tissue Typing it empowered some to build a new source of professional power which necessitated the exclusion of others. For doctors it posed a threat, yet could be accommodated. However, for MLSOs it had a much more extensive impact on their occupational role and professional status. What happened to the MLSOs indicates the limitations to some groups' ability to ensure that others share and legitimate their articulation of what value they bring to the organisation.

In considering why the occupational groups we studied had such different tactics in relation to PBS and ended up in such different positions, it is important to reflect on the influence of the variation that can exist in the level of prestige and power given to different professional groups. For the doctors, their professional position had a context that went beyond their immediate organisational environment and was further secured in legal regulation and statute. This gave them a more secure position from which to make their claims to knowledge and indeterminacy, and made available wider resources they could incorporate into their professional project in the laboratories. Using de Certeau's language they, in fact, could be strategic (1984). The MLSOs, in contrast, had only tactics available. They were more dependent on their immediate organisational environment and the occupational role that was 'allowed' them in the laboratory. This limited both the resources they could deploy and the tactics that they had available. In addition, the fact that MLSOs were testing patient samples for what were, at times, life-threatening conditions meant that there were clear limitations to how much they could actively resist the system. The MLSOs' own professional identity that entailed they treat safety as of paramount concern impacted on how they in the end would have to accommodate to the system. There was a need to secure the system and resolve uncertainty: a clear fear and issue during the early days of PBS in the laboratories was the need to remove any possibility that results could get lost or wrong results go out to laboratories or GP surgeries. These factors together left the MLSOs unable to police the boundaries that marked the resources – such as claims to knowledge and indeterminate skill – constructed as key to their professional status. Although, like the MLSOs, the clinical scientists in Tissue Typing were tied to a specific organisational environment, they were able, in a setting where no other significant occupational groups existed, to position themselves as indispensable to the laboratory's functioning. This gave them scope to perform professional 'labour' that confirmed their status and gave them a position from which to deal with PBS and alter its priorities into a set of organisational practices that rearticulated their project.

Professional identity helps actors to retain control and ownership over resources such as bodies of knowledge and skill that allow them to make claims to status and autonomy. The experience of the professional groups in Finlay suggests that knowledge can be a particularly important resource. Maintenance, surveillance and control over the flow and structure of information can help to retain security and ownership over what can be presented as a discrete body of knowledge. The close relationship between bodies of knowledge and the identities of professionals means that any disturbance to either of these is likely to lead to uncertainty. Rather than remain fixed, the solution for the professional is always to shift with the times, to deploy claims to the heterogeneity, indeterminacy and exclusivity of their knowledge to good effect. The concern then becomes how to establish strategies that will close the opened black box of their professional identity, to find a way back to security.

5 Organisational culture and technological change

Organisational culture has taken on increasing importance in analyses of technological and organisational change management. On one level we would agree that culture is an important element of understanding change. However, given our presentation of cultural dynamics in Chapter 1, we do not see the significance of culture as coming from attempts to control or direct it as a tool of change management. Instead the focus needs to be on how culture is lived and enacted by organisational actors (including central actors) during their day-to-day life and during change.

This chapter begins by outlining the problems with assuming that organisational culture can be a managerial tool for change. As an alternative we outline the ways in which organisational members enact and make sense of organisational culture, developing the initial points made in Chapter 1: in particular, our claim that organisations contain cultural dynamics rather than having 'a culture'. This then helps us describe how members' relationship to culture influences how they become involved in shaping new technology. We then use the Brodies case study to detail the ways that an existing organisational culture – as distinctively understood by various groups in the organisation – influenced how organisational groups interpreted the technology. In this chapter we focus on two of the occupational groups in stores, and on the division between large and small stores.

Positioning culture

Morgan (1997) argues that management academics became interested in organisational culture after the success of Japanese companies in the eighties. The distinctive culture of Japanese companies – in particular how it differed from that found in American companies – was seen as central to their success. A very particular version of what constitutes culture was presented in these analyses. As we suggested in Chapter 1, those looking at organisational culture focus on 'the values, ideas, beliefs, norms, rituals, and other patterns of shared meaning that guide organizational life' (ibid.: 7). Very quickly the new fascination with organisational culture within management literature became focused on identifying successful organisational cultures which managers could copy and implant into their organisations. This work was quickly criticised for its lack of sensitivity to the different types of culture required for different types of environment, organisational size and structure, product and organisational task. This led to a growth in literature that matched culture types to organisation types, suggesting that it was important that managers develop the right type of culture for their products, environment and staff. For example, Handy (1985) talks of four types of organisational culture – power, role, task and person – each of which matches particular types of organisation. Some sensitivity to variation was combined with an acknowledgement that successful organisations would have subcultures that would be integrated at some point within the organisation (ibid.).

In analyses such as that found in Handy, culture – whatever the type – is a tool managers should use to guarantee the success of their activities: 'The suggestion is that, if the appropriate culture prevails where that set of activities prevails, then that part of the organisation will be more effective' (ibid.: 208). Culture is presented as uniquely powerful in directing change, for, as Handy explains, 'the customs and traditions of a place are a powerful way of influencing behaviour' (ibid.: 188). Helpfully, many books emerged which promised to show the manager how to use culture. One by Hall (1995) makes the claim on its back cover that 'culture behaviour is manageable' and that 'you can learn how to manage culture'. In a variation of this, it was suggested that part of the work involved in directing change includes the construction of a new culture capable of carrying through the changes desired. This was because '[a]n established organisational culture, can . . . be a powerful block on the initiation of new cultural patterns' (Brown 1995: 129). Case studies emerged which detailed the successful completion of change through building and manipulating a corporate culture. Morgan summarised one such example of managed change with the comment that 'it is probably no exaggeration to suggest that, in this case, corporate culture may have been the single most important factor standing between success and failure' (1997: 132).

While we would not want to deny that higher management attempt to shape and manipulate organisational culture, this cannot fully encompass the cultural realm of the organisation or the role of this realm in change. As we indicated in our presentation of Martin's work (1992) in Chapter 1, organisational culture emerges from the social realities of organisational life rather than at the dictate of management. Organisational culture forms through the ways actors make sense of their own position and the organisation through the cultural symbols they help to create. One clear implication of thinking of culture in this way is that managers, rather than constructing culture, are constructed in culture.

If we think of the organisation as a 'reflexive social system' (Leflaive 1996: 25), we can regard all organisational members as participants in constructing the cultural terms through which they understand their position and role. Significantly, cultures become products of interaction, forming through the ways that different people within an organisation not only make sense of themselves but also make sense of each other. In the words of Gherardi, 'culture consists of the taken-for-granted and problematic webs of meaning that people produce and deploy when they interact' (1995: 12).

Cultural groupings

Focusing on organisational culture as a product of social interaction prioritises the role of organisational actors in participating in cultural dynamics. We have already seen that in various ways actors interact with each other and the organisation within different types of group membership: as members of different parts of an organisation in Chapter 3 and as members of professional groups in Chapter 4. Therefore, in understanding organisational culture we must consider how groups come to have distinct conceptions of culture and how this can create multiple interpretations of cultural meanings and values in one organisation.

As with Nonaka's notion of 'communities of interaction' (1994), we can suggest that different job roles or substructures of an organisation create clusters of meaning, forming a repertoire of symbols, language, action and identity that can be understood as a shared culture. In saying that shared meanings can develop along these lines, we do not claim that it is necessarily the job role or position within a substructure of the organisation that defines the interpretation that develops. Particular meanings and interpretations emerge in interactions within or between groups to produce the culture shared by group members. In addition, it is important to stress the influence of other aspects of people's group memberships – e.g. gender and ethnicity – in helping to shape shared meanings.

The potential danger of this approach is lapsing into a naive voluntarism that assumes that each group simply adopts a cultural interpretation that it likes or finds appealing. This would be to suggest that different groups are free to decide on their own interpretation of a wider culture. Such a position would ignore the fact that organisational space is immersed in power relations. The unequal distribution of cultural and material resources, including members' positions within structural hierarchies, is an important factor shaping these relations. Indeed, groups construct identities and articulate needs that help them secure such resources. There are important questions about, firstly, the circumstances that allow groups to form around values that are distinctive to, or even challenging to, dominant articulations of the culture of an organisation, and, secondly, how and why a group's articulation of culture takes on legitimacy among others. Why do some groups have more of an ability or opportunity to influence how other groups develop their interpretations?

Organisational culture and technological change

How are we to understand the relationship between organisational culture and technological change? It is clear that we are not presenting this relationship as

the adoption or manipulation of a particular culture in order to aid the introduction of a new form of organisational structure or a new form of technology,
as found in some of the approaches detailed at the beginning of this chapter.
Echoing the position of Bloomfield, Coombs and Owen (1994) we would
suggest that privileging either technology or culture is to miss the interaction
between both:

> The versions of determinism on offer are either a technological determin-
> ism in which organisations are seen as adaptations to the unfolding logic
> of technologies; or a social determinism in which technologies are seen as
> social products or reflections of particular constellations of social and
> organisational forces.
>
> (ibid.: 144)

However, we are still saying that culture will play a part in shaping change.
For we would agree with Coombs, Knights and Willmott's assertion that
'even the most technical of tasks cannot be undertaken without reference to the
meanings which underpin their formulation and guide their execution' (1992:
58). Johnson (1988) has stressed the ways in which a new technology or managerial strategy is interpreted through existing cultures and becomes invested,
like established routines and artefacts, with the myths and power structures in
the organisation. What we wish to stress as part of this is that:

- the process of culture mediating technology is not one that is driven by
  management;
- this process does not leave culture untouched – culture will be changed
  too.

Borrowing from Berg (1997), we can think of the relationship between culture and technology in times of change as being one of 'mutual adaptation'.
While groups may interpret 'technology' from within their existing cultural
assumptions, at the same time they will be developing new interpretations as
they interact with the technology and with others using it. It is these interactions as understood by each group that form the key theme of this chapter. The
mutual adaptation of organisational culture and technological systems is
framed by broader values associated with technology. As Chapter 1 indicated,
these values allow particular forms of speaking about technology, produce
particular exclusions and inclusions, and mediate experiences and interpretations. These cultural assumptions about technology can be supported by
instrumental discourses of efficiency associated with and legitimating management change. Together they are a resource and source of meaning distinct
from organisational culture, but one that can become part of the cultural life
of the organisation. Thus, innovation is about the interplay of norms and
assumptions associated with technology and organisational culture that result
in the rearticulation of both.

In light of the above, we would argue that technological innovation in an organisation needs to be addressed through the following questions:

- What characterises the cultural dynamics at the moment of change?
- How do such interpretations play a part in the innovation process?
- How are generalised values associated with the technical and the instrumental articulated in particular organisational cultures and in association with particular technologies?
- How do the meanings associated with the technology and with the cultural interpretation change as they interact?
- Do particular groups have a privileged position in developing the new organisational cultural and technological meanings emerging in the organisation?

The theme of cultural interpretations of organisation and technology is developed through examination of the Brodies case study and the Staff Organiser.

Brodies as family

Brodies, as we indicated in the Introduction, is a large, long-established retailer in the UK. During its long history a strong corporate culture has emerged that amounted to an organising narrative which underpinned management regulation and control over the scope of store and company operations.

One of the first things we asked staff in interviews – both at Head Office and in stores – was to describe Brodies. Initially we had expected responses outlining the structure of the company or the products they sold. While some answered in this fashion, the majority talked in cultural terms: they described a company unique in its operation and its relationship to staff and customer. One Head Office manager explained:

> [Brodies] is unique by virtue of its history and culture . . . Its history shapes its future . . . There is a particular type of person who is employed by the organisation.

Staff appeared keen for us as outsiders to recognise the culture within which they operated, one based on notions of 'family'. As the quotation above suggests, the mythology of the family was seen to derive from the ethos of the founders of Brodies. This culture had a clear shape for Head Office managers we spoke to. For them, the Brodies culture placed them in *paternal* authority over the extended family of the company: a language of obligation to the company, its staff and customers, combined with an unquestioned belief in management's right and ability to make judgements on behalf of others. As one senior Head Office manager put it:

In [Brodies] there is a culture that has been around for a long time where people have had very clear plans to follow and they follow it, they don't question why they do. Most people recognise that it is better than chaos and go with it.

Interestingly, many Head Office managers represented the family culture as a permanent defining feature of the company. Organising practices could come and go, new technology could arrive, but the family culture would remain unchanged and unchallenged. Others in the organisation supported the narratives of family that were expressed by Head Office managers. In particular, their right to govern was seldom challenged. In these terms the family culture did act as an integrative narrative that maintained a belief that Head Office 'knows best' and implicated store staff in the pursuit of common organisational goals.

Brodies' senior management worked hard to foster a corporate culture of togetherness and agreement and of commitment to the customer. It was secured in symbols throughout the company: shared canteens, uniforms for shopfloor workers and store management, and notice boards throughout the stores announcing profit figures, goals, tasks, company objectives and best employee awards. Slogans covered the back areas of the stores reminding the staff of company programmes and objectives. For example, 'Seven Ways to Keep the Customer Happy' was a prominent poster often placed close to the staff's entry point onto the sales floor.

Introducing the Staff Organiser

The Head Office managers who spoke eloquently about the heritage of Brodies also acknowledged that the company was changing. One explained:

> We are becoming leaner . . . Everything must have a cost-benefit justification that links to promoting sales, or reducing costs . . . The changes are about making it more efficient. Technology is one of the major ways of achieving that.

Interviews with Head Office managers pointed to shifting views of the organisation and of the role of culture in it. While some continued to draw on family culture as a source of meaning, others spoke the language of technology and technological progress. The significance of this split is that it indicates the way that more than one set of meanings and assumptions can develop amongst people sharing the same job role. It also reinforces our earlier point that culture is not just something which managers use to influence others, it is part of the process through which their own role comes to make sense to themselves and to others.

The quotation above comes from a Head Office manager more closely associated with the generalised values of technology. Such managers were relatively new to the company and this in itself marked them out as different. It is only in recent times that Brodies had begun to recruit senior managers from outside the company – including from direct competitors. Previously the tradition had been to promote from within – Head Office managers would recite long lists of stores they had worked in and positions they had held. The recruitment of outsiders broke with tradition and signalled the determination of those at the top of the organisation to change the way it operated.

Several of the Staff Organiser's management sponsors in the Operations Improvement Department (OID) were new to the company. They argued that technology was a powerful tool at the organisation's disposal that they would be foolish to ignore – after all, their competitors did not ignore it:

> In order to make it more efficient you need to introduce new practices, they can be new working practices . . . or they can be exploiting new mediums of delivery, information through technology.

They used a technical discourse in their construction of the Organiser's functions, capabilities and benefits that blurred a management agenda with a technological promise. From within this discourse and a discourse of instrumental rationality, certain priorities and assumptions were embodied in the system. These included legitimacy of formal representations of organisational life, and the goal of a standardised and predictable shopfloor environment. Together, their articulation of technical and instrumental discourses had the potential to hide the motives and politics underlying the system behind the cloak of imperative, necessity and progress. The generalised valuing of technology external to Brodies ('everyone is doing it', 'we must keep up with what so and so is doing') was an important resource to a group with little connection with the Brodies family narrative. It also helped link the technology in a mutually supportive way to the other operational changes that were taking place at the same time, including tighter staff budgets, increased performance management and alterations in distribution strategies.

Taking the Organiser to stores

For the Organiser to become part of store life, key groups there would have not just to use the technology; they would also have to adopt the logic of the system and begin to use the language of the new technical and instrumental discourses. However, this would happen through the complex interplay of these values and assumptions with the cultural dynamics of store life. This was a process that was unlikely to mean either that the technological values would be adopted wholesale or that the meanings associated with the cultural life of stores would simply be discarded.

The corporate version of the Brodies family was a key organising narrative with meaning for all company members. However, differently placed members of the organisation developed different interpretations of the narrative.

Therefore, in stores the family narrative went beyond the corporate story to form new narratives. In the following sections various different groups will be discussed, including their shifting allegiances both to the existing culture in Brodies and to the emerging technical and instrumental discourses which became conflicting sources of interpretation and value when the Staff Organiser was introduced. The first of these groups formed around occupational roles in stores.

There are various reasons why job role became significant in forging similar interpretations of family culture across the physical distance of different stores. Supervisors and store managers had broadly the same set of job responsibilities, whatever store they worked in. In part this was because large stores were remarkably similar in how they operated. In addition, the group identity of supervisors and store managers was fostered by the organisation itself. For example, Brodies would periodically bring both supervisors and store managers together at store visits and training events. Store managers met with other store managers in their local area once a month to discuss various aspects of company business. In addition, staff relations with each other were mediated through job role, as people interacted with each other and interpreted each other as sales assistant, supervisor or manager. An important symbolic example of this is that name badges included job title, and uniforms were specific to the different job roles. Aspects of the personal background of people in these two job roles also influenced the emergence of common narratives of family and culture. Store managers shared a common background due to their gender (male), class (middle-class), university education and career path within the company. Supervisors shared a common background due to their gender (female), their experience of balancing work with family responsibilities and their path towards limited power on the shop floor.

Established cultural interpretations of supervisors and store managers

Early interviews revealed the influence of the shared family culture for both supervisors and store managers, but they also showed that these groups had reinterpreted and rearticulated the culture through their own experiences and interpretations.

Supervisors' early interviews were peppered with the rhetoric of Brodies' family culture. What might, at first glance, appear as simple acceptance of corporate organisational culture was actually a subtle reinterpretation. Supervisors did not question the overarching patriarchal authority of the Head Office managers, and supported the dominant goals of the organisation. At the same time, however, they articulated a distinct version of family culture and of the organisation. The supervisors placed a high stress on ensuring the well-being of their staff – their 'girls'. One supervisor described her position in the following terms:

> I am the intermediate between the sales manager and the staff, I can see both points of view, and hopefully I can see it as fairly as possible. If the staff have a gripe then I put it to the managers, and vice versa. I think everyone works well together, because we all care about the environment we work in . . . I know that other retailers just don't care how they speak to their staff, and that doesn't breed loyalty.

From the early interviews with store managers it became evident that they articulated the family culture in similar ways to Head Office managers. This is hardly surprising, given that the culture placed both groups in an unquestioned position of power and authority. Store managers took great pride in their role in the organisation and in the heritage of the company:

Store Manager: I think it's always been regarded as a very paternalistic company, perhaps the younger employees don't recognise that as much as the older ones do, like all other companies we tended to move very slightly away from that sort of image. Not intentionally, it's just happened.

Interviewer: You say paternalistic, do you mean that's toward both staff and customers?

Store Manager: Oh yes. Very much so.

What this quotation also indicates is that this culture and, as a consequence, their role in the organisation were seen by many store managers as under threat.

Through the family culture, store managers positioned themselves as benevolent patriarchs, shouldering the responsibilities of power, while aware of the needs and interests of those below them:

> I am a leader of this band of more than a hundred staff . . . I have a small management and supervisory team, and through them and through the staff we deliver what the company wants. It is about making sure that the staff enjoy work – we have an element of fun . . . I encourage my management team to lead their teams, we are very open, very democratic . . . We drive that down to the staff and we do talk about empowerment, staff can take decisions, particularly when they are dealing with customers.

Both supervisors and store managers reworked the corporate culture and located it within their local experiences. It emerged from and shaped each group's interaction with others in the stores and with others outside the store from both Area and Head Office. It would also influence their interpretation of and role in the introduction of the Staff Organiser.

Supervisors' and store managers' early interpretations of the Staff Organiser

The first reactions of supervisors and store managers to the Organiser shared concerns and roots in cultural interpretations shaped by family narratives. All supervisors generally told the same story about the introduction of the Staff Organiser into stores. Initially the system was, as far as they were concerned, unworkable: it did not allocate the correct number of staff to tasks; it would pick the wrong people for particular tasks; it would give people inappropriate breaks; it would leave sales assistants doing the same task for too long and so on. To understand why supervisors viewed the Staff Organiser as unworkable we must turn to their interpretations of the family culture. Ultimately, supervisors' objections to the system rested on the belief that its logic and priorities were incompatible with the cultural assumptions by which their departments operated:

> I was very dubious of the Staff Organiser when it first came out, because I had a lot of problems. The strength that I found with the old system was that I knew my staff, I knew what they could do, and what they couldn't do, what they liked doing, which is a big difference . . . Whereas the Staff Organiser doesn't think like that. It doesn't know the individual.

Crucially, their understanding of their job role meant that the supervisors were highly concerned about the impact of the new system on their 'girls':

> Everyone is moaning, a lot of people say, 'I used to enjoy my job, but now there is so much pressure, I don't.' I think they blame a lot on the computerisation, it is telling you when you have to do things.

Another supervisor commented on her early impressions of what the system would mean for her staff:

> For some of the girls that I have, they have been here twenty years, and all of a sudden, they are given a sheet of paper that tells them what to do. I think they thought, 'well I know my job'. I think perhaps if they had been given some of the information which we had been given, about how it would improve the company, maybe they would have accepted it easier.

This early disquiet with the Staff Organiser and other changes is a reflection of the strength of the supervisors' allegiance to their cultural interpretation. As the quotation above suggests, however, a key element of that framework was loyalty to Brodies and acquiescence to the paternal authority of Head Office. This was to be a counterbalance to their critical interpretation of the Organiser and of the company's objectives in introducing it. In particular, supervisors rarely considered rejecting the system. Instead, much of their response focused on 'fixing' it. The most common response to teething problems adopted by supervisors was simply to write on the shopfloor plans produced by the system. By doing so, they attempted to give sales assistants more variety during their day and more say on when they took their breaks and worked on cash points. Many of the particular practices adopted by supervisors are discussed in more detail in Chapter 6. Overall, the Staff Organiser's plans were, in the words of several supervisors, treated not as 'gospel' but as an 'imperfect guide'. In so doing, supervisors reached an accommodation between the system and the culture of the shop floor.

The supervisors' strategies in regards to the Organiser were backed up and aided by the store managers. Like that of the supervisors, the disquiet of store managers owed much to their interpretation of the family culture. Store managers knew that supervisors were altering the plans on the shop floor and defended the need for them to do so. In one store the plans for an area of cash points in a particularly busy area of the store were printed off separately to allow the supervisors to make manual alterations. The store manager explained that the alterations were made to ensure that staff would not be on tills too long; that is, for the length of time that the Organiser thought appropriate:

> it is a small piece of paper . . . I don't believe that all the manual changes that we are doing on it – despite the implementer coming in and saying we are doing too many – I don't believe I could genuinely say that we are being less efficient by having more pencil marks on there. I am quite prepared to allow them to amend that as often as they need.

Store managers also allowed supervisors much greater access to the computer itself than had been intended by Head Office. In the majority of stores studied, store managers introduced times or specific occasions when supervisors themselves could change information held in the system to ensure that their departments 'worked well'; for example, altering the skills matrix so that it would change which sales assistants were allocated to which jobs at particular times of the day. Managers knew that the supervisors' definition of 'worked well' included a degree of looking after the sales assistants and accepted this as a justification. Protecting the morale of their stores was an often-quoted priority of store managers. It was used to justify their uneasiness not only towards the Organiser but also concerning other changes – in particular, the shrinking staff budget. As one store manager complained:

> It is not just that we are changing the way we do things, which has been significant anyway, it is the fact that we have had to reduce staff costs at the same time. That has had a significant effect on staff morale.

From within the security of the family culture, the managers, like the supervisors, noted what they saw as gaps and inconsistencies within the Organiser. Again, this went beyond discussion of 'bugs' in the system to a concern about the incompatibility of its underlying assumptions with the cultural realities of the store. What was inconsistent was that which seemed at odds with the values expressed in the family culture. The original core business of the company was a key area for managers: in part this was because to be a store manager you had to have worked in that area. For managers, the Organiser was particularly troublesome when in their eyes it hampered the operation of the core business. Crucially they felt that the Organiser harmed this part of store activity because much of what happened here, including interaction with customers, could not be found or placed within the formal representations held in the system:

> you've got a certain amount of downtime that they will allow you. However, how would you measure advice, and how do you time it, how do you compare one store to another? ... How do you put in skills that you can't measure, you can't quantify?

This manager's solution to the problem was to 'fix' the system by exaggerating trading patterns to increase the number of staff that the system would allocate to the core business: 'You have to build in the fact that you have put more [staff] time in than theoretically you're supposed to have.'

While supervisors and managers justified these alterations as being in the best interest of the efficient working of their stores, Head Office managers who had constructed the logic of the system based on their association with technical values and discourses deemed these actions 'resistant'. As far as the developers of the system were concerned, its plans and targets were sacrosanct; any problems with the Staff Organiser could and should be resolved by technical fine-tuning. During the introduction of the Staff Organiser, the roles that were played out by supervisors and store managers, and their understanding of what the organisation was, were highly significant. Supervisors and store managers smoothed the Organisers' acceptance by shopfloor staff by reinterpreting plans and data via the family culture; this ensured, they claimed, a greater sensitivity to the operations of stores. Without this localised interpretation, which could be called 'accommodating resistance' (MacLeod 1995), the system's introduction could have led to much higher levels of rejection.

Varied levels of belief in the system

We have suggested that by working with, rather than against, the Organiser the supervisors and store managers were reinterpreting and to an extent reshaping the system via the family culture. This did not, however, mark a decisive victory for their family cultures over the logic of the system. When we reinterviewed supervisors and store managers as part of the longitudinal part of our study, we found major shifts in their relationship to the Staff Organiser and, by implication, in their understanding of Brodies. What also became apparent was that the shifts in interpretation for supervisors and store managers were not the same.

On returning to stores, we were struck by evidence that supervisors increasingly accepted the plans, priorities and targets of the Staff Organiser. When they discussed their use and evaluation of the system, there was now little talk of the need to protect sales assistants or mediate on their behalf. After working with the Organiser for six months, one supervisor told how she had begun to accept the system as right and her previous forms of judgement as wrong:

> I now know the importance of priorities . . . We had a case where one girl was planned in to do some till work, but she didn't like till work, so instead of saying 'look it has got to be done,' we took the skills off her on the computer. Now I would say: 'That's a priority, you have the skill, you have to do it.' Before you were using personal feelings.

What a supervisor had once called her 'personal touch' was now reinterpreted as illegitimate emotion. Whereas previously supervisors had questioned the ability of the system to recognise the complexity and variety of tasks carried out by sales assistants, they now saw indicators generated by the Staff Organiser as proof of the amount of staff time spent 'usefully'.

The efficiency indicators produced by the Organiser, which had previously been disregarded by supervisors or massaged by management, were increasingly coming to represent organisational reality for them. An example of this was the way in which the measure of 'scheduling success' – an indicator of how well priority tasks were covered – had become the basis for discussions of performance within stores and between stores and Area Office. In every Brodies store, the supervisors and members of the management team met each week to discuss and evaluate each department of the store. Figures and plans generated by the system now dictated the form and content of this meeting. Supervisors reported that the accounts of the performance and needs of their departments offered by the system were privileged over their subjective, local knowledge and experience.

In the first round of interviews, supervisors often argued that a standardising system like the Staff Organiser could not appreciate the local realities of store life. In the later interviews this argument was rarely made. Supervisors had come, therefore, more and more to adopt interpretations and approaches embedded in the logic of the Staff Organiser. What encouraged supervisors to adopt these approaches?

One important factor that drew the supervisors into the orbit of the technology was their hands-on use of the computer system. Head Office had never intended that supervisors should have this form of access to the Staff Organiser. The officially prescribed role of supervisors was to use the plans produced by the system and provide information to keep it up to date; plans and reports were supposed to be produced by members of the store management team. Despite this, as we have already mentioned, during the introductory phase most store managers allowed supervisors access to the computer.

What a number of supervisors termed 'fiddling' with the Organiser –

exploring its possibilities and tinkering with the data on staff and store that it contained – initially allowed the system to become workable in the terms of the existing culture. Close contact with the computer was, however, also crucial to supervisors' eventual greater acceptance of the logic of the Staff Organiser: worries about the cultural and social consequences of the system were replaced by technical concerns about their own operation of that system and 'getting the system right'. The supervisors became focused on how well they were using the Staff Organiser – often assuming that any errors were down to their own inadequate use of it – and 'forgot' to question its suitability or legitimacy. They stopped wondering if the Staff Organiser was right for their store and instead they worried more about whether they were using it correctly. Tellingly, in the one store we studied where supervisors were kept away from the computer and left simply to use the plans it generated, they appeared closest to rejecting the Staff Organiser outright. In the other eleven stores, access had encouraged the supervisors to adopt the logic of both the Organiser and the other management changes being introduced at the same time.

The technical focus of supervisors' concerns were further secured by the store experts who were sent into stores during the early days of the system's operation. Developers of the Staff Organiser at Head Office were unhappy at what they saw as inappropriate use and adaptation of the system. To tackle this 'problem', Head Office appointed store experts (who were themselves supervisors and managerial staff seconded from other stores) who would go into stores and explain the 'proper' use of the system and stamp out practices such as over-writing on plans. What is significant here is that the experts involved store staff in the pursuit of the technical objective of 'getting the system right'. They were therefore effective in neutralising supervisors' reservations about the Staff Organiser by translating their concerns into problems of poor use that reflected inadequate training or understanding.

In the later interviews undertaken with store managers it was apparent that in some ways their changing positions were similar to those of supervisors. In particular, there was evidence that they were beginning to adopt the assumptions and priorities embodied in the Staff Organiser. The store managers were as keen as supervisors – and others in stores – to see scheduling success targets met and 'efficiency' gains 'proved'. Managers also talked about using the Organiser 'strategically' to predict store priorities and needs for the future. The Organiser allowed managers to play 'what if' scenarios which they used to experiment with what would happen if they changed their opening hours or altered stock deliveries. Playing 'what if' scenarios placed a significant level of trust and hope in the formal representations within the system to map out the future needs of the store.

As with the supervisors, managers' enrolment into the logic and assumptions of the Staff Organiser was testimony to the power of technical and instrumental discourses. Like the supervisors, the store managers were influenced by the ways in which those behind the Organiser ensured that discussion of making the system workable remained within a technical realm. A significant aspect of this was the continued technical improvements to the system. When we last interviewed in stores they were receiving the fourth set of upgrades to the Staff Organiser. These fixed programming errors and added to the functionality of the system. They also helped to exclude more challenging questions about the legitimacy and use of the information in the system. Rather than centring on the objectives of the system, most of the debates around the system revolved around the latest upgrade.

This cultural shift must also be understood in the context of changing forms of management regulation in the company (a factor that also influenced the changing attitudes of supervisors). Store managers talked of being under increased pressure to work within tighter staff budgets while obtaining increased profits. They saw themselves as caught up in a never-ending cycle of technological and organisational change: several managers suggested that all they wanted was a clear year when nothing new was introduced. At the same time, Head Office made sure that store managers were aware that the Staff Organiser was one vehicle they wished to see used to ensure that new priorities and targets were met. This produced a very real material incentive to comply with the figures and plans of the Organiser. To help this 'rational' response, one area manager we interviewed included Staff Organiser targets in the performance contracts of his store managers. He made clear to us, and more importantly to store management, that 'we're actually doing some very close auditing at the moment, to make sure that people are doing what we've asked them to do'. Area management would make unannounced visits to stores to evaluate how closely they were following the plans. One area manager explained that he would arrive in a store unannounced, pick up the Organiser's staff plan for a particular department and then ask the store manager 'It says on the plan that Flossie should be here between two o'clock and four o'clock, is she?'

While managers had adopted many of the assumptions associated with the Staff Organiser there are noticeable differences in how the store managers as opposed to supervisors continued to interpret both family culture and the assumptions embedded in the Organiser. Store managers continued to question the effect that the changes introduced alongside the Staff Organiser – reduced staff budget, increased opening hours, etc. – were having on their staff's morale and on the successful operation of their store:

> [b]ecause you're asking people to do more than they have done in the past, or deliver more, and that's where the pressure comes from. The downtime in any job is decreasing quite significantly. I happen to believe that if we are not very careful we're going to get to the stage where down time would have got so little, well we're already experiencing lack of flexibility . . . I can't conjure these people from thin air.

Store managers voiced this concern from a position of paternal authority over their charges. Very rarely did the managers present stress as a problem for themselves; it was their staff who, they argued, were suffering:

> [t]hey start to throw wobblies and can't cope themselves, we're coming to the stage where that is happening now. What we're asking them to do is getting more and more and we're seeing more and more stress, particularly at senior staff level. The general staff level are leaving, not because of what we pay them, but because they can't cope with the stress.

The continued allegiance to family meant that they continued to show a level of concern for their staff, a concern that in some ways supervisors had replaced with a concern for obtaining efficiency and ensuring the success of the Staff Organiser. The distance the store managers still retained from the technical requirements of the Organiser allowed them to continue to remain sceptical about the benefits and logic of the system. In particular, doubt was still raised about the legitimacy and accuracy of the formal representations of store life held in and generated by the Organiser:

> Perhaps we are expecting too much from the system and putting too much into it. If you work in M&S, they don't have a system other than one that tells them when tills need to be manned.

Why would the store managers continue to evoke their version of the family culture in the face of the drive towards standardisation and performance management? There is one important factor that separates them from the more accommodating supervisors. The store managers' version of the family culture had helped secure them independence and power within 'their' store. Over the years, Brodies' store managers had constructed and articulated this authority through the family culture. Store managers would defer to the superior patriarchs at Head Office, but in their store, in their immediate family, they had legitimate autonomy and authority. With this power came the responsibility to look after their staff, a responsibility full of gender symbolism that denied their largely female staff equal levels of power and independence. The discourses of standardisation and technical efficiency embodied in the Staff Organiser appeared to offer little support for this power. Instead they challenged the independence of store activity, by presuming that an IT system could predict store needs based on criteria set centrally. This sense of challenge to their patriarchal authority over their store and staff thus lay behind much of the distance store managers wished to retain between themselves and the logic of the system:

> I view very strongly the opinion that [the Staff Organiser] is there as a management tool, and that at the end of the day, myself and the management team must be responsible for the operation of the store. I won't allow the [Staff Organiser] to dictate what should be spent . . . I would regret

very much if the company then came along and said, 'you will be staffed to [Staff Organiser] levels', where would that then take my flexibility, and my management skills? It would take them away. I would be unhappy actually if I'm only allowed to staff towards what that paper says, there's no entrepreneurial skill attached to that at all, anyone could just feed a piece of paper in and take another piece of paper out.

Small is beautiful: small stores

In addition to job role, the structural distinction between small stores and large stores created groups formed around working in the two types of store that had a significant role in mediating people's interpretations of both culture and technological change. In part this is because a distinction between small and large stores is built into the structure and organisation of Brodies. Small and large stores have their own separate line management structure. In addition, while in large stores the number of permanent staff (part- and full-time) can reach over a hundred, in small stores staff numbers can be as low as five. In small stores the management team consists of a store manager and supervisors. In the smallest stores there is only one supervisor, who may be supported by an assistant supervisor. In comparison to large stores that have expanded into selling a range of goods unconnected to the original core business of the company, this area is still highly visible in small stores. As we shall see, it is this distinction, as much as the physical difference in size, that marks out the different cultural dynamics of small and large stores.

Both store managers and supervisors in small stores linked their descriptions of the organisation and culture of Brodies to the importance of the core business to the outlook and philosophy of the company. In the words of two of the small store managers: 'it's distinctive because of the [service] we offer and the way we deal with it. It's distinctive in our culture and philosophy' and 'I think that we are considered to be the nation's [provider of this service]. All the foundations are based on that; history, professional stance, ethics.' Small store staff positioned themselves as important players in the continuation of this heritage within the company. The manager who stressed the ethics of their approach also went on to say: 'Certainly the background in it, a lot of people primarily see us as [this kind of service], especially the small stores. The larger stores some people see as department stores.'

Before the introduction of the Staff Organiser the small stores had developed an informal set of working practices. One small store supervisor described it in the following way:

> We get a lot of co-operation from the staff in this store, and dedication, but we don't have rigid rules and regulations. We have the [Brodies] regulations and rules, but within the store the staff co-operate more.

The strong and distinctive articulation of the family culture was an important factor in how small store staff interpreted, identified and used the Staff Organiser. As in large stores, the Organiser was initially seen as problematic. Getting data entered correctly, generating 'usable' plans, and working on the skills matrix all took time and led to increased pressure in many stores. In small stores it was the supervisor who had to enter all the data into the computer and produce plans. This additional task was allocated because the role of the supervisor in small stores involved higher levels of responsibility and pressure than found in large stores – according to small store supervisors. Small store supervisors whom we spoke to were both proud of this and concerned about their level of responsibility. This context of stress and pressure influenced the negative perceptions of the Organiser that several of them had. In one store where there was only one supervisor, she worried constantly about how much time she should spend off the shop floor 'getting the Organiser right' and how much time she should spend 'doing my job':

> I think I'm spending a lot of time putting information into the computer, when I could go down there and say . . . I know that person's here, there or whatever and going to do it, and to my mind it's a lot of my time consumed sitting up here putting information in . . . I don't seem to have the time to sit up here for an hour and pick around the [Staff Organiser] to get it running up as probably it should be running, so to my mind it's just as quick to go down and say I know I want you there, I want you there . . . that's why I sometimes think it's not that good an idea for small stores as probably for a larger store. I mean there a supervisor is a supervisor. They just walk around.

This interpretation allowed the supervisor to define the Organiser as an intrusion into the distinct 'needs' of the small store. These were often the small store respondents' justification for arguing that the Organiser was not useful: it might fit large stores, but large stores were not the same as small stores. These respondents suggested that those behind the Organiser did not understand the environment or needs of the small store. One supervisor rejected the notion that the Organiser's formal representations could define or dictate the working of their organisation: 'This is God [the plans produced by the Staff Organiser]. As far as they're concerned this is law. I'd like one of them to come and work with me for the day.'

The valorisation of informality, responsiveness and co-operation by managers and supervisors in small stores was hard to reconcile with the logic of the Staff Organiser and the associated new company directives on staffing and store operations. In the words of one supervisor:

> the fact of we're more or less told what to do, rather than we used to do it at our leisure or at a time convenient to us. It's sort of – probably because of [the Organiser] I expect – you've got a certain amount of time to do a job and you do it and you do it at a particular time of the day, whereas

before we done a job and it didn't matter how long it took us to do it, we done it.

Many of the supervisors and store managers in small stores interpreted the Organiser as part of an attempt to draw them into practices of standardisation and regulation that they had so far been able to remain outside of. Again, the same supervisor:

> I think that's what [the Organiser] has done, it's brought pressure on to the stores, the likes of us, we've been plodding along for years OK, ticking over, but it's highlighting a few areas that we know that there is a problem there and we are going to have to do something about it because of [the Organiser].

Such interpretations led small stores to have a particularly informal relationship to the Organiser that entailed at the most producing plans and using them some of the time. A significant part of staff allocation by both store managers and supervisors still took place on the shop floor as was felt needed. In some small stores this meant that the Organiser was in fact barely used. One small store manager explained his perspective:

> I think we've got a good team and although, like now... we have the [Staff Organiser] but we don't actually use it. We use it as a sort of guide . . . so you have this piece of paper telling you you've got *x* amount of staff in this period of time, it doesn't mean a thing, so it's been there as a guide.

Small stores had a distinctive and strong bond to the family culture that led them to resist assumptions and priorities embodied in the system, and made them less open to a technical discourse as a way of understanding problems with it.

There is, however, one important caveat to this picture that gives further indication of the way that shifting interpretations and collections of meaning can become part of the resources not only of groups, but also of individuals. Store managers in small stores came in two categories: those beginning their managerial career and those aware that further advancement into large stores was unlikely.

One manager whom we spoke to was in the former category. He was just beginning his path towards advancement and was clearly ambitious to move to a larger store. He was keen to prove himself within the logic of the Staff Organiser and other operational changes being developed in Brodies. He asserted the notion that technology is a good in itself and believed the more of it the better. Such keenness appeared to rob him of any ability to criticise the company or the technology. Instead he worked hard – even with us – to find justifications for any problems that came along. When asked to evaluate the implementation process he argued:

If you talk to some of my colleagues, they will probably say that it's gone reasonably smoothly. There's an awful lot of constraints placed on the implementation team. The biggest of all is the time-scale because these people have often been taken out of stores and of course they're going to be needed back in stores soon, and the vast operation of it all. I think on the whole, it's come across as being rushed. I've spoken to a lot of the implementation teams, and I understand a lot of the problems that they've had, and I think that overall now, my view has changed somewhat to say that I think that it's been implemented the best they could have done.

This attitude indicates that one of the costs of adoption of this type of approved discourse is reduced opportunities to be critical, to see things differently. The technical and instrumental discourses articulated by this store manager closed off certain types of interpretation – such as 'this might not be that great an idea' – while encouraging others – 'it must be good' or 'it's the users' fault'.

Conclusion

Organisational culture flows from the multiple meanings various groups develop for what the organisation is and what their role is within it. The literature described at the start of the chapter argued that organisational culture is a management tool invaluable to directing change. As the Brodies example suggests, the problem with these approaches is that they represent only management as the producers of meaning. Management may believe that they invent, control and at times change a corporate culture but they are involved in the same processes of meaning construction as all other organisational members. What distinguishes particular groups of management is the material and symbolic resources that allow them to influence the interpretations produced by others.

The family corporate culture of Brodies involved an organising narrative that was used to sustain loyalty and authority, but it was reinterpreted in differentiated and localised settings. Many at Head Office viewed the family culture as something within their control – something to be exploited or discarded in the pursuit of managerial objectives. Those behind the Organiser saw the family culture as something they could choose to discard, replacing it with regulation via standardisation and surveillance. The introduction of their technology was, however, actually dependent on this supposedly outdated culture to aid initial acceptance and adaptation. Making the system 'workable' took place through interpretations of existing store culture. The accounts of culture we saw at the beginning of the chapter often portray it as either simply facilitating or blocking change. The interplay and adaptation of the family culture and the Staff Organiser over time was far more complex and interesting than these accounts allow. This interplay indicates how apparently 'resistant' behaviour can, in the long term, facilitate managerial objectives. The family culture, considered an obstacle to change and a source of resistance by those behind the Staff Organiser, meant that store staff did not reject the system outright but instead played a key role in its eventual establishment in stores.

Technical discourses flow from certain societal expectations and ways of thinking about the properties of technology which privilege certain meanings and speakers. The boundaries between 'technology' and 'culture' within organisations are, however, shifting and highly permeable. The process of groups moving towards the values of the technical and instrumental discourses embodied in the logic of the Organiser and other management changes was aided by changing sociopolitical contexts, such as the operational changes, that radically altered the relationship supervisors had with their sales assistants. These contexts helped to give legitimacy to the discourses, gained legitimacy from them, and suggested to different groups that the discourses held security and power.

The development of the Staff Organiser within Brodies' stores involved a number of different groups. The differing levels at which supervisors and store managers adopted and challenged values, associated, firstly, with the family culture of stores and, secondly, with the technical and instrumental discourses articulated alongside the Organiser and other changes, indicate that people do not belong to or adopt one set of values. Instead, they construct collections of meanings which come to make sense to them and order their relations with others. The different experiences also indicate that it is not a case of either the technical discourse or the family culture becoming the final source of meaning in the organisation. Meanings associated with each became resources that at different points and in different ways various groups used to secure their position, make sense of change and situate themselves with the technology and in power relations.

During the processes of change which took place in Brodies, both the technology and the organisational culture changed. The instrumental logic of the Staff Organiser was modified through localised interpretations. Users adapted wider discourses and meanings created elsewhere – either by a corporate culture or by a set of assumptions about the nature of technology. However, this process of adoption crucially included a localisation of these wider meanings to the everyday lives and practices that users were part of and interacted in. Therefore, the relationship between organisational culture and technology during change is about the mutual adaptation of interpretations, assumptions and values associated with each in the context of the other.

6 Gendering technological change

Femininity and the construction of skill

In previous chapters we have considered factors mediating the embedding of technologies in organisations. These factors have appeared predominantly to form either within the organisation (organisational structure or culture) or outside it (professional status and identity). In this chapter our focus on gender indicates that the boundaries between inside and outside the organisation are at best provisional and porous. Gender meanings form in and between the fictional distinctions made between public and private worlds.

Gender is crucial to understanding the working lives and identities of both men and women. Feminists examining organisations have highlighted the centrality of gender to all aspects of organisational life (Harlow *et al.* 1995, Itzin 1995), in particular to those aspects that create inequalities:

> To say that an organisation . . . is gendered means that advantage and disadvantage, exploitation and control, action and emotion, meaning and identity, are patterned through and in terms of a distinction between male and female, masculine and feminine. Gender is not an addition to ongoing processes, conceived as gender neutral.
>
> (Acker 1990: 146)

Many of the recent feminist analyses of gender in organisations have also stressed the role that organisations play in constructing gender norms, as opposed to seeing organisations as simple mirrors of pre-existing social norms. In the words of Gherardi, '[g]ender relationships in organizations not only reflect the symbolic order of gender in society; they actively help to create and alter it' (1995: 130). If, as these authors claim, all aspects of organisational life are gendered, then this includes technology acquisition and implementation. Elsewhere in the book we have characterised techno-organisational change as a process of mutual adaptation between sociotechnology and the existing realities of the organisation. In the same way the gender relations that inform organisational life influence the introduction of new technology and in turn are reshaped during innovation. This chapter explores the interplay of gender identities and technological values that takes place throughout the acquisition process.

It is important to stress here that when tracing feminine or masculine identities in organisations we should avoid treating women or men as homogeneous social groups with singular identities formed by social context. Aspects of people's lives such as race, class and sexuality fracture the identities that women and men form for themselves and for the things around them (Bradley 1996). As Spelman has argued, 'what one learns when one learns one's gender identity is the gender identity appropriate to one's ethnic, class, national and racial identity' (1993: 327).

Following on from the discussion of subjective regulation in Chapter 1, this chapter considers ways in which the gender identity of actors can be part of the process whereby constructing an identity, particularly during times of change, can be self-disciplining as well as enabling. Our contention is that, for women, the conflation of certain skills and abilities into 'feminine' identities is central to this. Self-discipline can be an outcome because the attribution of certain activities and attitudes to a feminine identity can make 'invisible' the skilful contribution which women make to an organisation and deny the challenge and significance of that contribution.

When considering these issues during technological change the issues become the following:

- How do existing gender identities for users influence their ability to participate in shaping the technology?
- What skills do men and women use with new technology and how are these skills gendered?
- How do the gender identities of users and the meanings of technology shift during the processes of innovation and change?

In this chapter we first discuss the relationship between gender and skill. The focus is on how women play a part in constructing gendered interpretations of skill and on identifying the factors that encourage these interpretations. We then return to our retail case study, briefly discussing issues associated with the changing role of retail supervisors before going on to describe the introduction of the Staff Organiser to Brodies from the supervisors' point of view. The core discussion of the supervisors' experiences relates only to the female supervisors we interviewed. In order to draw out the different experiences of the two male supervisors, these are discussed as part of a separate section.

Gendering skill

When examining technological and organisational change, to paraphrase Gill and Grint, we must consider the role of individuals in 'doing gender' (1995: 16). Gender is not something that just happens to people; it is an aspect of social meaning that men and women participate in constructing in particular settings. This can be related to analysis, discussed in Chapter 2, of the 'gendering' of technology. In this work, technology is understood as socially constructed in practices of identity formation (Ormrod 1995). For example, masculine notions of control and power find themselves operationalised in forms of technology constructed to enable control and power.

This same social constructivist position can be, and has been, used to understand the ways in which certain activities come to be seen as skilled and certain actors come to be seen as skilful. Feminist analysis of the relationship between gender and the social construction of skill began with investigations by writers such as Cockburn (1983) and Witz (1986) who highlight the ways in which men have denied women access to certain skills. This work has always included a subjective element by indicating that the ways in which objective strategies such as legal constraints have been secured is in assumptions about the inherent femininity and masculinity of certain roles and activities. An important aspect of the on-going maintenance of such exclusions is the social construction of certain male activities (e.g. engineering) as skilful, and female ones (e.g. communication) as natural attributes (Fletcher and Martin 1998). Tancred has developed this argument, asserting that women have 'invisible skills' in organisations (1995: 17).

The unskilled nature of many areas of women's employment is not therefore simply a reflection of their lack of skill: this would mean that resolution of the problem would require only the training of women in the skills that men possess. What is more significant is the way that activities where women do participate are deemed unskilled. If women take over an area of activity which previously had been seen as male and skilled, the interpretation of the 'skill' of that activity is likely to change. Retail work, for example, became viewed as low-skilled and low-status when increasing numbers of women moved into the sector. Broadbridge (1991) argues that the only retail workers who are still associated with skill are men working in specialised areas selling 'male' products. Women retail workers, on the other hand, are associated with a serving role, which, rather than forming a skill, is viewed as a continuation of their natural 'submissiveness' and caring role (ibid.: 45). Therefore, many women's activities in the workplace are rendered 'invisible' by assuming that they are simple extensions of those attributes associated with the feminine and the domestic:

> the 'socially constructed' nature of skill includes the assumption that women are born with certain 'natural' skills which require neither talent nor training and which are merely part of their 'natural', 'feminine' behaviour.
>
> (Tancred 1995: 17)

The portrayal of activity which has been learned as a natural attribute is, for Gherardi, a product of women's marginalised position in organisations:

> The attributes of femininity are ingrained in the subordination relationship: caring, compassion, willingness to please others, generosity,

sensitivity, solidarity, nurturing, emotionality, and so on . . . Since they are the attributes of the powerless, it is possible to occupy a feminine position, not because of biological destiny but because of a political and organisational social dynamic.

(1995: 15)

By focusing on one aspect of organisational life associated with women – emotion – we can see how the contribution of women has been misrepresented and devalued and how this impacts on the position of women. The emotional life of organisations is clearly gendered. The same behaviour by managers can be identified as assertive and good when observed in a man and overly aggressive and bad when observed in a woman. Women are more likely to be accused of being 'emotional' than men, yet women are also asked and expected to perform the 'emotional labour' (Hochschild 1983, Wajcman 1998) within organisations. Wajcman defines emotional labour as the work 'performed in dealing with *other people's feelings* in the public domain' (1998: 109; original emphasis). Women are trapped in a contradiction when gender norms place them in areas of employment where their 'attributes' of caring make them useful but poorly valued. This association with emotion also allows women's actions and perceptions to be second-guessed and challenged. As Hochschild suggests, 'women's feelings are seen not as a response to real events but as reflections of themselves as "emotional women"' (1983: 173).

Femininity as subjective regulation

Much of the discussion above reflects the way that gendered identities, in part, are the product of how people interpret the actions and attitudes of others as masculine or feminine. However, gender identities are also a product of how we see ourselves in the context of others' interpretations. This means that women are involved in the appropriation of activities as 'feminine' as part of their own attempts to secure identity in settings where gendered norms exist. They participate in the 'daily accomplishment' (Acker 1992) of gender and the construction of feminine identities. Why then would women participate in the construction of identities which label them as unskilled and that help to keep them in unequal positions in organisations and in the job market? In the words of Bartky, why would women be involved in the 'disciplinary project of femininity' (1988: 71)? In attempting to answer this question it is important to avoid presenting women as victims of false consciousness who mistakenly do not realise their own complicity in creating their hardship. Women's gendered identities do produce some sense of position and power. However, the identities are negotiated in an environment that is beyond their immediate control. This environment helps shape their subjectivities and their 'performances' in a way that can be thought of as both regulating and enabling (Butler 1990). Kondo captures the contingencies involved when she suggests that identity can be thought of 'as historically located, nuanced by ironies, and contextually asserted and reasserted within shifting relations of power' (1990: 257).

To understand therefore why women would be involved in self-discipline one has to be aware of the way such a move is encouraged by the particular 'conditions of possibility' women operate in. The types of employment women find themselves in, and the constraints placed on them by social realities and responsibilities outside the organisation, all help to shape the scope and context of identity formation. As a result, certain types of organisation combine with external myths of 'womanhood' to encourage 'femininity' as a 'chosen' identity. These organisations and myths combine to give that identity both power and limitation. There are particular aspects of organisational structure, practice and narrative that can contribute to certain forms of gendered identity which are ultimately problematic for women. Two such aspects, which we found to be particularly visible in Brodies, are discussed here, before we move on to the experiences of Brodies' supervisors.

Family relations

One way in which femininity becomes part of organisational life is through the association of organisation with 'family'. Pollert (1981) discusses how women have brought family relations into the workplace, for example, through much breaktime discussion being centred on family life. However, her analysis also makes clear the ways in which family relations are constructed *within* the organisation. By finding a source of their identity in family patterns, Pollert argues that the women she studied 'colluded with a sexist ideology which segregated the world into the private, female half, which it denigrated, and the esteemed public, male half' (1981: 135). Lown (1990) argues that these patterns of relations are particularly encouraged within 'family firms'. This usually means firms that are run by family members, but it can also include organisations that have strong notions of organisation as family. Kondo suggests that, in her words, the 'crafting of selves', via family relations which include a sense of femininity as service and obligation, results in both confinement and security: 'in company as in family the assertions of solidarity and warmth are in each case inseparable from the jural, disciplinary, and obligatory strands in this discourse' (1990: 198).[1]

In these family types of organisation and in certain types of occupation such as nursing, women become identified with and play out mothering identities which mimic the private role. In this way, the myth of motherhood 'silently attaches itself to many a job description' (Hochschild 1983: 163). Such mothering identities both secure a certain sense of self as caring and secure women's role as providing emotional labour:

> Women act as surrogate mothers . . . They do much, then, to foster a feeling of togetherness, of 'company as family' . . . Consequently, women strengthen their symbolic link to the household by recreating this role in

the company and continually set themselves apart from the central story of maturity through apprenticeship and masculine toughness and skill.

(Kondo 1990: 295)

At the same time, Kondo is clear that this same identity, in this same environment, does provide some – limited – position of power. She argues that the identity 'serves to make them [the women in question] important, though formally marginal, members of the company' (ibid.: 295).

Emotion versus rationality

Constructions of femininity and masculinity influence and are influenced by organisational definitions of rationality and knowledge. Both skill and technology are associated with masculinity. This has been encouraged by women's association with non-instrumental models of rationality, which, it is presumed, leaves them ill-suited to the use and appreciation of technology. Merchant (1980) argues that the associations between masculinity and rationality have been socially constructed over time in such a way as to deny the validity – particularly in the public sphere – of more context-specific (non-Western) notions of rationality. Again, such associations are a reflection of and give support to current power relations:

> The feelings of the lower-status party may be discounted in two ways: by considering them rational but unimportant or by considering them irrational and hence dismissible.
>
> (Hochschild 1983: 172)

The connected dualisms of masculinity/femininity and rationality/irrationality lead to the 'misnaming' of actions, skills, and activities, which could be understood as particular, situated and yet rational, as instead simply 'feminine' behaviour. Ultimately, the privileged status of instrumental rationality is secured in a gendered discourse. Mumby and Putnam argue that the organisational link made between rationality/masculinity and emotion/femininity inhibits the ability of organisations to recognise the value of emotion – whether exercised by men or by women. What Mumby and Putnam suggest instead is that by challenging the assumed obvious superiority of rationality over emotion, one 'debunks organizational efforts to reify certain experiences and behaviours as either masculine or feminine' (1992: 480).

When women are interpreted and interpret themselves as acting emotionally or being geared by maternal or caring concerns associated with femininity or family to produce a sense of identity, place and limited power, this may distance them from active roles in technological and organisational practices. This is not because technology or organisations require instrumentality but because of the dominance of the discursive link made between instrumentality, technology and masculinity in gendered organisational practices and narratives.

Retail supervisors

The role and identity of retail supervisors is closely associated with 'mothering'. As with the flight attendant supervisors discussed by Hochschild (1983), the retail supervisor both supplies emotional labour to those below her and ensures that her staff continue to supply emotional labour to the customer. However, the role of the supervisor is thought to be changing in service industries such as retail. These changes are part of the 'conditions of possibility' that informed the negotiations over role and status that supervisors had to undertake during the period of techno-organisational change at Brodies.

One source of change is said to be new technologies that – like our Staff Organiser – are thought to replace the regulating role of the supervisor (Dawson 1988). Delbridge and Lowe (1997) argue that the outcome of such technological change is not a product of technology. Instead, what happens is that the nature and role of supervision change when new technology is introduced. This conclusion flows from Delbridge and Lowe's definition of supervisors as actors involved in social processes of negotiation between management and workers. Therefore, the shape and role of supervision in organisations with new technology will form 'as part of a dynamic social process which reflects the embeddedness of managerial prerogatives, the character of workplace relations and the style of supervision' (ibid.: 424). In these negotiations, the gendered nature of the identity of the supervisor will be important in shaping the new role found for both the supervisor and the technology.

Another source of change is the techniques of 'impression management' which service industries are said to be pursuing. These monitor and control worker behaviour by instilling in workers a sense of self tied to the success of the organisation. For example, Garsten and Grey talk about the ways in which service industry organisations have adopted certain 'technologies of self' that 'lead to a certain type of self-formation' (1997: 221), revolving around the 'enterprising self'. Du Gay is perhaps the writer most associated with this argument in the retail environment. He argues that retailers are pursuing an 'excellence' project that attempts to mould in the worker a sense of self tied to the company:

> store managers and shopfloor employees within retailing, are increasingly being reconceptualized as 'enterprising' subjects: self-regulating, productive individuals whose sense of self-worth and virtue is inextricably linked to the 'excellent' performance of their work.

(1996: 119)

However, Du Guy fails fully to explore the influence of gender on the formation of the 'excellence' project. In addition, a problem he shares with Garsten and Grey is that their work contains little analysis of how actors make sense of and interpret these new discourses and forms of management. Retail companies may put forward an excellence project, but it is not predetermined that workers – including supervisors – will simply adopt such a discourse unchanged (Sturdy 1998).

In what follows we return to Brodies. This time our concern is with following through the introduction of the Staff Organiser from the perspective of the supervisors. How does their identity change; how do they 'perform' gender as part of their identity; and, finally, how is this different for the male and female supervisors?

The Brodies family

Chapter 5 indicated the importance of notions of family to the cultural environment of Brodies. Gender identities were a constitutive element of the articulation and maintenance of this culture for all of Brodies' staff, none more so than for the supervisors. As we have seen, supervisors prized what they saw as the particular traditions and culture of the company. This culture, while encouraged by the company, was one that the supervisors themselves manufactured collectively on the shop floor:

> I think they're quite a caring company, not just for the customers, they're caring for the staff . . . I like the people I work with, which has got a lot to do with it as well, that you get on with everybody around you. The fact that the atmosphere in the store is good, perhaps if I went into another store or another organisation you wouldn't feel quite so much of the team spirit, because you get on so well together, you socialise out as well as in store, we all pitch in and help one another.

While supervisors at Brodies can gain a qualification in supervision from the National Examination Board of Supervisory Studies, it is not a requirement for being a supervisor and was seldom mentioned in their descriptions of themselves, their skills or their role in the organisation. Instead, they placed priority on their relationship with the staff they supervised and their mediating role between their 'girls' and management. In the supervisors' descriptions of their relations with sales assistants, the supervisors appeared to adopt the role of 'mediating mothers', looking after their girls while deferring to the paternal authority of those above them. This supportive concern for the sales assistants can be thought of as confining and self-disciplining for both supervisor and sales assistant. It confines the supervisors by limiting their contribution to the organisation to one of caring. This makes it easy to represent their role as neither skilful nor an expression of good management. For sales assistants, it appears to reduce the possibility that they could be skilful and portrays them as passive and in need of help.

Supervisors were positioned within a paternal relationship with their store managers, to whom they showed loyalty and support. When supervisors spoke of their position in the organisation they showed a strong deference to higher authority. This was supported and legitimated by an assertion that the company was looking after their interests – that the 'father' (the masculine role in the company secured in knowledge claims as opposed to expressions of affectivity) knew best. A constructed vision of inclusiveness was produced which was self-disciplining in its denial of the possibility of contradictory or competing interests between management and worker, smoothed over by the gendered nature of the family culture on the shop floor.

There is a class dimension to the mediating mother identity worth briefly mentioning. The femininity constructed by the women supervisors showed the imprint of the particular types of deference, passivity, service and obligation that are tied to a version of femininity associated with middle-class women. Working in retailers similar to Brodies is acceptable for middle-class women. The class-bound notion of femininity articulated in Brodies is a factor in making it acceptable for middle-class women to work in a relatively low-status occupation, although it does not mean that all supervisors or sales assistants are middle-class. However, for the middle-class women who work there, the link to a middle-class version of femininity endorses, rather than confuses, their domestic gender identity. It is not a threat to their primary role of looking after husband and children, of being a proper middle-class wife. They continue to serve others while posing no threat to their husband as the primary breadwinner in the household.

The notions of skill that had developed in stores had done so within this gendered family culture. In so doing, the way different activities were represented as skilful or not both secured and helped construct the gendered identities of store staff. The paternal attitude of Head Office and store managers towards both supervisors and sales assistants cast doubt on the skills and abilities of the women – in particular their ability to cope with technology. This meant that the women were seen as a barrier, a problem for the 'father' to manage. The feminine identities of both supervisors and sales assistants only helped to encourage this view. It also gained authority from wider gender norms that question the ability of women to use and understand technology. Supervisors shared doubts about whether their 'girls' could cope with change and technology, but rather than articulating this as a barrier, this concern led the supervisors to talk of wanting to protect the sales assistants.

The supervisors' doubts about the ability of sales assistants to cope with technological change was encouraged by their own sense of technological inadequacy. One supervisor summed up her general discomfort with computers by saying: 'I'm always wary because I always think that I can't do it. That I won't be able to do it as well as anybody else.' This internalisation of the prejudice that women cannot use technology was particularly strong amongst the older supervisors, who believed themselves to be especially inadequate:

> I think, because of my generation, I think it's different for the younger generation – they're into computers, they're all keen and geared up for them, but if you get older as well it takes longer to learn anything.

Over time, supervisors had used the family culture and norms of femininity to carve out a particular gendered identity that underpinned their position in stores. This identity, on one level, provided security for their position. On another, however, it formed an account of femininity that cast doubt over their ability to use complex technology. This was to play an important role in the adaptation process of the Staff Organiser.

The Paper Planner and the change to the Staff Organiser

While originally the Paper Planner had been designed using central criteria and statistical calculations, over the years, supervisors had reduced the influence of these calculations on the plans. This had led to patterns of use that could be described as informal. One supervisor described the way she designed and used the plans:

> we didn't really stick to it. We had the basics of it. I used to do my plans for it when I first started, but the only thing we stuck to it for was lunches, tea breaks and important tasks that had to be done.

The flexibility to adjust the plans constantly was, for supervisors, a particular strength of the system. In the words of one supervisor: 'Its strength I suppose was that you could do that – manually over-ride the system and say right this happens.' The information that was placed on the plans was based as much on a collection of informal, local sources as it was on the statistics sent from the centre. The plans were written on acetate sheets that would be constantly amended and changed. The local practices and the paper-based system had developed together as a social process to create a malleable sociotechnical system.

The supervisors' use of the Paper Planner was influenced by their mediating mother identity. Through it they ensured that 'their girls' were looked after and the culture of family was maintained. Their actions could be described, in terms of the family culture and feminine identity, as attempts to mould the Planner to the social realities of their environment through the use of particular and situated knowledge and skill. It could be thought of as the inclusion of Mumby and Putnam's notion of bounded emotionality that allows for 'tolerance of ambiguity' and 'commitment to others' (1992: 474). As indicated before, the dilemma is that within the family culture of stores this approach was not articulated as 'management'. The skilful aspects of the supervisors' use of the Planner and the running of their department were made 'invisible' by the family culture through the portrayal of their activities as a natural expression of femininity.

One of the objectives behind the purchase of the Staff Organiser was to reduce the autonomy and control that supervisors had in staff deployment. The denial of hands-on access for the supervisors was a visible sign of their removal from decisions about how staff should be used (although, as we saw in the last chapter, store managers actually gave supervisors wider access than prescribed by Head Office). If the supervisors' role in organising staff was part of their identity then this would be unsettled by the reduction in role and responsibility.

From within the logic of the system its skilful use appeared to consist of two functions:

1 ensuring that store information was up-to-date;
2 manipulating staff and resources to produce measures of high efficiency – as defined within the system.

This is an instrumental model of skill, one at odds with the types of activity practised by the supervisors in the Paper Planner. This means that the activities and attitudes through which they secured their position and sense of role – the mediating mother role – did not match the instrumental skills that were operationalised in the Organiser. The previous chapter argued that the response of supervisors to the Organiser was mediated by their changing interpretations of family culture and technical discourse. There was both a gendered and self-disciplining aspect to these social processes, whose negotiated outcomes had implications both for the supervisors' identity and for the Staff Organiser.

Using the Staff Organiser: 'you can tell it's been designed by a man' (supervisor)

The previous chapter indicated that supervisors, as well as others in the stores, were unhappy with the Organiser when it first arrived. The most contentious issues were those which, for supervisors, were problems with the system because they altered the way that things happened in the department, but, from a Head Office point of view, were the objective of the system.

The first strategy many supervisors adopted when dealing with what they identified as problems with the Organiser was to ignore the plans and produce their own. Their justification was that to do otherwise would be detrimental to the department: 'I could show you our plans for today, and if we had done what it said then we wouldn't be functioning properly today.' However, as we have seen, the long-term strategy adopted by the majority of supervisors was to adapt rather than ignore or reject the system and its plans. In so doing, as users they took part in a reconstruction of the technology. One key thing that they did was to manipulate the information that they entered into the system, in particular information about the 'skills' of their sales assistants. This was done to ensure that the system, rather than reflect the actual skills in the department, had a model of the skills available that allowed a fair sharing out of the tasks that had to be done. So, for instance, although someone was seen as the best person on a cash point her skill would be underrepresented so she would not always be placed there by the system. They also found different strategies for working with the plans that the system produced for use in their department. In particular, the supervisors manually altered – often with store management approval – the plans that were presented to them for use on the shop floor.

In each case they justified the need to change things on the basis of their claim that each store and each department was different. A similar response was found in different types and size of store, but each based on a claim to particularity:

> The service and the customers are different from department to department. If you look at [Department X] they have till points to actually work with. We have four counters to take care of as well as the sales floor . . . I think it suits departments where people don't move about too much.
>
> also some priorities, although they [Head Office] might not consider them a priority, within our store they might be.
> (supervisor in a small store)

> I knew we'd have to change it because I know what our department is like. People will just ring up on the day and say 'can I have so and so lunch tomorrow, or can I have Thursday as a day's holiday because I need to do so and so'.

Part of the definition of what was right for their department included what was right for their staff, their 'girls'. One supervisor detailed how she instructed her staff to ignore much of the plans:

> I have said to them, basically as long as you know when you are supposed to be on the till or the gift shop, any other time come to me for direction or you get on with what you would normally do. They are happier with that.

For these supervisors the staff were not reducible to the categories and information held on them within the system:

> I know they have to be flexible, and they will do things that they don't like to do, but I would prefer where possible to give them things they like to do, because it is better for me, it is better for my floor.

The mothering dimension of this perception was explicit in favourable comments made by two supervisors for why they liked the Staff Organiser. One explained: 'It means I have more time to give the girls', and the other: 'The girls benefit because I am more available to them.' In rejecting the objectives articulated in the system, the supervisors did so on the basis of perceived legitimacy of their local priorities and the right they claimed to use their judgement to protect what they saw as the needs of their staff. For the supervisors this was their contribution to their department and the organisation. However, it was an invisible skill to both them and others. It was seen as just how they were rather than a conscious management style or approach. Articulated through notions of care, it helped secure their identity but limited the legitimacy of its practices.

In the next two quotations one supervisor justifies the changes she made to the plans on the shop floor:

> The strength that I found on [the Paper Planner] was that I knew my staff, I knew what they could do, and what they couldn't do, what they liked doing, which is a big difference. I know I shouldn't worry about that, but it is a big thing to me . . . Whereas [the Staff Organiser] doesn't think like that. It doesn't know the individual. It doesn't know that that person has a bigger section than that person, so I always give them less till work. It just doesn't seem to have a lot of rationality to it.

> Only I know, along with my sales manager and my assistant, my department. Only we know not to put two sales assistants together who hate each other. You have to have a happy work team, otherwise you don't get anywhere. I just put in that personal touch, if someone performs better at the end of the day, I will let them fill their department at the end of the day. If someone is not a morning person, don't put them on the till.

The first quotation indicates that the supervisor did not interpret her actions as outside rationality. For her it was the system that was not thinking rationally. Her claim to rationality was based on a sensitivity and awareness of the particular and local – in short, a different form of rationality to that exercised in the logic of the Staff Organiser.

The translation of system objectives into problems was part of an implicit claim which the supervisors made to have their knowledge included in the operation of the system and the store. The staff management practices inscribed into the Organiser did not match their understanding of their role and relations to other staff. Their feminine identity as mediating mothers distanced them from the assumptions and priorities of performance management being introduced with the Organiser. The supervisors did not at this point appear to articulate the types of value suggested by Garston and Grey or Du Gay's enterprising self. Given at the same time their acceptance of wider paternal authority as part of their feminised identity, the supervisors' perspective on the Staff Organiser occurred in a confined space that denied the possibility that they could reject it. At this stage, continuing to adopt feminine approaches to the Organiser secured the supervisors' identity as mediating mothers, and produced a reconstruction of the technology. However, it did not equate, for those in authority, with a skilful or legitimate use of the technology. In addition, because these continued practices were not articulated as skilful, even by the supervisors, but instead as the product of feminine attributes, they became easy to deny.

Changing identities

As already shown in the previous chapter, supervisors altered their approach to the Organiser and their use of it over time. This change marked their enrolment into the logic of the system and at the same time a devaluing of family culture. This process of enrolment was helped by the supervisors' desire to obtain a secure sense of position and identity. In pursuing this, the supervisors renegotiated the role and skills they defined as important. We have seen in Chapter 5 that supervisors criticised their former attitudes and behaviour for their basis in 'feelings' or 'subjectivity'. Their new emphasis was on getting their percentages right and ensuring that their staff were where the system said they should be. While they still thought that some manual over-writing on plans was legitimate, they were more content to be guided by the system and trusted the figures produced by the Organiser.

'Business needs' now dominated, and supervisors insisted that the sales assistants fit in with the priorities of the system:

> The computer is business oriented, and sometimes you get somebody quite cross because they've got 2–3 lunch, which is a heck of a late lunch. But if the business needs you till that time, then that's it.

A member of Sales Support who had responsibility for running the system recognised the shift in attitude amongst other supervisors:

> I think they're actually sticking to it because it is a new system that needs to be and it is going to stay. And I think they've accepted it now, and they're taking more notice of it now. And I think they're making sure that – even the people on the shop floor – they're making sure that people are on that till at that time. I think people are respecting it a lot more than what we did at the beginning.

The previous chapter considered the processes whereby supervisors came to adopt the technical and instrumental assumptions of the system. This was discussed primarily in relation to the cultural mediation of technological change. Being fully aware of this process of mediation requires an awareness of gender. In particular, we need to consider the influence of gender on the resources – subjective and objective – which the supervisors had available to respond with. The gender norms and identities in Brodies meant that in the discursive battles around the values of the Staff Organiser, the initial interpretations that were produced by supervisors were difficult to sustain. In part this is because their interpretation retained commitments to identity and practices defined by others and themselves as (1) feminine and therefore not skilful, and

(2) out-of-date. In response to this the supervisors lost some of their previous subjective commitment to the mothering role and its 'feminine' attachment to caring.

As Chapter 5 suggested, the previous gendered identity had been reaffirmed by an organisational culture that articulated the importance of family relations. The Staff Organiser embodied a new company emphasis on the importance of delocalised criteria of efficiency and success. The situated practices that the supervisors had developed had little support in the new technical and instrumental world of the Staff Organiser.

Over time, the supervisors' initial scepticism changed to enable them to link themselves both to the new technology and to the new management priorities. This involved establishing a new relationship with the Organiser that enabled them to claim organisationally accepted 'skill' and reposition their occupational identity as 'management intermediaries' enacting the logic and commands of the system. The benefit of this shift was that it enabled them to situate themselves with a set of skills that were accepted and legitimated in the wider realm of management practice. In the new language and assumptions of performance management and the 'enterprising self', supervisors renegotiated an identity and were able to perform a set of skills that had some status in the company and influence in the immediate environment of their store. Supervisors were rearticulating aspects of their identity that made sense in the language of technology and rationality, but other aspects of who they were, expressed in notions of femininity, remained too.

The new breed, the technophile and the strategist

So far we have treated the supervisors as a homogeneous group shaped by their gender and occupational position. In reality, this group varied in significant ways that included age and sex. This meant that the shifting relationships to gender identity, culture and technology of different supervisors are worth exploring.

The new breed

The supervisors who appeared to make the transition from mediating mother to management intermediary most easily were those who had made the least subjective commitment to the previous identity: new, young supervisors. For this 'new breed', the Organiser was a management tool that they could use to control their staff. One of our core group, an assistant supervisor, was representative of this new sub-group of supervisors. Although only twenty-seven, she had worked in the company for eleven years, joining straight after she left school. She had been an assistant supervisor for three years.

As a member of the new breed she did not appear to have the same level of attachment to the family culture. She expressed a level of individuality and questioning of conformity that did not fit with the family culture's exclusiveness.

For example, she queried the strict appearance code in a manner that supervisors comfortable with paternal authority would never have done:

> Sometimes it is silly things about jewellery, the colour of your tights, your shoes. Some things I don't agree with because I don't think that it changes your personality, how many pairs of earrings you wear, or if you've got a bracelet on.

Her lack of attachment to family narratives appeared to influence her interpretation of the Staff Organiser as a benefit to the store and to her. In her last interview she explained that the main benefit of the Organiser was that it helped guarantee that staff did what they were told. She noted that the plans 'will start meaning that staff will do the jobs at the right time. When it is written down people are more likely to actually do it and do it when they are supposed to.' For her, change – particularly technological change – was unavoidable and a symbol of progress. She recognised that operating with, rather than against, the Organiser was the pathway to security within the organisation. Supervisors such as her were quicker to negotiate an occupational identity in relation to the Organiser which was managerial, 'skilful' and legitimate:

> I realise now that there is such a lot of work that still has to go into the computer, it can't do everything. It needs the correct information before it can do anything. That is a major responsibility of mine now. Before the store can get it right, I have got to get it right. All this re-profiling . . . if I don't get my hours right, if I don't get my skills right, everything else goes to pot and the store as a whole suffers.

The Staff Organiser was a tool she could use to obtain power over staff. This new-breed supervisor did not see sales assistants as dependent girls. Instead, because of changing patterns of labour relations in the company which saw more use of part-time and temporary staff, her staff were distant, anonymous and transient. Her primary concern was to ensure that she had a mechanism that would give her authority and power. The Organiser was a vehicle for compliance and order:

> I was just thinking of our Saturday girls, we have four Saturday girls and they use the Organiser every Saturday, and it works really well for them because they have to hop on one island and then onto another for an hour or fill-up for an hour . . . We always like to know what they're doing, because often Saturday people disappear in the queues of people and you never really know what they should be doing.

The comparative ease with which she could adopt this occupational identity is an indication of the contextual and constructed nature of the feminine supervisor role in the family culture. The adoption of situated and particular modes of knowledge and rationality by most supervisors was not inherently about being female. This is made clear by the strategies used by a new-breed supervisor to adopt and use modes of instrumental and abstract rationality and knowledge associated with masculinity: highlighting the equally constructed bond between men and instrumental rationality. It also indicates the influence of the wider social environment. One reason why young women such as the one above were less at ease in a maternal identity is the wider shifts in gender relations that are taking place across the domestic and public spheres (Walby 1997). Changing patterns in education, work and family life all encourage women to limit motherhood as an aspect of their identity in the private and the public.

The technophile

We are arguing that femininity is socially constructed in a gendered organisation, and that this influences technology acquisition. Not all the supervisors who were interviewed were women. As indicated earlier two of the supervisors and assistant supervisors were men – how did their experiences differ? How did these men respond to the Staff Organiser? And what within their identity was unsettled and renegotiated?

Based on other organisational research we can posit two possible scenarios. The first response men can have to working in a feminine environment (meaning culture rather than numbers of women present) is to adopt similar feminine identities. In Ferguson's (1984) analysis of bureaucracies she argues that men were 'feminized' by the culture and power relations which existed there. The second response men can have is to create exaggerated masculine identities in order to demarcate themselves as different to, and often better than, the women they work alongside. An example of this is seen in the disproportionate number of primary head teachers who are male, in comparison to male primary school teachers. Taking on a leadership and managerial role in the primary school environment reclaims some element of masculinity within what would otherwise be seen as a feminine occupational role. Which strategies did our two male supervisors undertake? What we can show is that the men marked out their identities in relation to the technology in different ways, but for both the reference point was masculinity.

Our first male was one of the assistant supervisors. Like our female member of the new breed, he joined the company straight after leaving school and although only twenty-six he had already worked for Brodies for nine years. He was relatively new as an assistant supervisor and, again like the young female supervisor, his identity was not rooted in the family culture. He was very enthusiastic about the new management strategies and the new technology at Brodies. The large store that he worked in was beset with management difficulties. They were without an accounts manager, the person supposedly in charge of maintaining the Organiser. Supervisors were very unhappy with the system, which was being underused, and store information was not being kept up-to-date. The store manager was under pressure from Area Office to get the Organiser properly implemented in the store. His solution was to put one of the supervisors in charge of the upkeep of the system. He turned to the male assistant supervisor to perform the role.

With relish the young assistant supervisor took on an identity we suggest can be thought of as a 'technophile'. His ability to do so was helped by a culture which, when looking for someone to use technology, turned to the only male supervisor as the best person for the job. As a technophile the assistant supervisor could see nothing wrong with the system or the company. On the other hand, the older, experienced female supervisors were the target for blame for their poor use of the system. These women were, in his mind, holding back change by their continued and extensive practice of shop floor manual over-writing of the system:

> they wouldn't let the system run. They would just over-write it, rather than coming to me and saying 'this problem has come up, how can we solve it?' They were trying to keep it half the way they used to do it and trying to use half the computer system – that doesn't work.

The technophile gained purpose and sense of position and power through his privileged role in the management of the Organiser. Again, his ability to do this was helped by his immediate organisational environment. Of all the stores we studied his had the most exclusionary access to the Organiser terminals. Unlike the other stores, which experimented with various different levels of access for supervisors, here the technophile was the only supervisor with access to the terminals. This allowed him the space in which to construct a version of himself as different to, and powerful over, other female supervisors with more experience and knowledge of the store. Through the system he was able to position himself as important to the running of the store. The Organiser became a vehicle in which to articulate his identity, move forward and have a positive sense of self:

> There are certain applications that only certain people have access to. Implementers, managers, supervisors have different levels of access. They have now given me access to some of the management levels so I can do some of the tasks I need to do.

The strategist

The second male supervisor was one of the core interview group. Reading through the interviews with him over the three visits allows us to indicate the different processes of identity formation he underwent. His actions and narrative of himself throughout the three interviews positioned him as a 'strategist'. He was thirty-one and had been working for the company for twelve years.

From the first interview onwards he saw the role of the supervisor as a management one. Like the female supervisors he stressed the importance of taking care of the sales assistants, but unlike the female supervisors, he used a managerial discourse to describe it. This allowed him to identify his actions as skilful rather than as an extension of feminine attributes:

> I think that the role of the supervisor . . . is development, developing staff . . . we are more involved in developing, training and bringing people on and finding out what they would like.

This was the same activity as carried out by the female supervisors, but the 'development' language was that of management, of human resources, and allowed him to mark out the activity as skilful in a way the other supervisors did not. In the strategist's store, supervisors were given liberal access to the computer. There was even a timetable for when they could use it. The strategist saw his use of the Organiser as a way to secure his management identity. He envisaged using the Organiser to plan his department in more strategic ways and carry out more advance planning. However, this vision was threatened by two factors that he had to respond to. The first was that at the time of our second interview it had just been announced that supervisors were no longer to have access to the Organiser in the store (a move insisted on by Area Office). Instead Sales Support were to take over the upkeep of the system. This decision was one that he clearly resented:

> I was told a couple of days ago that we as supervisors rather than changing rota exceptions or whatever on the system we will be giving it to Sales Support . . . That is fine, but then I think to myself, if they are going to do that – which I am happy about – why do we have a computer in the office, why have we been taught to do it?

Not only was Sales Support to get the Organiser but staff budget was increasingly being transferred to this area as part of changing store operations. This meant that he was also losing staff hours to Sales Support and again he was resentful: 'It is obvious that more hours have to be put into Sales Support, but it is not so obvious that those hours should come from sales floor.' Part of his resentment flowed from his inability to control his department, his inability to be the manager he saw himself as. The second factor only helped to increase the feeling of impotence he articulated in the interviews. The staff budget was being cut and he no longer felt able to make decisions on how to use staff; the budget now carried out this function:

> It is the budget that is in control. A year ago I would be saying 'right I need this person in, I will ring them up', now I have to go to Marion and say 'I need someone do we have the money to do it?' Maybe she will say yes or no, usually no.

Budgetary control and withdrawal of access were threats to his identity. As a strategist, he planned his response not long before our final interview. In the second interview he had acknowledged the importance of Sales Support due to operational changes: 'Sales Support are more important in a way, they should have more staff than sales floor.' In this light his strategy was simple: transfer to Sales Support. From here his position in the game would be more central, here was where the action was, here he thought he could reclaim his management role in the strategic use of the Organiser. From here his vision of himself as management could take place. He described his plan to obtain budgetary control and through the Organiser play a role in the allocation of that budget:

> I think we would use [the Staff Organiser] . . . a lot more actively, we would be a bit more focused on the fact that we've got this money and we're trusted with it every year, we would certainly be more focused at getting things exactly how they should be.

The strategist's narrative of himself, the organisation and the events he was part of were filled with strategic language and notions of winning or playing the game. This was particularly clear when he explained his attitude to getting good figures in the Organiser. When asked whether he aimed to get good percentages in the system or ensure that his department was operating well he replied:

> You can see how we can get better percentage rates and that's what I'm looking for, because that's what they want. I do get into that, I don't know if it's the right thing, but I always have the feeling that I want to get that figure right, rather than the department.

Both the strategist and the technophile tell us vital things about the role of identity in Brodies. Both men appear to have had an easier time seeing themselves as managerial intermediaries than the female supervisors. They were distanced from the feminised account of the supervisors' role in the family culture. Using technology and having power and control were crucial markers of their masculine identities. Wider societal gender norms that assumed that they were the best people to use the technology, or to be in a position of power, were central to their ability to mark themselves out as different from and at times better than the women they worked alongside. The men faced similar challenges to their role and identity to those faced by the women, but they adopted different strategies based on the different repertoires open to them. At the same time, the new management intermediary identity being adopted by some of the female supervisors brought the male and female supervisory identities closer – particularly amongst the young supervisors. Both appeared to be articulating the values of the 'enterprising self'. The similarity was achieved through the exclusion of the skills associated with femininity and the privileging of those associated with masculinity.

Conclusion

When developing an accommodation with the new technology the supervisors in Brodies were active on several levels. Firstly, they integrated the technology into their environment; secondly, in so doing, they reinterpreted and to an extent reconstructed the role of the technology; and thirdly, in doing this they also reinvented themselves. The management intermediary identity to which the supervisors staked claim through an active role with the Organiser was not intended by the Organiser's designers and sponsors. Supervisors mapped out a role for themselves where they played a part in decisions about what went into the Organiser and what happened with its plans – helped by store managers supportive of this new role. By adopting this management role, the function and therefore the identity of the technology changed. As with skill, the ability to play an active role in technology's construction does not occur without costs and limits. Therefore, when highlighting the role that users can play in the social construction of technology it is useful to remember that this is a regulated process.

Initially, supervisors maintained practices and perspectives rooted in a feminine identity. By basing their actions and reinterpretation on these perspectives in an organisational environment that read femininity as subservient, they domesticated their challenge and denied the possibility of a more active, sustained rejection of the system. The feminine identification helped to deny that what they were doing was skilful and still legitimate to the organisation. The association of certain types of activity with femininity and mothering made them hard to defend against generalised versions of rationality and non-rationality. Mumby and Putnam (1992) suggest that organisations need to accept the validity of 'bounded emotionality' like that practised by the supervisors in the early days. However, what happened at Brodies suggests that this will require breaking the bond between the provision of emotion and the role of women in providing it. Processes of innovation would benefit from the levels of ambiguity and contextuality Mumby and Putnam associate with bounded emotionality. However, to be fully realised, this requires the removal of gender distinctions from the labelling of emotion in actors and actions.

By changing occupational identity, both male and female supervisors could be seen as successful: they protected themselves from a threat to their security and position. The women supervisors were able to use changing gender narratives to 'reinvent themselves, to present themselves, and to affirm themselves in a negotiative process' (Gherardi 1995: 109). However, we need also to consider the self-discipline involved in that reinvention. Supervisors constructed for themselves a new subjectivity and outlook acceptable within the environment in which they worked. From within the new discourses and values that produced authoritative meaning for the technology and the organisation, supervisors were able to construct a perspective that made new sense of their position in the organisation. They were on one level 'compelled' to do this by forms of regulation and influence that required they make some kind of response to the changes happening to them. The female supervisors were vulnerable to such a process because they were women in an environment filled with gendered norms that questioned their ability to be both skilful actors and users of technology. They appeared trapped in the paradox identified by Kondo: 'When women strongly assert their gendered identities on the shop floor, they constitute themselves and are constituted in ways that simultaneously reinforce their marginality as workers and paradoxically make them critically important creators of a certain work atmosphere' (1990: 293).

The denial of skill in the organisational activities of women helps to explain why women have difficulty playing an active role in techno-organisational change. Recognising the significance of gender to the processes we are discussing here ensures that we are sensitive to the ways in which gender identities for men and women secure the denial of skill in the practices of women during change. However, at the same time it also indicates the limited role that women can play in negotiating and interpreting their identities and the role of technology during such moments of change. The experiences of women in Brodies support the claims of feminist analyses of technology (Star 1991; Webster 1996) which argue that one benefit of looking beyond the design lab towards the users of technology is the greater inclusion of women in analyses of technological innovation. At times denied a role in design, women can nevertheless carve out roles in shaping techno-organisational change. While this occurs in reference to delocalised gender norms, the process is also influenced by the localised versions of gender identity which women play a role in constructing.

Note

1 Kondo's research is based on her time spent in Japan working in a small company. Therefore, the types of family confinement she suggests are specific to that culture and time. However, that family discourses are confining is a case equally valid in the West. What varies is the type and practice of confinement.

Part III

Comparative analyses of techno-organisational change

7 Developing value
Constructions of usability and utility

This chapter and the next take our analysis forward in two ways. First, we consider our case studies comparatively. The aim here is to think about the varied contexts of each setting and to consider how this affected both the similarities and differences we found in users' experiences. Second, there is an emphasis in these chapters on using the core interviews at each site – the people who were reinterviewed during the course of the study – to consider changing experiences over time. In both chapters, the focus is on how groups of users in the organisations came to incorporate the technology into their work, their relations with others, their group projects and their interpretation of what the organisation was.

In this chapter the focus is on the labour expended by groups of users to develop value in the technology. At the same time, we must also ask why and how users sometimes avoid or don't attempt to develop value in a new technology. Our argument will be that, for a new IT system to have value for users, they must be able to see the system as both usable and able to provide utility. The chapter begins with detailing these two crucial interrelated dimensions of value: *usability* and *utility*. Drawing from evidence from our three sites we then describe the ways in which differently placed groups of users constructed these values over time. In the following section the focus is on the factors that influenced these processes, notably organisational and technical complexity, regulation, knowledge, gender, and relationships between different technical systems. In the conclusion we draw out the significance of users' group projects to the ways in which they created paths towards usability and utility. We also suggest that the process of incorporation – explained more fully in Chapter 8 – is one which is influenced by both regulation and the conditions of possibility which shape what users find, develop and decide is either usable or useful, or both.

Constructing usability

Concerns with the 'usability' of new, complex information technologies have led to the development of design approaches whose focus is on including users in finding solutions to the quest for usability. 'Soft methodologies' (Checkland *et al.* 1996) and 'human-centred' or 'symbiotic' approaches (Benders *et al.* 1995a) talk of empowering and involving the user so that the end product is one that matches user needs and interests. Such approaches challenge the technicist notion that 'the human being is a source of unreliability and error' (Badham 1995: 78), replacing it instead with a notion that the human user is integral to ensuring that IT can work.

Much of the design work aimed at producing user-friendly IT concentrates on the system interface – the look and touch of the system. GUI (graphic user interface) systems and windows formats, for example, have become popular solutions to obtaining user-friendliness. Indeed in one of our sites – Brodies – users were seconded to the IT division to test new front ends and GUI formats for upgrades and new systems. However, usability encompasses more than just the look of the system and having attractive icons on a computer screen. Given that IT systems are sociotechnical, usability cannot be thought of as just a technical issue.

When users search for usability, they are looking for a way to work with the technology alongside other technologies, their job role and identity, and their place in the organisation. The narratives and practices that we have discussed throughout the book influence this process. These help guide or order the types of strategy that users develop to make a system usable and influence what aspects they feel it is important to make usable.

What then makes a system usable? During our first round of interviews we asked users about how they used the system, what aspects they found usable, what they would like to see different about the system, how they tried to improve it and how they would define what would make a system usable. We also asked them to describe their patterns of use, getting them to talk through the types of task they used the technology for. Two things came across strongly from looking through the pilot transcripts (see Appendix for how we did this). Firstly, there were multiple components that together made the system usable. Secondly, these components varied in meaning and significance for different groups in the organisation. In particular, people's job role appeared to be paramount in framing perceptions of usability. At this stage we developed the six criteria of usability that we went on to look for in all three sites. In addition, as part of the final interviews undertaken in each site we discussed our interpretation of usability with respondents. This feedback was useful in further clarifying our interpretation and validating our model of usability.

In presenting the criteria listed below we would not want to say that in all possible organisations and in all possible technologies these are the six criteria necessary for usability to exist: this would be to drift into a form of social and technical determinism. There are other possible ways of classifying usability. What these six do indicate, however, is both the complexity of usability and its sociotechnical nature. The criteria we have developed are summarised in Figure 7.1.

Each of these elements of usability can be understood within a techno-

Checkability:	The system has checks that ensure the correct information is going in and going out.
Confidence:	Users have confidence both in their capability to use the system and in the system itself.
Control:	Users have control over the operation of the system, particularly of the information fed into the system.
Speed:	The system can be used quickly.
Ease of use:	The system is easy to use.
Understanding:	Users understand the logic of the system and what it does with the data they input.

Figure 7.1 Elements of usability

organisational setting in terms of a variety of relations with users, practices and narratives, and other technologies. Thus, *checkability* is a factor of the importance placed within the practices and narratives of different settings, firstly on data being accurate, and secondly on users being trusted to enter data correctly. Users' *confidence* in either the system or themselves is related to social assumptions about different users' capabilities. For example, women and older people are often assumed to have difficulty using new technology and are soon identified as 'barriers' to successful implementation. Lack of *control* of a system can be connected to the way it can feel out of place with existing work practices, routines and technologies that have developed over time. A positive sense of control then comes from the routines and practices that secure a certain way of working. Users have to work, collectively, to maintain or regain that sense of control and security.

How adequate the *speed* of a system is felt to be is relative to organisational and occupational factors such as how much one has to use the system; whether one thinks that using the system is an important aspect of one's job; and whether it no longer seems out of place with the other tasks that are carried out day-to-day. In a similar way, *ease of use* develops from the everyday use of the system, the shared experiences of users and the way it begins to fit or not fit with other activities that are thought of as important to users. Finally, *understanding* a system is a complex issue that cannot be grasped without situating the system within the context of users' place in the organisation and their occupational identity. Users vary in what they think it is important to understand, and how that understanding can be achieved. For some, just being able to get through the routines of the system is enough; for others, understanding why or how the system works may also be important.

Job role and usability

Across the three sites it was clear that for many different users, making the system usable encompassed far more than whether the screen was 'user-friendly'. Usability involved such matters as how it fitted in with other aspects of their workplace, and its role in relation to what they felt they needed to do to complete their work. Thus, the way users defined usability seemed clearly related to their job position.

We are stressing job role for various reasons. Firstly, the priority placed on different aspects of usability varied with users' job positions. One reason for this was that the importance of the system varied for the different job grades in each setting. How much time did they spend using it? How much did they rely on it to do their job? Could they create some organisational space where they could avoid using the system? Secondly, the criteria were defined differently by users in different job roles: how 'control' was understood, as well as whether it was achieved or not, varied. Thirdly, users' evaluations of whether the system provided usability developed over time as they constructed a relationship between their day-to-day use of the system and the work practices and routines that helped to secure their occupational role and identity.

Tables 7.1, 7.2 and 7.3 summarise the data from our first round of interviews when we asked users in each site about issues related to the usability of the new system. There are two points relating to the structure and content of the tables that are important to explain. Firstly, the bold text signifies the component of usability that was most significant for that job role. Secondly, in Table 7.2 about Brodies, checkability does not appear. This is because respondents did not mention issues that could be linked to this aspect of usability. This helps stress the point that our six categories are not universal to all settings and technologies.

There are key trends worth highlighting from the tables. In Bancroft, most users shared a concern with a lack of ease with MAC. This issue was particularly strong for those who had to use it daily to do key tasks – secretaries and laboratory managers. The other common theme for regular users was finding the system slow. This was articulated in comparison to their previous systems. The perception that MAC was slow emerged from a familiarity with alternatives that both secretaries and laboratory managers thought were quicker. From very early on, users appeared to augment the usability of the system by turning to alternative sources of usability. A useful example of this was the secretaries' use of paper checks. While checkability was important to them, they felt it more productive to develop this outside the system. This was to become a common theme in Bancroft with the development of the Data Warehouse as a solution to usability concerns in MAC.

At Brodies, as with Bancroft, concern with the system not being easy to use emerged in early interviews. In particular, what is interesting is that while those in Head Office felt that if they could make the system easy to use, usability would be achieved, the only group in stores who appeared to share

Table 7.1 Usability at Bancroft by job grade

	Secretaries	Lab. managers	General support	DBAs
Checkability	Some retain paper as a double-check	**Checking in the area of ordering supplies is a particular concern**	Services keep a check on things in the system Finance no responses	**Believe that the system does contain checking capabilities**
Confidence	Lack of confidence in their use of the system and in the reliability of the system itself	Little confidence in the reliability of the stock and ordering information	No responses	Confident in their own use
Control	**A little evidence of lack of control of their data in the system**	No responses	Services and Finance feel they have little control of system and data	Some query their ability to control the type and scope of information produced by the system (not held by all)
Ease	**Ease missing; the number of keystrokes and screens is the main reason**	**Keystrokes are a serious cause of lack of ease**	**Depending on particular aspect of Support, some ease does exist**	Concerned about the lack of ease for other users, they find they can cope with the difficulty
Speed	Considerable unhappiness with slowness of MAC	Find the system slow for ordering stock	**Finance find the system slow; slightly better for Services**	Report writing particularly slow, helped by Data Warehouse
Understanding	System seen as difficult to understand	Doubts as to how easy it is to understand the system, especially for occasional users (academics)	Services believe that lack of understanding is widespread	**Believe they understand enough about the system, but worry about other users**

Notes
DBA: Database Administrator; General Support: Generic category for people working in Finance, Services and Estates. Since differences emerged for those working in this area, these are acknowledged in the table.

Table 7.2 Usability at Brodies by job grade

	Store managers	Accounts	Supervisors	Personnel	Head office
Confidence	Having to build confidence in computer after being used to and trusting paper	Initial difficulties have meant that confidence has taken time	Confidence has developed over time, damaged by early experience	Feel they have a crucial role in building confidence in plans with supervisors	Help Desk feel they lacked confidence in the early days
Control	Ensures managers gain clearer control over supervisor practices	Lack of control within Sales Support	Supervisors feel they had more control over previous system	Lack of control in beginning, regained using reports more carefully	No responses
Ease	Easy to use, complicated to get right	Computer itself easy to use	**Lack of ease came from unfamiliarity and terminology in the plans**	Layout of plans and reports has caused problems	**Ease seen as important to get right**
Speed	**Speed is a clear-cut benefit to stores, customers and staff**	Changes allow them to get the plans off a lot quicker	Quicker than previous system	Have had difficulties getting the particular reports they want off quickly	See speed of operation as a specific objective
Understanding	Want to understand how it can help the stores	**Worry about their lack of understanding means that they make mistakes**	Keen to have an understanding of how the system works	**Believe that their lack of understanding is a significant reason for the system not being used effectively**	See staff as needing different levels of understanding

Table 7.3 Usability at Finlay by job grade

	Doctors	MLSOs, MLSO2s and clinical scientists	Trainee MLSOs	Lab. aids/clerical officers
Checkability	Important and questioned	Concerns with how checkable PBS is in comparison to paper	Believe it to be checkable	Want the system to be checkable, believe that it is
Confidence	Growing from a shaky start	All have had to develop this, clinical scientists having the most difficulty	Have developed a confidence with what they do with it	Still being developed, shaky in some areas
Control	**Question over their control of the system**	Feel controlled by the system	**Sense of training being controlled by system**	Some concern with being controlled by it but not to a significant degree
Ease	Easy to use, but find that it does not fit easily into their job	All see it as an easy system – easier than the previous one	System is seen as very easy, more so than the previous one	**System is seen as very easy to use**
Speed	Takes time away from their 'real' role	**Find the system quick when they are using it day-to-day**	System is seen as considerably quicker than previous one	**System is seen as considerably quicker than previous one**
Understanding	Growing, but still limited, would like more understanding	Happy with a limited understanding	Happy with a limited understanding	Still building their limited knowledge

Note
The respondents used to produce this table came from Microbiology and Tissue Typing.

this concern to the same degree were supervisors. Ease of use was most important for supervisors because, in their job role, being able to use plans in the busy context of the shop floor meant the system had to be easy and clear. They explained this in the context of their role of looking after their sales assistants. They wanted the plans to be easy enough for 'the girls' to understand. In working to make the plans and the system easy, much of the supervisors' activity had little to do with changing the system itself. As in Bancroft, users looked to augment the capabilities of the system by drawing in other technologies and practices. For example, supervisors in different stores began to colour code the plans so that staff could see more quickly what cash point they should staff and when.

For those in the store management teams – in particular the store accountants and personnel officers – understanding the system appeared to be more significant. This reflected both the different uses they were involved in and their different job role. Both the accountants and the personnel officers felt it was now part of their job responsibilities to get the system working in stores. They felt under pressure to understand the system so that they could use it well. They also believed that their own misuse or lack of understanding was contributing to problems with the system. Again, this attribution of any lack in usability to failure of the user rather than failure in the system emerged as a common theme at Brodies.

In Finlay, ease of use rarely emerged as a strong theme. In part this was because few users felt that the system lacked ease. Instead, all groups apart from laboratory aids and clerical staff had moved on to other concerns. In particular, given that this was a group of hospital laboratories completing tests on patients, ensuring the system was checkable was a strong theme. One interesting finding that emerged was that although MLSOs used the system more than doctors, they found the system quick while the doctors found it slow. Their different attitudes related to the different value they placed on the time spent using the system. PBS was an unavoidable and significant aspect of the MLSOs' work in the laboratory, while for doctors, having to use it was something they perceived as time taken away from what they really should be doing – their 'proper' role.

The attitudes of the doctors and how they varied from others in the laboratories are a clear indication of the importance of occupational identity to how people defined and evaluated usability. A crucial aspect of doctors' occupational identity and their sense of professionalism was having control – control over what they did in the laboratory and control over how they spent their time. Therefore, having control over how they used the system was important to them. This is why control was the biggest issue for doctors: because it was essential to their sense of their role and identity in the laboratory. They had to believe that they controlled PBS; instead they felt at this point controlled by it. In terms of time, the doctors prized the discretion they maintained over how they divided up and spent their day. This discretion was interrupted by a system whose operation entailed doing things at certain times of the day.

The above summary indicates that users in each site became involved in attempts to find ways of making their system usable. However, when comparing our discussions with respondents about how they attempted to achieve this, variations did emerge. Users in Brodies – particularly those in store management – felt it important that they work hard to find the system usable even when they came across problems. At Bancroft, in contrast, faced with similar usability problems, certain types of user – especially academic secretaries – instead 'opted out' by continuing to use their existing systems. These contrasting attitudes are not due solely to technical weaknesses in the systems. Instead they reflect the different dynamics in the organisations. In particular:

- The organisational practices and narratives of Bancroft gave a sense of autonomy to academic departments. This belief in autonomy gave the secretaries the chance to 'opt out', with the implicit support of the academics to whom they considered themselves to be answerable. This situation was facilitated by organisational structures that left unclear the locus of any ultimate authority over users.
- Many of the store users in Brodies interpreted usability problems as problems of poor use rather than of the system. The 'it's my fault' interpretation at Brodies was 'encouraged' by the technical discourses associated with the Staff Organiser and articulated by the store experts who came to stores to show users how to use the system 'properly'.

Developing utility

In each site the early days of implementation were associated with different strategies aimed at making the systems usable. However, over time making the system usable was not enough for some (although as we shall see not all) users if they were to begin to think of the system as valuable.

For users to value a piece of technology requires that they move on from just finding the system usable (they can press the right button, it does things quickly) to finding it also has utility value (it can help them do *x*). Although developing usability may come before utility emerges, this does not mean that it is a purely linear process. Firstly, the perception that users will be able to benefit from the technology encourages them to 'find the right button'. Secondly, experimenting with finding the right button may lead to them finding new ways that the system can help them to do their job. Thirdly, certain users may not wish – or be allowed – to look beyond usability. As with usability, utility does not arrive fully formed with the technology. Those who are behind the system will have their own ideas about what it is for, and this will provide an important influence; however, utility will be worked out at the local level. In moving towards utility, users increasingly prioritise uses that provide benefits to what they consider to be group and organisational needs. As this occurs, new values and priorities for the organisation and for the group emerge. The distinction between usability and utility is illustrated in Table 7.4.

Table 7.4 The transition from usability value to utility value

	Usability value	Utility value
Checkability	Users feel the system has enough safeguards to make it safe to use	The system is used to check on the organisation and users and to check information
Confidence	Users have confidence in the system and their use of it	Users have confidence in their use of the system to change things in their organisation
Control	Users feel that they have control over the system	Users use the system to control their immediate organisational environment.
Ease	The system is easy to use	The system makes work easier
Speed	The system is quick to use	The system makes work or reaching decisions quicker
Understanding	The system is understandable	The system is used to make things understandable

It is important to stress various aspects of the transition from usability to utility:

- Systems do not achieve utility when they simply meet pre-existing user needs. Utility and user needs develop together over time.
- Users construct utility opportunities in their organisational setting.
- The impetus to find utility opportunities is encouraged by particular organisational contexts.
- Different users will have different utility values.
- Utility value emerges in the context of users' bond to both their group projects and the organisation. In some settings people will develop utility values that they associate with organisational needs and in others with needs they associate with themselves or the group.

Technical and organisational change

In each of our sites, different paths towards utility were taken and can be understood in relation to the different organisational practices, narratives and forms of regulation present in that site. Before going on to describe these different paths we need to reiterate the technical and organisational changes that occurred in each site. The intent is not to say that these technical and organisational changes brought about utility, but to suggest that they became both resources and conditions of possibility in helping to shape the developments towards (or away from) utility for the different users in our three organisations.

The Staff Organiser was not the only system being introduced into stores while we studied Brodies. A new system infrastructure was being introduced which networked stores to distribution depots, Area Offices and Head Office and upon which all system software – including the Staff Organiser – would sit. Alongside the Staff Organiser, other software was implemented at various points on the infrastructure. This included an email system, a computerised training package and a spreadsheet system that analysed till transaction data. During our time with Brodies, the Organiser went through three upgrades that dealt with bugs in the system, added management capabilities to it and reflected organisational changes. These included changes to the way stores operated and deployed staff as the company brought in new distribution strategies intended to reduce stock room space and minimise staff costs.

At Finlay, technical changes to PBS and the introduction of other systems influenced its further use and development. The most significant was the introduction of an interface with the hospital's HISS system. The HISS link-up led to two important changes. Firstly, laboratory staff could now access patient administrative and medical records. Secondly, ward staff, mostly junior doctors, could now request which tests they wished to have done on the samples sent to the laboratory, via terminals on the ward. In addition to the HISS link-up, as we concluded our study, the Virology laboratory was setting up an interface between PBS and new robots being introduced into the laboratory. Various changes were being made to PBS throughout the study, such as continued alterations to the menus and fields available on the screen. The majority of these changes were still about localising the system and dealing with bugs rather than adding to the capability or functions of the system.

Organisational changes for Microbiology came through the wider reorganisation of the PHLS at a regional and national level. At a regional level the responsibilities of the different PHLS laboratories were being altered. The biggest change was that rather than each laboratory doing a broad variety of tests and procedures, different laboratories would specialise in particular tests. The introduction of robotics technology was part of this shift towards a smaller core of procedures and tests.

At Bancroft, long-term problems identified with MAC led to continued attempts to upgrade and adapt the system itself. However, the major strategy was to use additional systems to deal with perceived inadequacies in MAC's ability to store and retrieve relevant data. As part of this supplementing strategy, the Data Warehouse described in Chapters 2 and 3 was introduced about three years after MAC's initial implementation. Data Warehouse was itself upgraded so that it could be of use to Finance as well as to Student Records.

Due to strong dislike of MAC among many key users, a number of strategies were set up at Bancroft to increase user involvement and acceptance. Some of these have been detailed earlier. The most important was the formation of an IT Steering Group, which included a department head and an academic secretary to act as user representatives, and others from central support and administration departments. Other categories of users, such as laboratory managers, were not included. Much of the future direction of system change came from this group.

The organisational structure of Bancroft was undergoing significant change during our study. Much of the trigger for these changes came from outside; in particular, wider changes in the structure of higher education. Senior management at Bancroft felt that the university's decentralised structure, outlined earlier in the book, did not match the new shape of higher education. A series of organisational changes was being planned and implemented which would introduce a level of middle management to the university, with responsibility for key areas of university business given to a new committee structure.

Contrasting paths towards utility

Examining the core transcripts across the three sites we have built up a picture of the different ways in which each site moved towards both usability and utility. Tables 7.5 to 7.7 summarise the usability and utility stories for each site, showing the continuing development of both usability and utility that took place during the time covered by the core group interviews. Although the tables are not structured around job role, much of what appears in each table still reflects processes that occurred due to the influence of people's association with a particular job role and occupational identity. In the discussions found below this will become clear.

In general, if we compare the three sites, it is clear that the transition to utility has been most significant for the users we studied at Brodies. Here users appeared to have constructed a usability relationship that allows them to discover utility values. While some doubt remained over the reliability and accuracy of some transaction data in the system, store users in different job grades were developing utility values associated with controlling their immediate organisational environment and using the system to measure, check and predict store operations. Interestingly, in both Finlay and Bancroft the utility that was constructed by the users was, for the most part, occurring with the aid of the other technology that linked to or supported PBS or MAC. In Finlay some utility was found through the expanded patient data that was available due to the interface with HISS. Both doctors and MLSOs commented on the value of this data in carrying out their work. This allowed the system to take on utility value as a source of understanding patients and diagnostic trends. In Bancroft, users hoped that in the future they could obtain some value from the management information that was being made available through Phase Two of the Data Warehouse. This data would allow the users to use MAC, in tandem with Data Warehouse, to check on the administration of their own – and other – departments.

In comparison to Bancroft and Finlay, multiple utility values were emerging for different users in Brodies. Supervisors argued that they now used the

Table 7.5 Usability and utility, Bancroft core group

	First interview	Second interview	Third interview
Checkability	Significant amount of double-checking going on due to lack of faith in the integrity of data in the system. Recognition that the system does allow some checks to take place	Checking problems still remain, being dealt with via paper, Data Warehouse and system change. Organisational issues mean that checkability important. In some areas, system being used to check departments	Greater belief in the accuracy of data in the system allowing it to be used by departments to check admin. matters. Concerns still remain
Confidence	Lack of confidence in the system, varied levels of confidence in different users' use of the system	Varied levels of confidence in the system; problems with data and report reliability a contributing factor to lack of confidence for many users	Still significant areas of lack of confidence in system reliability, data format and management of system and change
Control	Sense of little control over 'their' data once in the system	Conflicting views on control issues between centre and departments. Centre think they are giving control to departments, departments think control is being taken from them	Centre is keen to start using the system to produce management information reports to control local departments. Only possible through using Data Warehouse
Ease	System not seen as easy to use for most users; Data Warehouse helps in the areas that it can be used in. The number of key strokes and screens is the main source of lack of ease	Only area where ease is present is in Data Warehouse; since there are areas that does not cover, ease still a big problem. Warehouse preferred because format of data more flexible and retrievable more quickly	System is not easy to use and it is not easy to produce useful data. The only reason that ease has increased is because of the existence of the Data Warehouse
Speed	System slow; Data Warehouse helps in the areas that it can be used in. Warehouse cannot help order purchasing, which is a major problem for lab. managers	Use of Data Warehouse the only source of improvements in speed. MAC itself it still seen as slow, particularly in the area of data entry	Both MAC and Data Warehouse running more slowly. The problem seen to be too many users and stored data. Archiving held out as the solution, but there are problems with implementation
Understanding	General lack of understanding among most users; system seen as complicated to understand, particularly for occasional users	Lack of understanding of the inner workings and relationship between modules in the system. Added to this is a lack of understanding of the purpose of the data being entered	Complicated nature of the system makes it difficult to understand enough to use flexibly and effectively. Solution is to go to Warehouse. Some increase in understanding is occurring

Table 7.6 Usability and utility, Brodies core group

	First interview	Second interview	Third interview
Checkability	Any inaccuracy in the system blamed on user error. Supervisors check the accuracy of plans and change whatever 'errors' they find	There is an increased belief in the accuracy of plans; most manual changes now related to last-minute changes – for example, someone off sick	System now being used by supervisors, management teams, managers and Area Offices to check the efficiency and operation of shopfloor activity
Confidence	Initial store confidence low; management team realise the need to build confidence in the system	Users are confident about being able to use it, but not using it well. Store managers are feeling increasingly confident; supervisors still doubt the viability of the plans	Although confidence has generally improved, confidence in the system itself (its plans and data) is still lacking
Control	At first lack of control over system; supervisors feel their departments now out of their control. Managers and accountants want to retain control over staffing issues	Supervisors and management are beginning to control staff via the system, although both supervisors and managers aware of threat of being controlled by it	The stores feel that they are in control and are deciding what they can do with the systems. Using them as methods of controlling (particularly management)
Ease	Most store staff find the computer itself easy to use. Using it actually to plan store activity more difficult	System seen as easy; significant support for email helping ease of communication. For the Organiser, ease is not enough: 'does it help?' is a key question – still doubts	No responses
Speed	Speed is important. Apart from some problems with reports, system is seen as quick	Email seen as a quick method of communication, needed amongst management because of increasing lack of actual contact	The Organiser now a quick tool for supervisors (spend less time changing the plans) and managers (quicker than paper calculations)
Understanding	Most want – but have yet to achieve – a broad understanding of system, particularly accountants. Access important to understanding	Supervisors happy with their level of understanding; managers now anxious to understand it enough to use it strategically – in the process changing their understanding of the business	General levels of understanding have improved. Respondents still think there are areas that they are not so clear on, especially management

Table 7.7 Usability and utility, Finlay core group

	First interview	Second interview	Third interview
Checkability	Checkability important to doctors and MLSOs: they both question whether the system has sufficient checkability	Least improved aspect of the system. Paper still seen as more checkable. Fears over data and reports getting lost in the system	Multiple changes adopted to increase checkability: (1) working practice; (2) using paper; (3) HISS. Moves now being made to check work through PBS. Crucial issue
Confidence	Still in early stages but gradually developing. Users are confident in their own use	A big increase in confidence in being able to use the system. Still gaps in confidence in the system	Users are more confident about their own use than in the system itself. Doctors believe they have least confidence in the system
Control	Significant feelings of being controlled by the system for many users. Many feel lack of space or flexibility in the ways in which they can use it	For most, control of the system does exist. Others feel that the system is in control or that there are aspects over which they have yet to achieve control	Multiple definitions and views on control. Doctors want more individual control. MLSOs feel they have gained more control over the system, but that their work is controlled more
Ease	System seen as easy to use, but less easy to fit into patterns of work	Ease of use is there for most users; big issues remain for doctors relating to lack of fit with their working day	Ease there for most users, value being found in the ability to pull up patient data quickly and easily, especially useful for doctors
Speed	System is seen as quicker than previous system for all users apart from doctors, who feel it takes time away from their 'proper' role	Two reasons cited for lack of speed stressed: (1) it appears slow because they use it faster; (2) the HISS link is not working well and means additional users on-line	Speed acceptable to everyone bar doctors. System can get slow when there are lots of users. Beginning to be used to access data about patients and change nature of work
Understanding	Most users have a limited understanding; doctors are the group who most wish to increase their understanding	Most approaching a level of contingent, distanced understanding. There are still gap areas, particularly in what happens to data on the network	Some users' understanding a basis to explore greater utility of system; other users still exploring ways to make system more usable

Note
These responses reflect Microbiology: core interviews were not undertaken in Tissue Typing.

Organiser to control their staff and understand the operations of their departments. Store managers and others in the management team used the system strategically – in tandem with the other new systems – to plan change and structure present needs. Area Offices were using their access to the data to monitor store activity and to create performance targets for senior store staff. Across all the criteria of usability we could see that different users were making some transition to utility influenced by their position within the organisation:

1   For supervisors it had utility as a day-to-day staff planner to aid their work.
2   For the store management team it had utility as a strategic management tool to aid them in plotting long-term changes and projections in store activity.
3   For Area Office and Head Office users it had utility as a regulatory system to monitor and direct store activity.

Explaining the different experiences

A straightforward IT management account would argue that the Staff Organiser was simply a more usable and useful system than the ones introduced at Finlay and Bancroft. It would commend the ways in which implementation took place. It would suggest that success was due to user involvement and the successful integration of organisational and user needs into the system. Such an account would argue that at Brodies we have a model of best practice which organisations like Bancroft and Finlay could learn much from. Some management and change approaches are better than others; however, the variation we have seen in the sites is not just about 'good' or 'bad' acquisition and implementation management. Instead, it is about differing organisational practices, narratives and forms of regulation.

Why and how did this process of reinvention take place for users in Brodies? What factors at Finlay and Bancroft made utility construction more problematic for users? The best way to discuss these issues is by distinguishing factors that varied in their significance and effect in the different settings.

Organisational and technical complexity

As we have already argued, groups develop utility over time. Users will work to find utility if they can identify clear ways in which incorporation of the technology into their group projects makes sense and helps secure their position in the organisation. For some of our users, their perception of organisational and technical complexity meant that the labour involved in developing utility appeared too great and, at best, of ambiguous benefit.

Users we spoke to at Bancroft felt surrounded by a complex system and a complex organisation. The sense of complexity and confusion was exacerbated by uncertainty and ambiguity about the future organisational shape of Bancroft. This feeling was shared by many different users at the university and influenced their approach to MAC and to their interpretation of their place and function in the organisation. On a basic level, they felt that MAC was simply difficult to understand. Entering data and accessing information required numerous keystrokes and multiple screens that had to be gone in and out of repeatedly. For users such as academic secretaries or laboratory managers, what previously had been thought of as simple tasks – such as entering data – had been turned into what they felt was an irrelevant test of endurance. Developing utility was restricted by difficulties in constructing a usable system. A feeling of lack of ease and understanding was created by a mismatch between the priorities set in the fields and formal representations in MAC, and the priorities and needs of the users. Many users found no value or significance in the amount of data they now had to enter into the system:

> There is information that I put into MAC and I haven't a clue what it's for . . . I don't know how it will be used subsequently, and therefore I don't really know how important it is.
>
> (Academic secretary)

They found it difficult to enter the data, and had a limited understanding of why they had to go through the difficulty. In that context, there was little incentive to figure out 'why'.

At this point two different things could have happened. Firstly, the fields and formal representations found in the system could have been altered to match the needs and priorities of users post-implementation to make it more understandable and easier to use. Secondly, users could have adapted their priorities and needs to match those maintained by the system to make the work appear more worth while and easier. However, for the groups we spoke to there is little indication that either of these responses happened. In part this stemmed from the organisational complexity of the university, which made it difficult to incorporate the myriad of different priorities and needs which had developed within a culturally diverse and devolved organisation. This complexity was reflected in the management structure of MAC itself, with confusion surrounding who was responsible for MAC and the varied roles of the different committees that had been set up. This confusion was even shared by those within the committees:

> there's an IT Steering Group, but the IT Steering Group also answers to the, now I've got to remember what we're all called again this week. There's the Information Committee and there's the Computing Committee, which I think is the one I sit on. Yes it is. I know I'm definitely not on the top one.
>
> (Estates manager)

The complexity of the committee structures reflected the competing interpretations of needs and values that cut across the organisation. As a result of
this:

- Users were left unsure about what management had identified as problems
  and when or how these problems would be resolved.
- There was an organisational space through which certain users could initially 'opt out' of the system and simply carry on using existing practices.

For key users in our other two sites such an 'opt-out' space did not exist. The
need to engage with the system meant that users in both Brodies and Finlay
had to increase their understanding and come to some sort of accommodation
with the system. This effort meant that they had less of a perception of it as
complex. One element of this was that system changes were made to reduce
the number of keystrokes needed to enter and access data in both sites through
upgrades (Brodies) and adaptations (Finlay), helping ease of use to increase.
Another reason was that users were able to learn and introduce short cuts due
to their increased understanding of the system. At Finlay and Brodies, the
result of mismatches between the formal representations in the system and the
organisational environment led to different results to those in Bancroft. At
Finlay, doctors were able to put pressure on management to change the formal
representations to match their pre-existing definition of needs. However, they
did make some accommodations to the system, as witnessed in their changing
approach to the validation issue discussed in Chapter 4. At Brodies, over time,
as discussed in Chapters 5 and 6, the users' perceptions of the organisational
environment began to change to reflect the formal representations of the
system. Both these processes reduced feelings of complexity and confusion,
ensuring utility opportunities could be found.

Knowledge and utility

As discussed in Chapter 4, group projects can construct knowledge as a
resource securing their status and position. In all our sites, knowledge and its
link to group projects based on occupational identity were influential to the
varied levels of utility constructed for the different systems. Three forms of
knowledge contributed to how groups developed utility:

- knowledge of the system;
- knowledge produced via the system;
- knowledge produced independently of the system.

In Brodies, the Staff Organiser was not just part of the working environment:
it became over time central to defining the day-to-day operation of that environment. Knowledge produced via the system was increasingly valued. Users
of different job grades in stores were keen to show expertise and knowledge of

the system. Younger supervisors saw expertise in the Organiser as important to future promotion and status in the stores. Both Area Office and store managers identified an ability to work with the Staff Organiser as a skill that assistant supervisors must have before being moved up to supervisor. Knowledge of the Organiser had become an organisational credential at Brodies. At the same time this meant that knowledge that was outside the system – the type of local and subjective knowledge discussed in Chapter 6 – was devalued by both the organisation and users themselves.

This contrasts strongly with Finlay, where key users – especially doctors – had the resource of professionally secured knowledge that was recognised as valuable and could be used to dictate the shape of PBS. To take on utility for these users, PBS would have to acknowledge and reflect this professional knowledge. In contrast to users at Brodies, the doctors were able to use the professional narrative of occupational identity to aid their efforts at getting their knowledge included in the system. Where this was successful they began to construct some utility on their terms and incorporated PBS as a work tool. For example, one doctor was using the system to pull off infection control reports helpful to his role in monitoring any spread of infectious diseases within the hospital. Here there are signs that such doctors were using the system to develop and construct their understanding of the patient and their environment.

Validation was always the cornerstone of the disputes doctors had with the system. Using their professional status and knowledge was crucial to the doctors' position on this issue. One of their main complaints about validation was the time that it took on the computer. Short cuts and adaptations did reduce the time taken, but doctors still felt that it was not a good use of their time and knowledge. The eventual solution was to turn over validating negative results to MLSOs. Doctors would focus on the positive results. This altered the professional boundaries between MLSOs and doctors. Ultimately, it secured the sense of the doctors as having knowledge that was (1) more significant and valuable than knowledge of or within PBS and (2) a basis on which to judge the utility value of PBS. Because of their position and identity the doctors could find some value in the system, but also retain some distance from it. Much of what they understood as their job and the role of the laboratory remained outside the system or its influence.

The relationship between the MLSOs and doctors was mediated by boundaries of knowledge affected by other aspects of the running of the system. Ward-ordering was intended to increase the utility of the system by allowing doctors in wards to order specific tests before a sample was sent to the laboratory. MLSOs saw in the introduction of the ward interface a devaluing of their knowledge and role in the laboratory. They rejected the assumption that the junior doctors on wards would be best placed to decide which tests to perform. For once, managers supported the MLSOs' assertion and changed the system to allow them to make some alterations to the tests asked for by doctors on the wards. The experiences of MLSOs and doctors indicate that knowledge independent of the system if secure and acknowledged by key members of the organisation, can give those associated with that knowledge a privileged position in shaping the values for a technology.

Regulation and utility

It is important to be aware of ways in which users or groups can be compelled to search for utility in a technology and in their use of it. Wishing to incorporate a new technology into their projects may be evidence of their recognition of the privilege given to the technology and associated management priorities. On this level, the process of valuing is influenced and shaped by the patterns of management and subjective regulation that we have discussed throughout the book. In attempting to respond and make sense of changing patterns of regulation, the system can become a resource to aid users' attempts to control their position and their environment.

In Brodies the variety of store users all appeared increasingly keen to develop utility within the Staff Organiser. Supervisors began to use the Organiser to dictate staff activity and worked to ensure that staff did what was laid out on the plans. They found the Organiser particularly useful in their relations with temporary staff, using it as a method of control over a group of staff with whom they had less well-developed relations. This approach to staff and to the technology was linked to the conditions of possibility created by the changes in staff relations and store operations introduced at the same time as the Staff Organiser. The Organiser had become a potential resource in securing the supervisors' position in a changing environment. The supervisors had made a transition from believing that the system controlled them to believing that through the Organiser they could control others.

Store managers were also active in seeking out utility opportunities. Their focus was on demonstrating that they could use the system to generate utility values recognised by the organisation. One store manager liked the email system because it meant he could monitor his management team by sending them tests that they would have to respond to. The upgrade to Version 3 of the Staff Organiser, which allowed managers to play 'what if' scenarios that tested out the implications of a change in opening hours or a shift in store profile, was identified by store managers as a key improvement in the utility of the Organiser:

> we can do 'what if' scenarios. We can project in any changes we might want to put into any of the systems – staffing levels etc. – and let it run. It will come out with what will happen if we do that, and even compare that with what we normally do. So in a business sense we can plan much more easily what will happen as a consequence of any changes that we make. That has been a definite benefit.
>
> (Store manager)

Both the management and subjective regulation that we have witnessed in Brodies were important to producing a context that compelled users to develop utility values that they believed were organisationally approved. Management regulation was witnessed in the importance that the company placed on the system and its operation, alongside the other operational changes taking place. Store staff of all ranks recognised that success within the company was to a significant degree marked out by success with the Staff Organiser. This view was encouraged by Brodies' post-implementation strategies. The store experts who came in to help users with the Staff Organiser did more than show them how to make the system usable. They stressed the potential for utility, the need to find utility and the value of the priorities set in the system as defined centrally. This is where regulation becomes more subjective. Users were encouraged to see value in the Organiser through the regulatory influence of the technical discourse associated with the system and articulated by store experts. They adopted the values and assumptions provided with the Organiser, while at times devaluing previous values and assumptions associated with their local culture and occupational identity.

These processes of regulation did not go unchallenged. Brodies was an environment that had other sources of meaning. Store users recognised that the company was placing a great deal of emphasis on the Staff Organiser, but did not always support that emphasis. Managers still had a significant bond to the 'family' narratives that were part of their account of organisational culture. This culture gave them a significant amount of authority over the running and well-being of their store. From this position some questioned the utility constructed by the sponsors of the Organiser and saw instead a threat to their position and status. This challenge continued, and perhaps increased, throughout our time studying Brodies. One store manager commented when we spoke to him the second time:

> I view very strongly the opinion that [the Staff Organiser] is a management tool, and that at the end of the day, myself and the management team must be responsible for the operation of the store. I won't allow [the Staff Organiser] to dictate what should be spent, but I view it as a very useful tool. I would regret very much if the company then came along and said, 'you will be staffed to Staff Organiser levels'. Where would that then take my flexibility, and my management skills?

In both Bancroft and Finlay, different patterns of regulation allowed some – although not all – users to remain distanced from the system. This gave them a stronger base from which to develop utility values distinct from those stressed by those behind the technology. Significantly for some users at Bancroft, this distance also gave them the chance to refuse to work to construct utility value. The organisational complexity of the site and the relative strength of the varied narratives of autonomy gave some users the chance to decide not to seek utility opportunities for the system. Instead it was the people behind MAC who had to provide features within the system through which significant users such as academic secretaries could find utility. Those behind the technology could not rely on the types of regulation we saw at Brodies to enrol users in the objectives of the system.

At Finlay, key users had authority with which they could resist any regulation that appeared with the technology. Doctors felt little need to prove that they could use PBS or find utility opportunities that matched new organisational priorities of performance management and clinical audit. They had control over their environment irrespective of PBS, and it appeared to provide few new avenues to promote control. MLSOs and others in the laboratories, in common with clerical staff at Bancroft, had no choice but to use the system, and in addition had less authority from which they could dictate what they thought should be of value in it. While some MLSOs were beginning to find value in the patient data, the organisation was happy for these users simply to use it. Managers did not view it as important to the success of PBS for MLSOs to develop utility for it. At the same time, staff at Finlay were aware of the increased potential for management regulation from local and national organisational changes. The increased monitoring of laboratory activity and the routinisation and automation of testing were viewed as a threat to professional claims to autonomy and expertise. The threat of regulation that came from these new organisational perspectives replaced in many users' minds their concern with possible regulation through PBS.

Gender, confidence and utility

Confidence is an important aspect of both utility and usability. Users can feel confident in their use of the system and/or in the system itself. When users focus on a lack of confidence in the system itself, there is less of an incentive for them to labour towards developing utility. On the other hand, if users feel a lack of confidence in their own use they may feel unable to question the abilities of the system. In this context users may work hard to prove to others that they can find utility in the system. What then becomes important is considering what factors influence how confidence is attributed. In our analysis, the different gendered cultures of the organisations and identities of the different users were significant in creating the forms of utility that developed over time.

In both Bancroft and Finlay, users gained confidence relatively quickly in their ability to use the system. In Bancroft, even though users found the system difficult to use and understand, they were confident it was not their own use of the system which was creating the difficulty or the errors that occurred. Users in Finlay, even when they did not like the system, felt they could use it easily and with confidence. This growing confidence was important for three reasons at Bancroft and Finlay. Firstly, it gave users confidence to blame problems on the system rather than on their own use. The focus instead was on a lack of confidence in the system. Secondly, recognition that the systems could be at fault meant that they remained sceptical towards technical discourses associated with them. They continued to question the supposed benefits, purpose and capabilities of PBS and MAC. Thirdly, the belief that they could use the system and could understand its weaknesses made them able to voice demands for change:

> it is just a shame it's taken a year and half to do it, but now we understand more how the system works and what we can expect of it, we can start having our own expectations, and we can ask now if we want certain things doing.
>
> (MLSO, Finlay)

In contrast, in Brodies users were willing to blame themselves for system problems throughout the study. Any notions that the system was too complex for store activity, that it was unable to accommodate to local needs, or that it was unsuited to the store environment were eventually drowned out by the repeated assertion that 'we are not doing it right'. Supervisors in particular blamed themselves and were blamed by others. The supervisors often categorised themselves as incompetent: 'I'm always wary because I always think that I can't do it. That I won't be able to do it as well as anybody else.' Those higher up the store management team responsible for the upkeep of the system often blamed themselves too. One store accountant was convinced that she and her team must be responsible for the mistakes. When she was pressed on whether some of the liability could lie with the system she replied: 'I don't really think it is the system to be honest. I think it is getting used to it and getting the right information into it.'

Confidence in respondents' use and understanding of the system did increase, and indeed supervisors and others were surprised at their ability to learn how to use the Staff Organiser and find new uses for it. However, their early fear and worry left a legacy of assumed inadequacy amongst many users. Unlike staff at both Finlay and Bancroft, supervisors and others in the management team were always willing to place blame on themselves rather than on the Staff Organiser or on those behind the system.

An important reason for this difference lies in the particular type of *gendered* organisational culture that was present in Brodies. In the context of the family narrative the notion that a female, middle-aged workforce would have difficulty using technology was easily formed. The paternalism and maternalism of local store culture, which expressed itself in notions of 'looking after the girls', merged with wider social narratives that cast doubt on the abilities of women to use complex technology and created a focus on looking for and finding individual blame. The efforts of store experts also helped to encourage this view. The favourite IT phrase, 'if you put garbage in, you will get garbage out', was often repeated to store staff by the experts who travelled to stores to fix 'problems', and subsequently repeated to us in interviews. The focus on individual blame had two consequences:

- Other explanations, in particular that the system was at fault, were excluded.
- Rather than questioning the assumptions embedded in the system, supervisors worked hard to prove that they could get the system right, focusing on finding utility opportunities in the assumptions enshrined in it.

Women were significant users in both Finlay (MLSOs and doctors) and Bancroft (academic secretaries), but the notion that women in these occupational roles would find it hard to use the new systems appeared to be less influential. There were various reasons for this. Firstly, academic secretaries at Bancroft and MLSOs and doctors at Finlay were already using computers or other sophisticated pieces of technology. Since using such technologies was already a significant part of their working environment and occupational identity, social narratives of the technical incompetence of women would be unlikely to carry much weight amongst the women in these occupational groups. Secondly, while both Finlay and Bancroft had their own gendered narratives and cultures, the absence of the family discourses of paternalism and maternalism ensured that users' interpretation of their own abilities did not take on this particular gendered association.

Constructing utility with other technologies

Technology rarely operates in isolation. A single system often works in a context of other systems, including those which:

- are designed to link with the system;
- have been introduced to deal with a perceived failing in the system;
- exist to deal with completely separate areas of the organisation's activities.

All three of these different types of system existed in our sites, and were important to users' attempts at finding utility.

In Bancroft, MAC interacted with another system – the Data Warehouse – that had been introduced to help solve its apparent weaknesses. Rather than make MAC more usable, the strategy of system managers was to look for utility elsewhere. One of the goals behind that strategy and the later version of the Warehouse was to provide certain key users (first relating to Student Records and then to Finance) with flexibility and ease of use. It was hoped that these criteria would enable users to think of Data Warehouse and MAC as together providing a single service that was useful to them. For example, once Phase Two of the Data Warehouse was in place it was hoped that departments would start to draw off management reports and data, and become more responsible locally for monitoring their budgets.

In Finlay, continued concerns over PBS's ability to check its own accuracy and fears over users entering data incorrectly led to the introduction of new checking procedures in some laboratories. In particular, in Virology an increase in the volume of tests and difficulties with the interface with the new robotics system raised fears over the accuracy of data entry. The problems with the interface meant that test results were written onto paper and then entered into PBS. This led to fears of transcription error, needing further checking procedures:

> So we've evolved a system whereby, because it's obviously possible to make a transcription error, when you're putting the results from paper onto PBS. So we've evolved a system whereby a second person always checks that input, to make sure it's accurate.
>
> (MLSO2)

In both these cases we could see the adoption of other technologies, or the introduction of additional working practices, as 'failures' in the technology – the failure to secure utility value in the technology itself. In the same way, the manual over-writing of Staff Organiser plans on the shop floor could be seen – and was seen by system sponsors – as an example of poor use of the technology. However, there is another way of understanding the relationship the systems formed to other technologies in their environment. If we treat each system, each technology, as an individual artefact, then the only way to measure its success or failure is as a single entity evaluated on what it alone provides. However, as we have made clear, that is not what happens during the embedding of new technologies into organisations. Organisational technology is the collection of systems and working practices that form over time, not one individual system. In this understanding, the link to the Data Warehouse at Bancroft, the reintroduction of paper checks in Finlay, and the use of pencil to amend the Staff Organiser's plans in Brodies are not evidence of technological failure. Instead, they are examples of the construction of utility through the integration of different technological artefacts to create a successful *sociotechnical ensemble*.

Conclusion

The different experiences at each of our sites show how the consumption of technology in organisations involves the production and maintenance of usability and utility values for the technology. While utility does not require the pre-existence of usability, there appears to be a strong relationship between the two. The development of these two values occurs in shifting organisational settings and tells us something about the shape and influence of organising practices and narratives, organisational cultures, and patterns of regulation. The place of users in the organisation and their externally developed identities will influence whether reaching a usable and useful relationship with the technology is important to them and to the organisation. For some users, usability is enough. In some cases there is little incentive to labour towards developing utility opportunities and values. The decision not to incorporate a technology into a group project can be evidence of the security of other resources that continue to sustain that group project. It can also result from a lack or failure of forms of regulation to compel users to incorporate the technology.

At the same time, those behind the technology wishing to enrol key users do attempt to encourage such users to develop utility. Once the technology becomes an integral part of staff promotion, once performance contracts reflect targets and values within the system, users can feel little option but to be involved actively in turning the system into a 'useful' tool. Therefore, at least some of the utility values that users find for technology flow from the patterns of regulation they are part of. In understanding the conditions of possibility that inform the development of utility, the goal is to see the emerging utilities as products of the strategies and negotiations that users are part of. These negotiations are attempts to retain or obtain power and position in the organisation and help explain the labour undertaken to incorporate new technologies into the group projects of users. It is important to consider users as active, as well as constrained, in seeking to turn use of the system into a resource that can help them secure their position and identity within and beyond the organisation.

In a context that appears highly regulatory, the utility values that users develop to secure their position will be strongly informed by the values they see stressed by system sponsors and actors higher in authority in the organisation. Where instead the context is one of structural or professional autonomy, users may find they have the chance to develop their own utility values distinct from those defined by others, or even decide that they have no need to find utility at all. Connected to this, if certain users can rely on existing resources to support their status and power – for example professional or occupational identity – they may be able to resist organisational allocations of value and priorities in the system.

This chapter has looked at the changing relationship between users and technology. How does this relate to broader processes of stabilising the technology and embedding it within the organisational setting? This question is considered in Chapter 8.

8 Ending the acquisition process
Stabilisation and incorporation

Our analysis of the introduction of MIS in Bancroft, Brodies and Finlay is very different from the conventional managerialist accounts of technology acquisition discussed in Chapter 1. The complex, messy and drawn-out processes considered in Chapters 3–7 seem many miles away from the portrayal of acquisition as the matching of technological solutions to pre-existing organisational needs. Running through this book has been an argument that the specification, selection, implementation and consumption of new technology in an organisation are not complete, self-contained moments but rather form a process of on-going, intertwined organisational and technological change. Related to this is another recurrent theme – the differentiated and often difficult relationships end-users develop with systems.

Given these conclusions, in what sense can we talk of the end of a technology acquisition? As discussed in Chapter 2, Social Studies of Technology SST offers a potentially important concept for understanding this. The term *stabilisation* is used to refer to the process by which designs and meanings of artefacts and systems become cemented. This involves firstly, the jostling among different groups for the power to determine the meaning of the technology, usually resulting in the eventual dominance of one interpretation; and secondly, an increasing monitoring of its shape, role and relationship to other technologies. The result, for Bijker and Law, is an embedding within social structures of a *sociotechnical ensemble*, which is progressively entrenched and hence increasingly difficult to dislodge – in other words, it becomes an *obdurate* sociotechnology (Bijker and Law 1992a, Bijker 1995).

From an SST perspective, stabilisation takes place primarily in the initial development and design of technologies. As we suggested in Chapter 2 and have demonstrated in later chapters, however, the introduction of a new technological system into a particular setting involves some degree of *de*stabilisation of both the sociotechnology and other elements of organisational life. Whilst the system has been blackboxed by its designers and managers, the black box is bound to be reopened before the technology can settle down and become (temporarily) stable. Our case studies show how technology is subject to scrutiny by a wide range of organisational actors, to be altered by some of them but to remain impervious to the attempts at alteration of others. Thus we should consider how, on what terms, and to what extent the systems and organisations we have analysed were *re*stabilised. Doing so requires a different approach to stabilisation from that normally found in SST. Our account of stabilisation:

- is focused on how technologies are established locally rather than on the formation of generic technological conventions;
- views stabilisation as continuing, fragile and partial;
- is not based necessarily on the establishment of common understandings of the technology but rather on the meeting of different positions and perspectives.

This last point can be explained further with reference to Chapter 7. In that chapter the emphasis was on the varied ways in which differently placed organisational actors constructed value in systems. The discussion of the interviewees' development of usability and the transition to utility suggested that, over time, their relationship to the systems changed. It also, however, outlined a highly variable and fragmented set of accommodations between users and technology; so much so that it is quite difficult to see how these might add up to a single coherent process of stabilisation.

Again following Chapter 2, we would argue, therefore, that discussion of *stabilisation* should be complemented by consideration of *incorporation*. As we said in that earlier chapter, there are parallels between organisational actors struggling to establish a relationship to new technology and domestic consumers who reappropriate mass-produced goods and integrate them into their lifeworld. Consumption studies use the concept of *incorporation* to understand how goods become part of everyday life and hence invisible as commodities (Silverstone *et al.* 1992). Associated with this is *conversion*, the way that goods come to mediate social relationships such as those within the household and between the household and the outside world. This approach – looking at the incorporation of new technology into an existing constellation of objects, meanings, relations and projects – can be adapted to understand the position of users in techno-organisational change. In particular, it adds a number of new dimensions to the discussion of stabilisation:

- Incorporation allows us to understand the participation of end-users in stabilisation, focusing on the labour that users put into integrating the technology into their life within and beyond the organisation. In doing so they may or may not ultimately contribute to the shaping of the system as a sociotechnology.
- The account of stabilisation offered by SST implies the development of a high degree of agreement across an organisation about the properties, form and purpose of the technology – incorporation does not. Here the emphasis is on how technology becomes part of a multiplicity of individual and group projects.

- From an SST perspective stabilisation is never final. Focusing on incorporation provides further insight into the contingency of any stabilisation within an organisation. There is an inherent fragility and open-endedness to the process that spring from the ever-changing array of artefacts, meanings and relationships into which the technology must be incorporated by various interested groups.

Thus, in discussing the ending of acquisition, this chapter will explore both the *stabilisation* of the MIS as sociotechnologies and their *incorporation* into the lives of people in organisations. Our contention is that it is in the interplay between these two sets of processes that some sort of completion of technology acquisition occurs. This interplay also means, however, that closure is never final: any of the elements that comprise an organisational sociotechnical ensemble may be reopened, again destabilising it.

The chapter explores these issues using data from our three research sites, often drawing together and consolidating examples and arguments already raised earlier in the book. It is divided into four sections. The first begins the discussion of ending by considering the responses of our interviewees. To what extent and how is it possible to identify from their comments a sense of the three systems settling down, and the acquisition reaching a conclusion? The next section moves from these subjective experiences to develop a broader analysis. Here the key theme is that any account of stabilisation must include a range of elements beyond the system itself and be located in a wider account of techno-organisational change. The third section examines the relationship between this stabilisation of the three systems in our study and their incorporation by users. The chapter concludes by asking how a technology can become embedded in an organisation while different users attach different meanings to it. Our contention is that this is as much about the ability of the systems to act as *boundary devices* between the different social groups in the organisation as it is about the standardising of meanings, technology and usage.

Signs of ending

Our interviews, particularly those conducted with our core groups later in the study, revealed a number of diverse ways in which people came to see acquisition as being at an end: these are set out in Figure 8.1. Rather as consumers, through a process of acquisition, eventually come to see goods as personal objects instead of as commodities, for many users the systems in question lost their 'newness' over time and became part of their organisational 'furniture'. This sense of completion is, however, as we shall discuss below, a diffuse and ambivalent one.

Milestones of closure and projections of completion

As part of their planning, early in the acquisition, managers make projections about when a new system should be stable. They set a series of milestones that

Projection of a timeframe for completion

Passing of milestones

System ceases to be seen as 'new'

The old system fades from memory

The new system becomes integral to daily routines

The realisation or dashing of expectations

Problems must be lived with rather than resolved

Figure 8.1 The ending of acquisition

seek to mark progress in the acquisition process and the development of closure around the shape and role of the system. Early milestones, before a new system has even been physically installed, would include:

- the identification of system requirements and specifications;
- signing a contract with a supplier following the tendering process;
- signing off the system as acceptable, following test procedures;
- the moment of 'going live' with the system.

As other chapters have shown, however, at each of these stages questions about the eventual shape of the system remain; also the very act of 'going live' unleashes a whole new raft of uncertainties and problems. In response, managers establish other milestones after implementation that signify the closure of the system and debates around it. The production of localised manuals and standard operating procedures, for example imply that usage has stabilised enough to allow work routines to be set out formally and adhered to. Milestones of this kind, whether embodied in formalised routines or simply expressed informally, can be seen as strategies that aim to mitigate uncertainty and instability by setting the process of acquisition within a bounded, rational framework – in effect, a plan for completing the project. They are an important way in which managers seek to promote systems to their staff.

Formalised plans form only part of the activity of management planning in organisations, which must be understood in situated, localised terms in order to account for the apparent mismatch between planned goals and contingent 'reality', which rarely matches objectives (Dant and Francis 1998). Managers and their staff in each of our sites identified points in time that they regarded as marking both milestones in the process of MIS acquisition and the final endpoint. Nevertheless, the ways in which these milestones were deployed indicates the flexible role they can play as strategic resources. An important aspect of this is the way that the ultimate completion of the acquisition is usually projected some time into the future. For example, the IT manager at Finlay hospital responsible for the implementation of PBS set out in our first interview with him a timetable by which he expected the implementation process to be complete. By the second interview this programme had slipped by about six months, but he felt, aside from that slippage, that it was still on course. By his third interview, however, his interest in this issue had subtly changed. He was no longer looking towards a stable system; instead he saw the *use* of the system as becoming stable, but he saw the context of the system remaining fluid as new, associated applications were being brought on-line in the hospital.

Stability is not, then, even for those managing acquisition, a clearly defined and fixed entity, even where it is presented as an organisational objective. To underline this point, at Bancroft University we were presented with a range of conceptions of stability. An MIS manager framed stabilisation in terms not of system or use, but of *acceptance* by users. In contrast, the head of the IT Steering Group felt an indicator of stabilisation would be that the Steering Group would be no longer needed; whilst the Project Manager for the Finance module felt that stabilisation was more functional, that it would have occurred when the module was running smoothly and reliably. This flexibility and debate over what constitutes stability also maps onto the varying organisational dynamics at our research sites, in that at Bancroft no one group could easily claim control over meaning because of the university's diffuse authority structure. At Brodies, in contrast, there was greater centralised control over meaning and development of stability: the variation came in the object of stabilisation – for supervisors it was a day-to-day staff planner, for store managers it was an aid to strategic planning, and for Area and Head Office managers it was a system to monitor stores.

From the novel to the mundane

Although of significance to users, management milestones and projections of completion sat alongside the considerable anxieties and uncertainties associated with the introduction of systems. We can, however, chart a number of indicators that show that in each of our sites, over time, the novelty of the technology diminished – it ceased to be 'the new system' – and became increasingly mundane. Interlinked with this were the changing status of recollections of what things had been like prior to the introduction of the new system. Memories of a previous system can themselves inhibit closure around the new system, acting, in Mort and Michael's term, as a 'phantom intermediary' that reminds those who remain of paths not taken (1998). As memories recede, users find it hard to envisage what life in the organisation would be like without the new system.

In this respect, again, there is a split between the experience at Bancroft and those at the other sites. At Brodies and Finlay, the novelty of the system progressively faded away. A series of quotations from the three sets of interviews with our Brodies core group illustrates this nicely:

Interviewer: Could you imagine going back to [the previous system]?
Personnel officer: We could do it, I don't think we would have a major problem, apart from having to retrieve all the figures . . . It would be possible.

(First interview)

Interviewer: Can you imagine going back to a time when you didn't have [the Staff Organiser]?
Store manager: We are used to it now, if it was to disappear we would be 'Oh my God'. The staff use the plans, they are used to those, if we were to start writing them again I think they would be surprised.

(Second interview)

Supervisor: I look at it every day, it's just a way of life now.
Interviewer: Could you imagine going back to [the previous system]?
Supervisor: No.

(Third interview)

At Finlay, the progression was not so slick, but it took place none the less. Although there was a stronger sense than at Brodies of problems left unresolved, by the third set of core group interviews it was evident that the system had become a relatively mundane part of the daily routine – as an MLSO said, it was now 'part of the bench'. Integral to this was the forgetting of the previous system: in the last round of interviews one MLSO could not even remember the name of the old system.

At Bancroft, although MAC was now part of everyday life for many users, the sense of it superseding previous systems was much more tenuous. Some users, notably the academic secretaries, were still using pre-existing systems in tandem with MAC. Finance users had no choice but to switch to MAC and stop using its predecessor, KOREA, altogether (except in relation to unpaid invoices). But there was no risk that users would forget KOREA's name:

> People still talk about [KOREA], you hear the name mentioned, things like this. [MAC] hasn't phased into a system that is just there that people use and don't really think anything about. It's still talked of because there are a few glitches still in it [MAC], it [KOREA] tends to be talked about anyway. So from that point of view, I wouldn't say it's settled into obscurity yet here, people still do talk about it, so from that point of view it

does keep it foremost in your mind that it is still a relatively young system to us.

(Management accountant, third interview)

Thus at Bancroft the shift from the novel to the mundane is less clear cut than elsewhere, but it was also far more differentiated, between different modules of the system and between different groups of users.

From expectation to accommodation

As earlier chapters have suggested, the introduction of an IT system into an organisational environment is in itself destabilising of *both* the system and the environment. One important aspect of this is the expectation engendered by the arrival of a new system. The hopes and fears projected by users onto the system can be a problem or a resource for those managing its introduction. In either case, however, they are indicative of a high level of uncertainty and inter- pretative flexibility around systems when they first 'go live'. Initial expectations and later reconstructions of these expectations have an important influence on the course of acquisition. At Brodies, for example, a number of the users we interviewed felt that worries prior to going live had proved unfounded, making the implementation a smoother experience than was expected. At Finlay, in contrast, high expectations of the system prior to going live later resulted in some disappointment; this may have been a factor hin- dering the implementation. In Bancroft, managers reported that they had 'over-sold' the MAC system, raising expectations that were hard to meet. Certainly academic secretaries contrasted their problems with the system with the high hopes they had had of MAC prior to implementation.

As the systems became more established in each of our research sites we could see a shift from (positive or negative) *expectations* about the potential of the new system to a series of *accommodations* to the reality of it. A notable finding across the sites was the degree to which the new system would, ini- tially, be given the benefit of the doubt by users. This was supported by management entreaties to make allowances for the system while it 'bedded down'. In Finlay and Brodies especially, the systems were initially seen to need considerable improvement, but users exhibited faith that problems would be ironed out and the technology would settle down. Early expecta- tions about the potential of the systems and, in particular, the resolvability of problems were dented over time. Thus while some problems were resolved post-implementation, those that remained took on a new significance for users, and their attitude towards them changed. In Finlay, for example, issues regarding validation became more, not less, irksome for medics over the course of our three sets of interviews. While laboratory working practices had been adapted to address their concerns, it became clear that the system itself was not going to be changed. This became seen as a progressively greater setback, compounded by the suppliers' unwillingness or inability to resolve it. Thus, in this case, what had been at an earlier stage a potentially resolvable technical problem was now part of the way the system 'worked'.

One aspect of the ending of acquisition is, therefore, the stabilisation, rather than the ending, of problems. They must be lived with rather than resolved and this is indicative of users reaching an accommodation with a relatively stable system. The sense of the passing of time can also, however, lead to the outright rejection of the system – users lose faith that the system will ever be workable. Users, for example, saw the Finance module at Bancroft as persistently problematic, or 'flaky'. Even at the end of the module's first year of implementation, the module leader for Finance presented us with the following analysis of the situation:

> My view is that if this system by Christmas is looking reasonably stable and we've got Data Warehouse working properly, then we'll live with what we've got and I would push it another year at least. If it's still flaky and not working properly then I think we've got to seriously look at next year starting to tout around, if we were going to move in 1999 we'll have to start early next year.

This evaluation of the system at the management level referred back, then, to the timeframes for stabilisation already discussed, throwing open the question of whether the Finance module would *ever* stabilise.

Stabilisation and techno-organisational change

The section above discussed a number of indicators of users experiencing the end of the acquisition. In the limited acceptance of management timeframes and milestones, in the decline of novelty, and in the adjustment of expectations, we can see:

- the shape and role of systems becoming clearer to users;
- users establishing a relationship with the system and it becoming part of their organisational lives.

Our contention, however, is that to appreciate fully the *destabilisation* and *restabilisation* of technologies in organisational settings we must widen the focus. Discussion of users' changing relationships to the technology must be placed in a broader account of techno-organisational change. Chapters 3–7 have addressed this in different ways. Taken together, they highlight a range of interconnected components of techno-organisational change (see Figure 8.2). Each of these components of an organisational setting contributes to the forms in which systems are stabilised as sociotechnologies. They also, however, are potentially *themselves destabilised by the introduction of a new system*. We outline below some of the ways in which these processes can be found in our study.

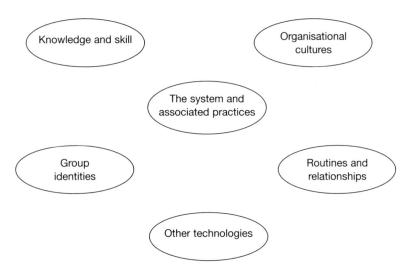

Figure 8.2 Elements of techno-organisational change

Knowledge and skill

We can see existing claims to knowledge and skill influencing the stabilisation of the systems in our study. Most notably, the claim of doctors at Finlay to a privileged understanding of patients and samples led to their concerns being built into the development of PBS both before and after its introduction into the laboratories. It is striking, however, how technology acquisition can, intentionally or unintentionally, also challenge claims to knowledge and skill. At Finlay many of the MLSOs experienced the arrival of PBS in terms of 'deskilling'. Brodies supervisors initially saw the Staff Organiser as a challenge to their special local knowledge of their particular store or department and 'their girls'. During acquisition, they reinvented themselves as management intermediaries, partly through the development of new skills and knowledge associated with the system and the interpretation of its outputs.

Group identities

The divisions between different groupings within organisations and the identities of those various groupings play a significant role in shaping and positioning new systems as sociotechnologies. In our analysis of Finlay this was discussed primarily in relation to professional identities and their clash with managerial objectives. In Bancroft we focused mainly on the divisions within the university between academic-related and administrative staff and the strong loyalties users felt to their local departments. In Brodies we were struck by the particular, gendered identity through which supervisors understood the organisation and their role in it. Across the three case studies, therefore, group identities mediated the ways in which users reached accommodations with the systems. It is important once again, however, to note that the acquisition of new technology does not merely reflect divisions and identities; it can also disrupt them. While doctors at Finlay were able to resist any threat to their professional status, MLSOs had to accept a degree of destabilisation of their professional identity. The supervisors' accommodation with the Staff Organiser also involved significant shifts in their group identity.

Routines and relationships

The acquisition of new systems in each of our sites demanded some acknowledgement of the power of existing work routines and organisational relationships. The acquisition of MAC, for example, brought to prominence the distinction at Bancroft between the university's administrative centre and academic departments. Initiatives such as the Data Warehouse could be seen as an attempt to make MAC workable in the context of departments' current practices and assumptions about their relationship to the centre. Examples such as this should, however, be taken alongside others that point to work routines and organisational relationships being redeveloped during acquisition. Chapter 6 tells how the relationships of Brodies supervisors with shopfloor staff and management altered during the introduction of the Staff Organiser. Equally, PBS meant that MLSOs at Finlay changed not only their working routines but also their relationship to samples and patients. Even the doctors at Finlay had to alter the structure of their working day to fit in with the validation requirements of the new system.

Organisational cultures

A theme running through our analysis is that technology acquisition requires the embedding of new systems into the cultural dynamics of the organisation. Once again, however, it is important to understand that these dynamics are themselves disrupted by the arrival of new systems. We can illustrate this by considering the part played in acquisition by organising narratives – accounts of the nature and purpose of the organisation. At Finlay, for example, a prominent narrative portrayed commitment to patient welfare as a key organisational priority. On being asked who were the main beneficiaries of PBS, many respondents said that patients *ought* to benefit even if they were not yet doing so – as one laboratory assistant told us, 'if it is going to be a benefit to the patients, that needs to be our main aim'. This patient-centred focus both worked as an organising narrative across the site, and overrode any willingness among users to reject or resist the system (underpinned, of course, by the life-threatening nature of some of the illnesses staff were dealing with). It consequently played an important role in ensuring the acceptance of and accommodation to PBS across the whole organisation. A similar, but more complex, situation occurred at Brodies. The introduction of the Staff Organiser was driven in part by a desire on the part of senior management to replace existing organising narratives (the Brodies family) with a new emphasis on efficiency and standardised measures. The stabilisation and embedding of the system, however, took place thanks to those 'outdated' narratives.

Other technologies

Another dimension of stabilisation is the way new systems are joined with other elements of the organisational *sociotechnical ensemble*. At Finlay, the hospital information system (HISS), which went live in the hospital several months after PBS, regularly threatened the stability of PBS in the Pathology laboratories, as staff began to rely more and more on links between the two systems. When working, HISS significantly reduced the requirement, for example, to input patient data within Pathology, since this had usually already been entered into HISS. On many occasions, however, HISS or the connection between HISS and PBS was not functioning; this caused problems in the laboratories as clerical staff would have to take on extra work, and MLSOs and medics would have to process specimen tests without much of the information usually provided. The interaction of another, less stable, technology with PBS was thus able to destabilise the use of PBS and the routines of users. A contrasting situation was the way in which the introduction of the Data Warehouse at Bancroft was crucial to the stabilisation of MAC Student Records. As we showed in Chapter 3, prior to Data Warehouse users of Student Records saw MAC as a system that was necessary for the university but not of any value to themselves. Whilst this could, as we have argued, form the basis of a stabilised system, bringing in the Data Warehouse to enable the extraction of data from MAC in ways that could benefit certain users led towards a very different kind of stabilisation. This related technology impacted on routines and relationships, then, but in much more positive ways than MAC itself. Data Warehouse for Finance, too, although not yet stable when we last visited the university, was showing similar potential for helping MAC Finance and its associated practices to restabilise.

To conclude this discussion, we make no claim that the list of different elements of techno-organisational change is in any way definitive: patterns vary greatly across sites and we acknowledge that the factors distinguished above are intertwined. Our purpose in establishing this typology is, however, to highlight the variety of elements of techno-organisational change *beyond but related to* the stabilisation of the system and associated practices, in order to show something of the complexity of any stabilisation. Technology is subject always to the influence of other organisational factors that can both promote and constrain its stabilisation. Each of the various elements of techno-organisational change that we have identified can become destabilised and restabilised in ways that impact on other elements. Thus while discussions of stabilisation have technology at their centre – as either the object or cause of instability – this ultimately rests on the gross simplification that technological change is the only source of uncertainty within an organisation. The implementation of new technology is an arena through which interlinked destabilisations across a constellation of organisational elements often come to be understood – this can overstate the role of technology in wider, non-technological destabilisations. This theme will be developed further below in a discussion that looks beyond organisational influences to consider how techno-organisational stabilisation is affected by *extra*-organisational factors.

Contexts of techno-organisational change

As we have shown, the arrival of new technology in an organisational setting can destabilise identities, knowledge and skills, organisational cultures, and routines and relationships, whilst these things can at the same time destabilise apparently impervious technological trajectories. This argument adds more weight to the case against technological determinism (MacKenzie and Wajcman 1985, Edgerton 1993). Our analysis of case study material has reiterated again and again the point made in Chapter 1 that techno-organisational change is not simply driven by external imperatives – technological or otherwise. Nevertheless, again following Chapter 1, we can see the importance of a broader set of contexts that offer *conditions of possibility* for the stabilisation of sociotechnologies within the particular settings of our case studies. These contexts – or rather the ones we have focused on in our analysis – are set out in Figure 8.3. As with our discussion of the elements of techno-organisational change, it is important to recognise that, depending on the circumstances,

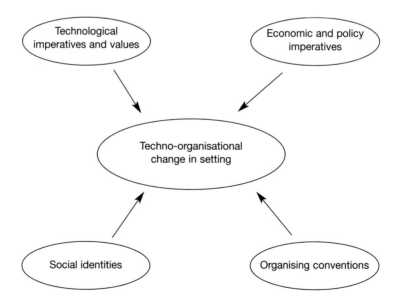

Figure 8.3 The contexts of techno-organisational change

these contexts can contribute to the stabilisation *or* destabilisation of a sociotechnology in a particular setting.

Technological 'imperatives' and values

In each of our case studies, managers and users made sense of their local acquisition in a broader context of general, on-going technological development. One way in which this is manifested is in a sense that such development is taking place broadly across the sector in which the organisation is located. Discussions of technological change in Brodies amongst senior managers and more junior staff, for example, were predicated on the knowledge of the general shift towards computerisation in the retail sector via developments such as EPOS and EDI. Comparable local interpretations of wider changes also take place in public sector organisations, but there is an added dimension in the way sectoral trends are prescribed by regulatory agencies. At Finlay, there were NHS procedures that 'had' to be followed, whilst at Bancroft the goal of computerisation was successively translated across several policy and sectoral levels. In all three cases, though, the sense that organisations had to respond to wider technological developments was an important factor behind the adoption of new technology, and contributed to its stabilisation within the organisational setting. The notion of sectoral trend is supported by powerful assumptions about the inevitability of technological change – such as the general 'project' of computerisation across a wide range of fields (Kling and Iacono 1995).

Sectoral trends and the general valuing of technology may promote the acceptance of new systems but they can also act as destabilising influences. At Bancroft, for example, the widespread shift towards a Windows-based PC environment within and beyond the university was a key factor in rendering MAC out of date in the minds of most users. This wider technological development destabilised the relationship of MAC to other systems on people's desks, and consequently destabilised their working routines through the extra effort needed to shift between different kinds of system. More generally, belief in the inevitability of perpetual technological change can raise hopes and fears among users that are hard to contain during acquisition. They are also destabilising in offering the promise of a newer, better system over the horizon that will soon supersede the existing one.

Economic and policy 'imperatives'

In different ways across our three sites, we can see the notion that systems are responses to external economic pressures or policy dictates contributing to stabilisation by smoothing the acceptance of the system among users. Store staff in Brodies, for example, frequently premised their assessments of the Staff Organiser on the need for the company to remain economically competitive. Wider economic and policy change can also, however, have a destabilising effect. The MAC system was destabilised in its early stages, before it even entered Bancroft, by a number of policy changes that resulted in a need for retrospective 'workarounds' (Pollock 1998), either by the system's programmers or by subsequent organisational users. For example, screens in Student Records had to be revised following the replacement of UCCA with UCAS as the national undergraduate applications agency, since the new agency's application form – which fed into the MAC system – ordered its information slightly differently. Changes in legislation around ethnic monitoring similarly led to a need to adapt MAC's Personnel system.

Organising conventions

Wider conventions about how organizations should be run are a more nebulous but important influence on the stabilisation of a sociotechnology in a particular setting. One aspect of this evident in each of our sites is the impact of new philosophies of management. Discourses of organising influence not only managers but also other organisational actors to find value in technology via instrumental notions of rationality and efficiency. As Chapters 5 and 6 described, a key element of the stabilisation of the Staff Organiser in Brodies was the difficulty that supervisors had in defending evaluations and practices rooted in their localised experience against a new system represented as the embodiment of a delocalised rationality.

Social identities

Brodies also provides us with a fine example of some of the ways in which the stabilisation of a sociotechnology in a particular setting is influenced by broader patterns of inequality and identity. We have seen how the location of particular organisational actors within these patterns frames their incorporation of the technology and ultimately how the technology is embedded across the organisation. To understand how and why supervisors in Brodies worked hard to make the Staff Organiser work, despite the apparent threat it posed to their position and skills, we have to understand their tenuous position in a gendered labour market and their enactment of feminine identities.

Thus, to sum up, the stabilisation of sociotechnologies in organisational settings takes place in the context of a diverse set of conditions of possibility. Recognition of this, and in particular of the ways in which these conditions may be a source of uncertainty inside an organisation, further highlights the likely complexity and fragility of any techno-organisational stabilisation.

Stabilisation, incorporation and conversion

From the SST perspective epitomised by Bijker (1995), stabilisation marks a (temporary) ending to sociotechnical change. Bijker understands this in terms of the closure of meaning around a particular artefact, where fixity of meaning comes to constrain how people think about and work with that artefact. Its subsequent stabilisation within a broader sociotechnical ensemble of related artefacts then proceeds as a playing out of micropolitical interactions among and within 'relevant social groups'. This both solidifies these constraints and disciplines the groups' members with regard to technological practices such as problem-solving strategies, design methods and usage (ibid.: 262–4). As we have already indicated, however, our analysis goes beyond the commonly drawn boundaries of SST by, firstly, extending discussion past the design and specification stages and into particular settings of technological change and, secondly, demonstrating more fully the extra-technological aspects of sociotechnical – or techno-organisational – development. This leads us to amend Bijker's account of stabilisation.

In the analyses of Bancroft, Brodies and Finlay set out in previous chapters, we saw how various individuals, groups and interests attached particular meanings to the new IT systems, which then jostled for influence across the organisation. In the context of this struggle, management attempted to gain compliance with and support for systems on the basis of the benefits they offered to the organisation, whilst certain users often refused to comply with that interpretation of the system as long as they faced severe difficulties using it. Where we differ from Bijker in our analysis is, however, in the assumption that such struggles necessarily result in closure – that is, in a fixity and sharing of meaning – and that this closure is an essential precursor to the stabilisation of an obdurate sociotechnology. We argue, on the contrary, that a piece of organisational technology can achieve a degree of obduracy whilst different meanings co-exist, and that this diversity of meaning is, indeed, often integral to stabilisation. This is not to say that there is no struggle over meaning, or that one meaning might not dominate over others as a result of such struggles, but simply that meanings which are less powerful do not necessarily cease to exist as they do in Bijker's case studies (1995). Alternative meanings can, rather, co-exist alongside dominant ones, with the potential to play a role in destabilising them again at a later date.

Thus, to reiterate, in our usage stabilisation of a system is indicated by the ways in which users of a new organisational technology increasingly regard it as no longer new or open to change. There is no reason to assume that this closure of the acquisition process brings an end to alternative meanings. What it does bring, though, is an acceptance among users that there is little further prospect of resolving outstanding problems with the system. It does not, in any way, presuppose that users regard the technology positively, but unless they are at this stage going to reject it outright (which for most is not an option), they must find some accommodation with the technology, whatever meanings it holds for them. As Chapter 7 demonstrated, this accommodation can take many forms depending on users' location within and beyond the organisation. As Chapter 7 also suggested at a number of points, to understand fully how users develop their particular relationships with a technology requires a broader appreciation of how the technology is contextualised into their organisational lives. This theme will be developed further below, through discussion of the concepts of *incorporation* and *conversion*.

Incorporation

As we stressed above, users can come to an accommodation with new technology without believing it is inherently useful, and without liking the way it impacts on their work. In addition, this does not necessarily involve a closure of interpretations around the technology even for one particular group of users. Doctors in the laboratories at Finlay Hospital, for example, held simultaneously two very different understandings of PBS. On the one hand, they regarded it as a highly inadequate and poorly implemented system that caused considerable problems for their work. At the same time, they accepted and endorsed the management definition of the system as a powerful means of integrating information across the Pathology Department and the hospital as a whole. A doctor who was highly critical of the way the implementation of PBS was managed nevertheless found its integrative capacity of great value:

Medic: I didn't realise how integrated we were going to be with the wards . . . I didn't have any concept of that really. I'd heard in theory about computer links with general practice, and all the rest of it, but to actually see it working for the first time I found quite impressive. You know when we go down to intensive care if I haven't got a result with me I can tap into the computer down there and actually have a look and see what's going on the specimen which is a complete change of practice really, rather than having to phone up and find someone to come to the phone.
Interviewer: Is that a positive change?
Medic: Very, yes, it's a good thing. Very useful.

This polysemy of technologies, even as they achieve a degree of obduracy within a setting, is further compounded by the very different social and organisational locations of users. These locations set the conditions under which users can reach an accommodation with the technology; so that while the doctor quoted above could bring many professional and cultural resources to bear during acquisition, other users experienced the system very differently.

Laboratory assistants at Finlay and clerical staff at Bancroft were the two groups we interviewed that had the least scope for effecting any changes to their respective systems. Members of both groups were highly critical of the technology and to some extent of management too, and it would be fair to say that they would have liked to open up and change some aspects of their respective systems. Their organisational positions, though, made this impossible. To the extent that they opened up the black box of technology, they had no option, having peered inside and disliked what they saw, but to replace the lid as they found it. Nevertheless, despite their feelings towards it, they had to find some way of living with the new system. For clerical staff in the Finance Department at Bancroft, this was achieved to a large extent through mutual support and a collective sense of grievance. However, short of resigning or refusing to work with the new system (which would almost certainly have led to sacking), staff in all our sites in this lowly position within the hierarchy had little option but to accept the presence of the system, and seek out the least problematic ways of working with it.

We view the incorporation of technology by users as a key element of the transition from a sociotechnology being stabilised in a particular organisational setting to it becoming an obdurate feature of that setting. Users' incorporation builds on their gradual acceptance of a new system: they move from first conceding that the presence of the technology is a 'fact' of day-to-day organisational life, to eventually building it into their daily routines and ways of thinking about their work and their workplace.

As the examples above suggest, the conditions under which users incorporate new technology vary greatly. They also suggest, returning to a theme discussed in more detail in earlier chapters, that incorporation can be highly regulated. Given the many cross-cutting factors and interests that influence incorporation, it would be quite legitimate to examine it at the level of individual users. The sections in Chapter 6 on 'The new breed', 'The technophile' and 'The strategist' show the potential of an analysis that considers how each of our interviewees incorporated the technologies into their own particular biographies and work and life projects. Our analysis will, however, continue the theme developed throughout our case study discussion by focusing primarily on how incorporation is differentiated by membership of occupational groupings. Consolidating the arguments of earlier chapters, Figure 8.4 illustrates our understanding of how occupational groupings are differently placed in technology acquisition. A group's location includes its technological environment, organisational routines and relationships, and the claims to knowledge and skill that help define its competencies. Its members are also situated in relation to cross-organisational identities and relationships such as those of professionalism, and to wider social divisions – notably those of class, race and gender.

Conversion

As Chapter 2 discussed, in consumption studies the notion of incorporation is closely associated with *conversion* – a term used to describe how goods, through a process of appropriation, become integral to consumers' relations with others. We can adapt this concept to understand how users have incorporated technologies on our three sites. Over time, in different ways for different users, knowledge and/or usage of systems has become integral to users' understandings of the organisation and their place in it. We have already highlighted a number of examples of this, as outlined below.

Figure 8.4 Locating an occupational grouping within and beyond the organisation

Knowledge of the system becomes part of group identities

Chapter 6 told how Brodies supervisors moved from initial scepticism towards the Staff Organiser to accepting and enacting the logic that underlay it. This was part of a shift in their identities and their relations with both shopfloor staff and management. Understanding and usage of the Staff Organiser and its outputs became part of a new group project in which supervisors repositioned themselves as management intermediaries.

The system comes to mediate users' relations with others

In Finlay many of the laboratory staff's initial unease with PBS was rooted in a belief that it ended their connection with the 'whole' patient that they had constructed via paper records. However, over time some users began to develop a different vision of the patient in the data held in PBS. One MLSO explained:

MLSO: It allows easy access to, for example, different specimen types on
             the same patient, you don't have to go and look through forms,
             you can just do patient searches.
Interviewer: Does that help you in your work?

MLSO: Yes, it can do, it brings it all together as a whole picture rather than just one specimen. It can make it more of a patient as opposed to one specimen.

The system becomes part of users' redefinition of organisational time and space

The introduction of the Staff Organiser was only one of a raft of changes taking place at Brodies. These included radical alterations to the length of the store day; so that, for example, most stock handling and shelf replenishment now took place outside opening hours. Members of store management teams told of how, as a consequence, it was increasingly difficult to set up times to have meetings or pass on information. Another associated development was the increased reliance on temporary staff. Supervisors talked of knowing less and less about their staff as a section of them became increasingly transient. Within this changed environment, users turned to the Staff Organiser as a way of retaining knowledge and control of store life. Supervisors monitored their transient staff through the plans of the Organiser. Likewise the store managers monitored and communicated with their dispersed management team through the system. Thus in this case, *conversion* involved users coming to depend on the system to know and manage the changing contours of organisational time and space.

Uncertainty and incorporation

As the last point suggests, one important impetus to incorporation is users' desire to limit the uncertainties of their organisational life. Of course, the introduction of new technology is itself one such source of uncertainty. We have seen how, in various ways, users labour to make systems workable in their local settings. The quest for certainty underlies much of this activity. MLSOs at Finlay, for example, co-operated with the fine-tuning of PBS, despite serious reservations about its impact on their job role, in part out of a concern to ensure that no test results were lost or erroneous. Similarly, laboratory managers at Bancroft held highly negative views of the MAC system but still made a substantial *investment* in the system to develop its usability and utility. They helped establish coding structures for the Finance module; they learned along with their secretaries how to input financial data; they held meetings to share and then pass on their feelings about the system; they sought ways of overcoming the absence of reports in the early stages by developing their own reporting facilities; one laboratory manager also developed routines to make the Student Records module more usable for his departmental secretary. Like the Brodies supervisors, these laboratory managers were enrolled in a process of technical problem solving that was likely eventually to lead to their incorporation of MAC, despite their antagonism towards it.

The introduction of a new computer system may be a key element of organisational uncertainty at the time of implementation, but over time other sources of uncertainty will become more prominent. In our case studies there were a number of examples of users who, confronted by other changes and problems, began to treat systems as source of *certainty*. At Finlay, for example, by the end of our fieldwork problems associated with PBS drifted into the background as staff faced new uncertainties brought about by the regrouping of the PHLS laboratories, the resulting requirement to shed jobs, and the prospect of privatisation. Similarly, as we have already suggested, in Brodies the Staff Organiser became a source of certainty that users deployed to cope with new uncertainties such as changes to the store day and the setting of tough new targets for sales and staff costs.

Conclusion: technology as boundary object

This chapter has examined the ways in which the acquisition processes in our research sites reached some sort of conclusion. It has portrayed the stabilisation of systems as a multi-faceted and fragile endeavour involving a diverse range of organisational and extra-organisational elements. It has suggested that at each site in our study, the systems in question achieved a degree of obduracy in their organisational setting. Our discussions have, however, provided a different account of the nature of that obduracy and how it is achieved to that one would normally find in SST. In his discussion of stabilisation and obduracy, Bijker claims that closure around the meaning of a technological artefact is 'generally, but not absolutely, irreversible' (1995: 271). Our view is that when technologies enter an organisational setting, they must make sense across a variety of groups and therefore closure of meaning is not the key factor ensuring irreversibility.

Throughout this book we have highlighted the work users put into embedding technology into their working practices and into their individual, group and professional projects. These incorporations of technology take many forms and involve contrasting evaluations and attributions of meaning. Particular outlooks on technological change can result from the occupational or professional grouping people belong to, from their spatial or structural location within the organisation, from the relationship they have to members of other groups, and from their class, race or gender position within the organisation and beyond it. A sense of the diversity of position and experience is expressed in the following quotation from an academic secretary at Bancroft:

Interviewer: Do you think as the system begins to settle down, do you think that legacy is still hanging over it or is it possible to move beyond that?

Academic secretary: I think it's hanging over in the sense that we still feel that it's them and us. I don't know what could be done to prevent . . . there's been too many corners, there's been [the Student Registry] which has been concerned, they're the ones that I've related to directly, they've been concerned

> to implement student records in particular, but I think [a manager there] was put in charge overall of introducing it and then there's MIS which has actually had the hands-on problems of trying to make it work, and then there's the departments who've been either resisting because of academic freedom, or resisting because they're frightened of it. Then there's the secretaries who have been trying to actually make it work.

How then do these different perspectives contribute to a broader process leading to the obduracy of systems? In other words, how can we bring together the two levels of the consumption that we have been addressing in this book – the acquisition of technology by an organisation, and the incorporation of that technology by a variety of communities of interest? One way to do this is to borrow the concept of *boundary objects*, developed by theorists to understand the multiplicity of networks and meanings in scientific and technological work (Star and Griesemer 1989, Fujimura 1992, Star 1991).

Star explores how certain artefacts can act as a focus for co-operation on a specific set of tasks among diverse actors all with their own priorities and agendas. A boundary object mediates among these otherwise divergent social worlds, providing enough of a shared framework to allow the tasks to progress, but still allowing flexibility of meaning across those different social worlds. Pollock (1998) suggests that there can also be *boundary subjects*, individuals whose work makes them into intermediaries alongside boundary objects, and he puts forward the term *boundary devices* to cover the variety of different kinds of intermediary.

Our contention is that systems in organisations achieve some obduracy and users are able to develop the usability and utility of those systems to the extent that these can balance standardisation with multiple interpretations and incorporations. In other words, perhaps aided by other boundary devices, the IT system comes to act as a boundary object. Fujimura (1992) develops discussion of boundary objects further, viewing them as part of *standardised packages* which also include *tools* that ensure uniformity in the way boundary objects are used in different social worlds. As Fujimura's argument implies, the parallel incorporation of a system such as MAC, PBS or the Staff Organiser into the projects of differently placed users across an organisation does not guarantee that incorporations will be in perfect alignment across all groupings.

The development of a boundary object is the product of *enrolment* and *compliance*. We can see across our sites attempts to develop standardisation of use of the system. These include management prescriptions of how to use the systems and prescriptions for use that were built into the systems themselves. These standardising tools may have ensured standardisation of use and thus coherence of data across the different organisational groupings, but for incorporation to take place other factors needed to come into play. At Bancroft, for example, management realised that standardised practices and procedures needed to be supplemented with other tools and resources to bring about any degree of compliance by users. Hence the establishment of the IT Steering Group and the Consultation Forum to obtain some input from users into the management of the system. At Finlay such consultation procedures, like the standardised operating procedures, were recognised as necessary but always presented by management as something they *intended* to implement in the future. At Brodies, implementation staff returned to stores to revise/reinstall the store model alongside store management staff and supervisors, thus drawing them into the process.

The tension between standardisation of practices and localised incorporations also suggest that the regulation of technology acquisition is a complex business. We have described the high degree of *regulation* at Brodies; while *management regulation* attempted to ensure the standardisation of system use, it was the *subjective regulation* of store staff that was crucial to how the Staff Organiser was embedded into stores. At Finlay it was the concern for patients' welfare rooted in users' professional identities that ensured that the opening up of the black box of PBS never went so far as to jeopardise the daily routines of the laboratories. At Bancroft, there was a degree of subjective regulation that compelled users to some extent to co-operate in trying to achieve stabilisation of Student Records so that students would not be affected by problems such as examination halls not being set up properly. Likewise, with Finance, laboratory managers ensured their secretaries were inputting data into the system, even though they could not be guaranteed adequate reports, because it was their own departments that would suffer from unreliable data.

What we have in each of our sites, then, is a boundary object, the management information system, which is intended to bring about co-operation in relation to specific organisational objectives among a wide range of organisational groupings with often conflicting goals and understandings. A number of tools and resources exist alongside the boundary object for standardising how people use it. A coherence of stabilisation and incorporations *across* an organisation depends to a large extent on how effectively these tools and resources work.

We discussed earlier the fragility of any stabilisation of sociotechnology given its location within a broader constellation of organisational and extra-organisational factors. Once a system has achieved a degree of obduracy, however, users will have an investment in maintaining its value. This is further supported in users' attempts to construct systems as a point of certainty rather than uncertainty. Nevertheless both stabilisation and incorporation require on-going maintenance by both managers and users.

Conclusion

In this Conclusion we shall review some of the main themes that have emerged from our exploration of the valuing of technology and consider some of their wider implications. We begin by highlighting some of the key points we have made about the complex and multi-dimensional process of techno-organisational change. We shall then go on to explore some of the practical implications of our argument for those involved in acquiring and implementing technologies. Finally, we will conclude with some considerations of the ways in which our overall argument contributes to contemporary debates in social studies of science and technology.

When new technologies enter organisations, both the technology and the organisation get shaken up: new technologies bring new uncertainties, instabilities and unforeseen problems for those who buy them and for those who use them, while the technologies themselves are reworked and rebuilt by users as they endeavour to build local values into them. Organisations are, we have argued, always subject to instability and uncertainty, but at times of techno-organisational change become – at least for a time – visibly *dis*organised. Not surprisingly, there is a powerful drive, especially from those senior managers who are responsible for this disturbance, to try to reduce uncertainty and re-establish a sense of managing an 'organisation' through established procedures, practices, forms of social regulation and bounded identities and roles. The attempt to construct technological certainty is then paralleled by the attempt to reconstruct organisational certainty.

Our accounts of the introduction of the Staff Organiser in Brodies, MAC at Bancroft and PBS at Finlay show how those who acquired and used the systems had to invest considerable amounts of organisational labour to make them 'work'. In each case the new system carried within it various assumptions about the management of information, informational needs and informational criteria, which to a greater or lesser extent conflicted with the existing organisational structures and cultures of Brodies, Bancroft and Finlay. The process of implementation that followed was one which involved both organisational and technological change: the organisation, the system itself and the users were reconstructed as the technology was stabilised and incorporated at each of the sites. But this was no singular convergent process across the discrete groupings we found in each organisation: multiple, localised stabilisations occurred as groups constructed usability and utility for the systems. Groups also varied in the manner and extent to which they found technologies more or less usable or useful, and varied too in their capacity to challenge and redefine the value of the systems; in Bancroft, for example, this was reflected in the capacity of some, but not all, to deploy a narrative of 'autonomy' to establish the terms on which they would engage with and subsequently incorporate the system.

This variation in the ways in which different user groups embed technology in their local settings directs our attention to the degree of interpretative flexibility associated with new organisational technologies, and is core to our argument that the standardisation of use of IT systems which enables information and data sources to be integrated should not be regarded as a process involving singular *common* forms of stabilisation. Software systems that are predicated on integrative data management do not necessarily become, by virtue of that integrative capacity, immediately and intrinsically valuable to those who use them. Users make systems workable at the local level, and only through their localised envaluing can systems gain any wider organisational currency as working technologies. This raises, of course, the question of how to understand the relationship between the processes through which individuals and groups develop value in a system and a wider process through which organisations develop value. We shall return to this point in the second section of this chapter.

There are important differences between the occupational groups we found in the organisations we have explored that are related to status, occupational location, professional claims to knowledge and skill, and gender identities. Users within different occupational groups had distinct informational needs which were constructed and reconstructed over time. In developing value, these groupings expressed alternative and sometimes competing definitions of both the technological systems they used and the organisations in which they participated. At the same time, we have tried to show how the boundaries between and identities of the different groupings are not permanent. We have seen how new alignments between users who were once quite separate can develop, and at the same time new disjunctions and boundaries can emerge between and within groups.

Groups varied as well in terms of the degree of organisational 'space' they had through which to maintain some distance from the position of senior management. Professional claims to knowledge also mediated the terms on which a system would function in its local setting, though not all groups were able to deploy professional resources to the same extent. Gendered identities, in part derived from wider discourses on gender and technology, were able to shape some users' engagement with and sense of control over the IT systems. However, they too were not static but reframed and expressed in new ways at the local level as the systems stabilised.

The 'conditions of possibility' that shape action within an organisation need not be limited to the political, economic and technical contexts described in

Chapter 1. A wider, external social narrative about women's (in)ability to handle technology was seen as one important example of a number of broader conditions of possibility that set the context within which our three organisations had to operate. The interpretation and articulation of the meaning of this wider context by organisational groups gave them a sense of their identity and function in society and a sense of the changes and threats to which they 'must' respond. Conventions of organisational success which ascribe major importance to the continual adoption and upgrading of IT systems act as especially strong 'imperatives' for organisational actors. This clearly makes for increasing demands on the managers of change, who, on the one hand, may hope to see a stable and standardised IT regime prevail within their organisation, yet must attend to new software systems which competitor or collaborating organisations adopt. In all of our case studies, managers were looking ahead and considering what new IT developments would be needed, which would mean, of course, that new organisational changes and new forms of user enrolment might be required.

In general, therefore, constructing value for the different systems was never simply a matter of 'getting it right', of ironing out technical problems, of ensuring the computer interface was 'user-friendly'. As we have shown, finding usability is a sociotechnical rather than just a technical problem. While technical issues were important in helping to create systems that were eventually usable, they were only the first necessary steps before the users could begin the much more complex process of finding utility in the systems. Some in fact never found, and in some cases did not feel the need to find, utility values in the MIS. This suggests that Woolgar's (1991b) argument, outlined in Chapter 2, about the requirement for system builders to configure the user, takes us only so far down the road of understanding the relation between users and systems: its focus remains firmly on the designer fashioning the user–good relation. Configuration does not allow for the ways in which users actively construct the value of goods or technological systems, nor does it show how this process varies according to the different 'group projects' (related to job role, profession, gender and so on) that we have explored in the substantive chapters of the book. In short, the notion of 'configuring' fails to register the sense in which the development of technological systems is far from complete when they enter an organisational space.

At the same time, we have acknowledged that the localised meaning that users bring to envaluing systems cannot be read simply as reflecting an empowering of users, as a form of agency which displays users' capacity for mediating the terms on which they 'consume' the technology. For we have also said that users incorporate new technologies in part through forms of *self-regulation*. Both self-regulation and managerial regulation exert an influence over the processes of value construction.

The extent to which management can be said to regulate users varied across our three sites. Much depended on the dynamics of the organisation and the structure of organisational relationships, but this does not imply that localised narratives and practices are inimical to the successful implementation of systems. Even in the case of Brodies, which exhibited the strongest form of managerial control from the centre, local practices were the medium through which eventual regulatory ordering was secured.

This raises the question of how far, in real terms, we can regard localised practices as a form of resistance to new technologies; frequently, initial resistance by staff to new technology turns out to have facilitated the ultimate stabilisation of a system. That resistance can have such a paradoxical effect does not imply that it will always be so. In the case of Brodies supervisors, resistance was framed in a particular (domesticated) gendered narrative – by both managers and the women themselves – which worked to limit its potential to challenge. Elsewhere, the resistance of medics at Finlay to the new procedures built into the PBS, while involving some flexible accommodation on their part, was sufficiently strong to ensure the system was modified to meet most of their demands. The reason for resistance has to be understood, therefore, in terms of the conditions of possibility that favour or constrain different groups' projects.

There is a case also for speaking of a resistance in the technology itself: inasmuch as the system becomes stabilised it becomes a boundary object which, while acting as a site where different interests can be expressed, takes on a growing 'obduracy' as a sociotechnical phenomenon through which organisational members must pass and through which their daily lives are structured. Once this occurs, the system not only loses its novelty but occupies a position in the organisation which any new system would have either to articulate with or seek to displace. In our three sites, the Staff Organiser and PBS became powerful media through which the daily routines of the store and lab. staff became orchestrated. In part, this reflects the commercial and clinical drivers behind the systems, which demand high levels of standardisation to generate profit on the one hand and safety on the other. It also reflects the specific organisational narratives and practices which left limited organisational space through which alternative practices might be sustained. MAC, on the contrary, struggled to secure a central place in the work practices of the staff located outside the centre, precisely because the narrative of autonomy at local departmental level was better accommodated by the systems that pre-dated MAC.

Implications for managing IT systems

The factors which determine the effectiveness and success of a technological system do not lie solely in the technology itself but depend on the acquisition and implementation process. It is clear from our argument that the acquisition and implementation of new IT systems within organisations is a complex affair. Management notions of identifying user needs, designing these into systems, and then rolling out the systems bear little relation to the contingencies, variation and cultural mediation that implementation processes must confront. Yet our argument does have important lessons for change management practices.

Firstly, it is important to approach the introduction of new technologies as a process which inevitably will require both the enrolling of the user and the reshaping of the organisation. The so-called 'roll-out' of systems may begin as a technical exercise but, as we saw in the case of the Staff Organiser at Brodies, increasingly becomes more a marketing exercise. Yet one of the problems associated with enrolment is that managers may try to sell the system in terms of benefits that can be regarded by organisational actors as rather nebulous or yet to be developed: at Finlay managers felt much of the disenchantment among users was due to the system being over-sold prior to 'going live', while at Bancroft there was initially little suggestion of benefits and this made it hard to enrol users. A more reflexive process of 'change management' would need, therefore, to explore the structure, culture and group projects that are expressed within the organisation in order to see whether there are ways in which the acquisition process can be sensitive to user interests.

Secondly, the two notions of usability and utility must be clearly distinguished, as we have argued in Chapter 7. The criteria which we describe – checkability, confidence, control, ease of use, speed, and understanding – provide a guide to the ways in which different users will envalue technology. Enrolling the user is not, therefore, a once-and-for-all process structured into the design and marketing of the new technology: enrolment requires engagement with a variety of (shifting) user needs which may be unevenly met at acquisition and subsequently. Usability and utility values are not pre-given but develop over time in local settings. Consequently, we can never regard systems as finished, or completed, but instead, a successful system is one that can enable a variety of users to develop a 'usable' relationship with it. While, from a practical perspective, this may be regarded as causing complications, it might also be regarded more positively, since it means that a provisional map of different users' 'utility opportunities' within an organisation can be constructed during the acquisition process itself. This would be quite distinct from the conventional notion of 'operating requirements' which presume a stable and sustained set of needs in terms of which the user–technology relation can be configured. Our analysis suggests, as we said in Chapter 2, that matters are much more messy than this, that organisational 'requirements' or needs are reformed and reconstructed as part of the *on-going* process of techno-organisational change. Such an approach means that a rather different form of organisational labour would need to be expended by managers, but this is likely to 'add value' not only in the conventional economic sense but also in a genuinely social sense: indeed were it not the case that value is constructed and added through the activity of users at the local level, we would suggest that any economic gains would be very restricted.

Thirdly, as has been illustrated in each of our case studies, during the stabilisation process the various IT systems were never closed off, blackboxed, once and for all. There were many ways in which the systems were reopened and reshaped. This continual reopening of the black box not only means that 'things can always be otherwise', but also that attempts to close the lid will only be successful where managers recognise the distinction between standardised use and integration of the system, and local versions of its stabilisation by different groups. The first is central to any integrated information system that presumes coherent management of organisational data; the second is central to embedding the system within an organisation. To the extent to which it is possible to distinguish in practice between these two objectives, we might expect to see managers be more accommodating to localised practices that users deploy to make systems more usable.

This of course immediately points to a fundamental tension that managers have to resolve: there is the move on the one hand to standardise systems, yet on the other to respond to the requirement to localise systems. This tension is more pronounced in those organisations, such as Bancroft, where standardisation and localisation are most acutely at odds. In such a situation, as we saw, any degree of successful standardisation requires on-going maintenance by central managers, who must engage in continual techno-organisational labour to achieve this end.

At a more general level, the question arises whether it is possible to cultivate utility-building opportunities in new systems. This may well be a means through which some staff become empowered in ways that their more junior positions have prevented before. Clearly, this shift would involve political choices by senior management about the role and status of staff in the organisation. On the other hand, we have also indicated how, as in the case of Brodies, the new utility values that supervisors derived from the Staff Organiser helped reinforce the overall policy of management. The cynic might, therefore, regard this as no more than a sophisticated form of political enrolment via the technology, rather than as a genuine empowering of the staff on the ground. Yet one might find that these staff are more able to voice their interests in any subsequent acquisition of new systems because of their engagement with the present one.

However this is perceived, the embedding of a system within an organisation is closely related to its being valued according to the 'group projects' of different organisational members. This is clearly far removed from the more conventional 'instrumental' criteria through which the success of an MIS is typically measured. Such criteria imply a self-evident improvement in the technical specification, operating practices and organisational pay-offs brought by any new MIS. Such a view can only be sustained when one assumes a standard set of needs that can be met, once and for all, by a specific MIS design, where users are regarded as an undifferentiated group. In many ways, this view lay behind the ambitions of the MAC system, which was the product of innumerable national and 'family' committee meetings where the 'generic needs' of universities were hammered out, and where over many, many months the basic structure of a system was developed that was intended to meet these, reflexively and exhaustively articulated, needs. Yet, of our three sites, this was probably the most difficult, and perhaps the least 'successful', MIS implementation.

The question this poses is whether the contingencies that bring value – and so success – to a system can be made a little less contingent, or at least drawn on in such a way as to facilitate better implementation. Can an awareness of the envaluing process be accommodated within the language and practices of an instrumental approach to MIS? This seems unlikely: after all, instrumentalism is based on rationalist assumptions about organisational ends being met by informational means. Such ends are expressed in a multiplicity of ways, as 'mission statements', brochures, forward plans, 'bottom lines', and so on. What we need to understand is how these 'ends' are translated and transformed at the level of organisational membership and, in this particular matter, how they articulate with localised needs that are constructed among end-users of IT systems. This translation and articulation process means that needs and utilities cannot be built into a system in any fixed way from the outset, though clearly, certain parameters in terms of core requirements of a system can be agreed upon, without which the system would have neither usability nor utility.

Beyond these aspects, the acquisition and implementation process can focus on the criteria of usability and utility we discussed in Chapter 7 and differentiate these according to distinct groups. This will lead to a recognition among change managers of plural, and not always harmonious, conceptions of the 'system' . However, these should not be forced into a false homogeneity simply to secure standardised practices. As noted above, standardisation is possible within the context of diverse forms of stabilisation, but it is the latter not the former that opens up systems to a more effective and creative use by different groups.

Outside of MIS implementation, how far might these arguments apply to other technologies which are introduced into organisations? Other technologies that have been introduced into organisations – such as biotechnology research and development systems – while less subject to rapid change than IT, bring their own disorganising influences. Thus in the late 1980s the US corporation Monsanto endeavoured to restructure its research laboratories by refocusing scientific efforts via a biotechnological lens. This caused a major disruption to the existing research disciplines and practices, such as traditional chemistry. Creating utility values that require a major paradigm shift in the competencies and knowledge base that staff deploy is a more demanding organisational problem than even those experienced at our three sites. Nevertheless, the same arguments can apply, since the eventual stabilisation of biotechnology R&D at Monsanto depended on an intra-organisational negotiation which, crucially, opened up some organisational space and time for value in the new systems to be constructed (Chemistry and Industry 1985). Similar developments can also be witnessed today in the emergent bioinformatics companies, which require a hybridisation of informatics and biotechnology, each carrying very different 'business models', different professional claims to expertise, and different relations to extra-organisational markets. Reshaping these new organisations through the technologies of bioinformatics is likely to require what Badham (1995) calls 'configurational intrepreneurs' – those who build and try to ensure that novel production systems (such as those required by bioinformatics) do not collapse.

Whatever kind of techno-organisational change we are considering – the introduction and implementation of biotechnology or MIS, or the emergence of a completely new techno-organisation, the bioinformatics firm – in none of these cases does the utility and efficiency of new ways of working speak for itself. Considerable organisational labour has to be invested in securing stabilised and incorporated systems, and in sustaining such systems. In our three cases, we have shown how end-users are actively involved in this. But we must also recall that this process was one which reflected inequalities of power and resource among the different groupings we found in our three settings; whilst some were 'net losers' in the process, others were able to incorporate new systems without any erosion, and indeed sometimes with an enhancement, of their position.

Implications for theory

Our argument throughout this book has sought to build on and conjoin the insights of social studies of science and consumption studies. A single phrase which might be said to bring these two together is that both see technologies in *relational* terms: for the first, technology is constructed as a result of the relations between the negotiated (and negotiating) positions of different social actors; for the second, the value of any consumer good lies not in any intrinsic property it has but in its relation to other goods. This stress on relationality also points to the ways in which these two perspectives draw our attention to the relations between elements of a sociotechnical ensemble; that is to say, to the *boundaries* and *identities* that social actors construct and deploy in their concern to sustain local (and perhaps more distant) control over their individual and collective practices. These boundaries are expressed in part through the localisation of technological goods, whereby their consumption can be understood as a process of 'objectification' (Miller 1995a).

Unlike some positions within SST, however – perhaps best represented by the strong relativism of Grint and Woolgar's work (1997) – we do not subscribe to the view that the construction of technologies takes place solely through language: the components of the various information systems we have seen in this book have a material quality as objects which cannot be constructed and reconstructed in an *infinite* number of ways. This point relates of course to both of the principal perspectives we have drawn on throughout this book: on the one hand, SST enable us to see how systems are constructed, but on the other, the lesson of consumption studies is about the ways consumers live with and construct value for things *not of their own making*.

Moreover, in organisational settings, the process of constructing value for new goods is more evidently regulated than consumption in the domestic, private setting. This does not mean that the process of stabilisation is predictable because of the shape, size and speed of an IT system: each of our systems was stabilised in a variety of ways. As such, we saw the creation of multiple systems. Yet the initial *sociotechnical* framing of the technology that was acquired constrained the terms on which subsequent stabilisations and incorporations could be built: in a sense, we might refer here to how, as Douglas says, such constraints 'serve to contain the drift of meanings' (1992: 12).

While acknowledging that sociotechnical constraints impinge on the stabilisation process, our argument that the same technology can engender a variety of differently stabilised forms goes beyond the arguments advanced by Bijker (1995) in the social construction of technology. He argues that stabilisation is favoured around one specific construction of the technology while other constructions are marginalised or abandoned as a process of closure begins to bite. The sort of closure we see in our three cases is quite variable in range and extent, and even in Brodies, where closure around a particular framework – the technical one – became exceptionally strong, there were still members of the organisation who were able to resist or at least complement this framework with alternative ones. That we accept a greater degree of closure at Brodies than at Bancroft, and to a lesser extent at Finlay, indicates our belief in the need to relate technological closure and stabilisation to specific organisational cultures and structures.

This points to the need to explore the sociotechnical relationship between new technologies and the organisation that acquires them, to see how technologies are embedded into the organisational fabric. In the case of MAC this relationship was extremely loose and not one which could easily be tightened up, precisely because of the culture prevailing in the organisation. In the case of Finlay hospital, the US-originated PBS became only partially convergent with the professional structures and networks that prevail in UK pathology labs; here, the organisational culture allowed both for a reconfiguring of the technology and for users to help shape a more effective implementation and, crucially, integration across the labs.

These observations on the relative disjunction between system and user indicate our own theoretical disjunction with actor-network theory (ANT), which we discussed briefly in Chapter 2. Unlike ANT, we argue that members of organisations construct group projects and identities that they use to frame their relationship to other groups and to the system itself: these are not simply the product of relations within that network, as ANT would hold, important though these are. Thus, we have argued that the professional project of the doctors at Finlay was able to claim extra-organisational warrant from the professional associations to which they belonged. A similar claim was made by the MLSOs but to a much lesser effect. Resources of this nature are frequently deployed in organisational settings by occupational groups: that the doctors' claims were given more recognition than the MLSOs is not simply a reflection of their greater competence as actors in the Finlay network. It also reflects greater stocks of institutional capital built up elsewhere over the years.

Similar arguments were advanced with regard to the role of external discourses on gender identities (both masculine and feminine) which were then mediated within the organisational setting. As with claims by certain groups in Finlay to professional standing, discourses on the gendering of skill and occupational identity were drawn on by both men and women in Brodies to make sense of or justify localised narratives and practices. That these were not solely a construct of the organisational setting itself is evident from our account of the new female supervisors whose identity and role in the store reflected changing 'conditions of possibility' for women in the wider society.

In addition, in contrast again with ANT we have tried to convey a much more complex notion of the enrolment of users: ANT's position is that users are enrolled by their being drawn into furthering the enroller's interests within the network. This *translation* makes users subject to the position and interests of the enroller, the network-builder. While we acknowledge that this can occur, we also want to give a more active role to users, who are sometimes able to translate the enroller's meanings of the technology into their own localised accounts and practices, and indeed to invest their own meanings in the system. In other words, our concept of enrolment via relocalisation of technological goods allows for a much more active translation of the technology within the meanings set by the user(s). ANT might say that this would mean that these users were not thereby effectively enrolled in the network. In response, we would say that firstly, this presumes a highly singular, homogeneous notion of which meanings can be sustained within a network; and secondly, if, for the moment, we regard our organisations as made up of multiple (group-based) networks, it is only because of the multiple restabilising of technological systems at the local level that the techno-organisational 'network' can be sustained.

Our thesis that technological systems are envalued leads us to ask how the same systems can be destabilised and so lose value and utility. In Chapter 8 we suggested a number of ways that this might happen, though we also pointed out how techno-organisational inertia can build up in systems once stabilised, and thereby encourage most organisational members to confirm the utility of the existing system. Labour process theory might argue that systems would lose value (for owners/managers) when they no longer generated the return expected of them (by deskilling or cheapening labour); our approach would be to see the value ascribed to technological systems in terms which are more sociocultural – it is not the labour, but the broader process of acquisition, incorporation and conversion, that determines the valuation of technology. This is not to deny that economic arguments are likely to be used by senior management to justify decisions about techno-organisational change, or that the acquisition of new technology can have serious impacts (both actual and perceived) on the labour process. But such decisions do not in themselves show us how technologies come to have value over time in organisations. Whatever role techno-organisational change plays in relation to economic or other organisational decision-making, all staff, as organisational actors, will only be able to build value in a new system if they can integrate it and the practices it requires within their localised sociotechnical setting. It is through this that utility and value are constructed.

Appendix
Methodology

This Appendix provides a discussion of our research methodology and experiences. In common with much sociological research, this project centred on qualitative methods based on semi-structured interviews with a wide range of respondents, accompanied by a small amount of observation in our research sites. This approach was felt to be the most effective method of achieving our research objectives, which centred on understanding the experience of the users of organisational technology following the acquisition of new IT systems, and the ways this experience developed over time. The Appendix describes how we went about selecting research sites in which to study this, and then sampling respondents from those sites; how we then structured our interviews and periods of observation; and the techniques we used to organise and analyse our data. It also considers our relationship as researchers with the individuals and organisations we were researching, and how this relationship developed over the course of the study. Finally, we try to put across something of the flavour of doing research – of being 'in the field' (Burgess 1991).

Selecting the sites

The project's starting objective was to examine the acquisition and implementation of management information systems (MIS) in three distinct settings. It was therefore important to identify research sites with strong comparative potential, with regard to both the organisations and their workforces. The three sectors we chose for the study were the health service, retailing and higher education, which provided the opportunity for comparison across a number of organisational characteristics:

- between public and private sector organisations;
- between different kinds of services;
- across a variety of organisational structures and hierarchies;
- across different organisational groupings, gendered divisions of labour and contrasting professional identities.

Table A1 indicates the main structural and management characteristics of our three research sites.

Table A1 The three research sites

Site	Core activity	Organisational structure	Management of MIS
Finlay Hospital	Microbiology and Pathology laboratories	Eight laboratories managed independently, but linked contractually with the Hospital Trust	System implemented and managed by Project Team of laboratory managers
Brodies	National retail chain	Stores managed locally but answerable to Head and Area Offices	System implemented and managed centrally by Head Office personnel
Bancroft University	University	Decentralised structure, with administrative offices and academic departments each working largely towards their own objectives	System implemented by central managers, and managed by a Steering Group with cross-university representation

Identifying research sites, negotiating access with gatekeepers and carrying out the research were staggered across the three sectors over two years, from summer 1995 until summer 1997, beginning at Finlay Hospital and ending at Bancroft University. This allowed a manageable division of labour and use of time of the four members of the research team. The first stage in the project involved securing agreement with managers in the Bacteriology and Virology laboratories of Finlay Hospital to pilot the project there. This pilot study, which was subsequently extended to a full study of three labs, was intended to pilot not just our interview schedules but also the coding and analysis of the data. The pilot thus fed into both the more detailed study of Finlay and of the other sites too, providing us with a template for our later interview schedules and for the coding structures we established within NUD•IST (see below for further discussion of this).

The pilot consisted of eight face-to-face interviews with a cross-section of laboratory staff, who then became our 'core group' of respondents. We interviewed this group again six and then twelve months later to track developments in their use and experience of the new system. In the third interview with the core group, we also took the opportunity to present some of our provisional findings, in order to generate more reflective discussion about the issues, to gain some feedback on our analysis from those we were researching, and to give them a sense of why we were doing the research. This pattern was repeated with the core groups in our other two sites.

As well as the core group, we also interviewed the managers of the other Pathology laboratories who formed the Project Team that directed the implementation, plus a further twenty-five members of staff within the Microbiology and Virology labs. In addition, the entire staff of eight (including the manager) in the Tissue Typing laboratory were interviewed. Finally, we undertook three half-days of observation in one of the laboratories, spending time with three different groups of staff there.

Whilst the pilot was getting underway at Finlay, efforts were begun to identify a retail site. Retail is an underresearched area, particularly in terms of our research questions, and is hard to gain access to. A large number of retailers were contacted, with some interest expressed by a few companies. One in particular, Brodies, was especially keen to collaborate because it was in the process of introducing a suite of IT systems across its stores nationwide. Brodies contrasted with Finlay (as would any retail chain) in being highly dispersed geographically and having a very clear-cut company hierarchy. This meant that we had to negotiate several layers of 'gatekeepers' before we gained access to respondents. Firstly, we spoke with senior Head Office managers, who gave us initial access to the company and then worked with us to decide which specific system would be studied. Then Area Office managers helped us to identify which stores to study, on the basis of criteria that provided a variety of experience and length of time using the system. Finally we liaised with store managers, who had to give us permission to go into their store, and then help us identify the specific people we would speak with in each store. This process of negotiations led us to select a sample of stores, six large and six small, within two of the company's area groupings. Within each store we interviewed a representative group of users of the system, covering store management and supervisors. We also interviewed staff in Head and Area Offices, as well as key managers behind the purchase and design of the system, and computer specialists responsible for system support.

Gaining access in the university sector was again a complicated process, in part because our starting point was not the sector itself but a nationally developed MIS – the MAC Initiative. Discussions with two key national players in MAC led to approaches being made to several universities, initially with the aim of interviewing across a variety of institutions. The uneven ways in which MAC had been adopted and implemented at different locations made this option impractical, so agreement was secured to interview staff in just one university, Bancroft, whose decentralised structure meant there were essentially no gatekeepers controlling access as there were elsewhere. Whilst we followed the suggestions and advice of our initial contacts at Bancroft, we were free to approach for interview any member of the university's staff that we wished, on the understanding that nobody would be made to feel compelled to speak with us. Interviews were thus conducted across the different parts of the organisation in ways that made the study more comparable to the other sites than it would have been if several universities had been included.

Sampling and confidentiality

The model established at Finlay of interviewing a core group sampled across the organisation, plus managers and system support staff and a broader representative sample, was also adopted for our other two sites. We used 'purposive' sampling methods to select respondents, aiming to achieve a representative selection of users of the relevant system. How we identified and selected the sample varied slightly across the three sites. At Finlay, our pilot sample (later the core group) was identified for us by the laboratory manager. We then selected a representative sample of all staff in the Microbiology laboratories according to job role, based on a list of staff we were provided with.

At Brodies, we selected stores to represent store size and the time they had spent with the technology. This was assisted by area management, but management did not know which stores we had selected. No management in any of our three sites knew the identity of any of our individual respondents, except for the core group at Finlay, whose identities were known by one laboratory manager. However, as in all our writings about the project, all quotations have been anonymised so that no individual respondent's comments could be traced back to them.

Brodies management did define which categories of staff should be interviewed, according to whom *they* considered to be users of the system. Hence we did not get the opportunity to interview general assistants in the stores, as we would have liked, because they were not regarded as 'users'. This was not something we were free to challenge, and raises interesting questions about the different definitions of users, and about the compromises entailed when negotiating access in organisational research.

At Bancroft our access was mediated only minimally by gatekeepers. We identified an initial group of respondents through discussions with system managers in one central department, again keeping the identities of individual respondents confidential. We combined these interviews with a degree of 'snowballing'; that is, asking each respondent whom else they thought we should speak to. We thus built up a sample of the main groups of users of the system modules we were concerned with, supplemented with some more marginal users or users of other modules.

Care was thus taken in each site to spread the interviews across the different structural components of the organisation, and to interview as far as possible a sample that was representative, either of all staff or of system users (by whichever definition). The breakdown of groups of respondents in each organisation is given in Table A2.

A key issue with social research is confidentiality. As we have indicated, senior managers in each research site were guaranteed confidentiality for the organisation as an element of gaining access, whilst within each site we made it clear that the identities of individual respondents would also be kept confidential, and that all quotations would be anonymised. This benefited the project first in providing us with insights which we would not otherwise have been allowed – several interviews included comments about colleagues or about the organisation for which we were asked to switch off the tape recorder, or were at least told this was 'off the record'. Aside from this, several staff in each site were either concerned that what they said might get back to management, or were simply uncomfortable being interviewed. At Finlay, for

Table A2 Respondent breakdowns in the three sites

Site	Core group	Project management and support	One-off interviews	Key job roles[a]	Observation	Total
Finlay	8 across Microbiology and Virology (24 interviews)	8 managers from different laboratories (2 of these in core group)	25 (Microbiology and Virology) 7 (Tissue Typing)	6 doctors 9 MLSOs 7 clinical scientists	3 half-days in Microbiology	62 interviews
Brodies	8 in two large stores (21 interviews)	7 Head Office 3 Area Office	23 (large stores) 16 (small stores)	12 store managers 14 other store management staff 21 supervisors		70 interviews
Bancroft	11 across the university (29 interviews)	3 Steering Group 2 database administrators (others in core group)	13 (academic departments) 11 (central departments)	10 academic secretaries 4 laboratory managers 5 clerical staff (3 interviews)	Informally during some interviews	58 interviews
Total	27 respondents 74 interviews	21 interviews	95 interviews			190 interviews

Note
[a] These are the key roles in relation to our analysis. Some respondents here will have been interviewed more than once, as core group members.

example, one of our initial contacts refused when it came to the interview to speak with us, whilst another said very little throughout the interview, looking away from the microphone with her hand over her mouth when she did speak. In contrast, there were a few cases where confidentiality was not an issue for our respondents. Following our observation in the Finlay laboratories we sent copies of our notes to each of the staff that we had accompanied in their work. On a later visit, it transpired that one group of staff of similar grades in the same laboratory had exchanged their 'confidential' notes to compare how they had been quoted. Whilst it is crucial always to offer staff confidentiality, then, there is no certainty that it will always be taken up.

Whilst our interviewing programmes in each of the sites went mostly very smoothly, there were a few setbacks. During the course of the study we 'lost' a small number of our core group members in each site. At Finlay, one person had left the laboratory by the time of the second interviews. At Brodies we lost two core group members who were unavailable when we tried to meet them for subsequent interviews, but gained another. At Bancroft, one core group member proved unavailable for the third interview, whilst another – away on maternity leave – was replaced by a colleague with similar responsibilities. Of potentially more concern, at Brodies we lost a key sponsor of the study at Head Office when he moved on. These cases were unfortunately unavoidable, but thankfully did not pose a substantial threat to the integrity of the study or of our core group cohorts. They certainly did not negate the positive value of maintaining a longitudinal dimension to the study, despite the additional work involved in keeping track of core group members.

Interviewing methods

It was a key research objective to gain access to respondents' interpretations and experiences of technology, things which are hard to quantify. We therefore used qualitative interviewing techniques that aimed to draw out these themes. Interviews with respondents took the form of semi-structured in-depth interviews, lasting approximately one hour per interview. Without rehearsing here well-established debates about qualitative versus quantitative methodology (see Silverman 1985), this approach allowed the users of technology to define the issues and concerns that were important to them, rather than being defined either by the researchers or by management gatekeepers. It also allowed different kinds of user perspective to emerge, since our interviews were designed not to constrain responses.

Most interviews were one-to-one, although in some cases two of us would interview together – this was the pattern in particular for the pilot study, and for many of the more senior staff we interviewed in each sector. Working together had benefits in allowing each interviewer more freedom than usual to reflect on and follow up responses, but this approach was more demanding on time, and was not feasible for nearly two hundred interviews. There was also one case where two of our *respondents* insisted on being interviewed together.

Each interview was taped, with the permission of the respondent (in some cases with the tape recorder placed out of their line of vision to help them forget it was there). Our interview schedules were initially developed – for the pilot study – through discussion among the research team, based on the objectives of the project and set against our knowledge of Finlay, the pilot research site. We consequently developed a pilot interview schedule that dealt with the following themes:

- the respondent's own organisational position and professional background, including IT experience;
- their views and any experience of the specification and acquisition of the new system, or of the decision-making process behind acquisition and implementation;
- their experience of using the system following implementation, including issues and problems that had arisen, and whether and how these had been resolved;
- their evaluation of the system, and of how the change had been managed.

We also asked respondents for any additional comments they wished to make, and for any suggestions as to whom else we should talk to. This schedule was then revised and tailored to each of our research sites, bearing in mind, for example, the particular position a respondent might hold.

We interviewed respondents within their organisational settings, in a variety of locations. Most interviews took place in a quiet room, either the respondent's office or a meeting room. Occasionally this was not possible, and we would have to use whatever space could be found, sometimes causing problems for us later when transcribing an interview in a noisy work area.

Whilst we tried to ensure that each of the topics on the schedule was covered with each respondent, we allowed the flow of interviews to be directed largely by the respondent's own interests. Only occasionally would we fail to cover an issue, usually due to pressure on the respondent's time. However, something that happened quite often was that somebody would tell us they did not have much time, but would then give us far longer than we expected, sometimes even more than the standard hour. For example, one doctor at Finlay, who was highly critical of the new system and of the way it placed pressure on his time, quite justifiably resented the further pressure which our interview presented him with. However, when the interview had finished, he expressed surprise that it was over so soon, probably because he had valued the opportunity to express his feelings about the system.

Once completed, interviews were transcribed and then returned to the respondent for checking. This was done partly as a means of underlining our commitment to confidentiality, partly out of respect for respondents' right to have some control over how we would be using what they said, and also to reciprocate in a small way the contribution they were making towards our research. Several respondents expressed an appreciation for the opportunity to review the interview, and to correct what they saw as mistakes. The return rate for transcripts was high, and we assumed that failure to return a transcript meant it was acceptable to the respondent. There were few substantial revisions, mostly reflecting people's surprise at the difference between spoken and written language, and a desire to make their speech read more coherently (the same could also be said of the interviewers). However, respondents also made valuable corrections in relation to specialist terminology and organisational procedures. This process of allowing respondents to correct transcripts raises an interesting issue around which version of the interview is then treated as 'accurate' – a question we did not resolve during the study since it affected such a small part of our data.

The reciprocity that we tried to build into our relationship with respondents in this way also emerged in a few cases in other forms. With our core group respondents, especially, we developed a longer-term relationship than might be usual. We would not want to place too much significance on this – none of us, for example, has developed a lasting friendship with any of the people interviewed. However, we did on occasion get asked our advice on issues around IT and organisational change, and one respondent at Bancroft asked if we could send her a copy of her transcript to give to a student who was studying IT and change.

Coding and analysis of transcripts: valuing NUD•IST

Corrected transcripts were coded for use with the qualitative software package NUD•IST (which stands for Non-Numerical Unstructured Data – Indexing Searching and Theorising). NUD•IST is a package which facilitates the handling of a large quantity of textual material, by allowing the user to organise data both by groups of respondents, and also according to different themes, or codes. Any code can be attached to specific blocks of text within transcripts, and then searched across different combinations of respondents. This means that every reference to, say, 'a bug in the system' could be called up from all interviews at Finlay, or just from all doctors.

We used a fairly complex coding method, combining codes for relevant empirical and conceptual themes with a demographic code for each respondent. The themed codes allowed us to use NUD•IST to search transcripts according to specific issues raised in the interviews. The demographic code would then allow us to identify the source of a quotation by gender, age group, job role, and so on, which helped make up for the fact that no individual member of a four-person research team could ever know every respondent by name. A related problem that we found with such a complex coding structure was the question of consistency in how we each interpreted the codes, and how we interpreted and prioritised the issues raised. This made it necessary for some double-checking of coding, and for one individual to ensure consistency of coding for each site.

As stated above, the codes were initially identified during the pilot study, covering ten broad headings, with a variety of sub-themes to allow quite specific searches to be carried out. These headings covered issues such as the main purpose of the system, the different aspects of usability discussed in Chapter 7, the different kinds of need the system was felt to serve, and the sources and motivations for change. As our coding moved on to the other sites, new sets of codes were established that had not been relevant at Finlay.

Once the considerable work of coding and indexing documents in NUD•IST had been completed, we were able to analyse the material. NUD•IST makes it possible to generate reports of all references to a certain issue across a range of respondents, something which is often essential to understanding the data. Another benefit is that it allows a systematic analysis of material across the entire database, and can thus help confirm – or indeed counter – hunches and assumptions developed through the process of conducting interviews. However, we found it important in some parts of our analysis to go back to the transcripts themselves, in order not to disengage specific statements from their broader context. This was especially helpful in analysing issues that carried across the three core group interviews. The fact that this could be extremely time-consuming did not detract from its value in understanding the site, for which we found familiarity with the transcripts was crucial, with or without the addition of NUD•IST printouts.

Our analysis did not, therefore, begin and end with NUD•IST, but developed through interaction among the researchers, and between the researchers and the data. NUD•IST played an important – but not the only – role here. Analytic and substantive themes emerged and developed throughout the study, as part of the on-going research process. This led, for example, to occasional revisions to our interview schedules, and more importantly to the development of new schedules for each new set of core group interviews.

As with the research itself, the analysis developed over the course of the project. Certain aspects of the research process itself necessitated some analysis of the data at a fairly early stage – the need to evaluate our pilot study, and the feedback reports we produced for Finlay and Brodies, for example. The opportunity to present conference papers likewise meant that some analysis of the data was taking place before the fieldwork had been completed in all sectors. This had the benefit of informing later stages of the study, and of generating feedback from other academics about our analysis whilst it was still taking place.

As a final note on NUD•IST, this package gave us considerable pause for reflection on our own experience of technology acquisition and consumption. Both the package and the computer on which we ran it caused us innumerable problems, which we of course constructed as technical problems whose cause lay with either the NUD•IST suppliers or Apple Inc., rather than being problems with our own use of the program. Either way, this affected how usability, utility and value were constructed in our own organisational setting for NUD•IST, involving numerous emails sent back and forth between us and the suppliers, and between us and our computer services department, dealing with the consequences of programming errors, and of the whole system regularly crashing, and frequently vowing to revert back to coding up our transcripts using coloured felt tips, scissors and Sellotape. We eventually acquired for this project a Beta version of the program, which had its own implications regarding certainty and stability. Quite how we have *incorporated* the package into our group project as qualitative researchers remains to be seen – at best we are somewhat cynical users, who nevertheless find some value in using NUD•IST in our own idiosyncratic ways.

Feedback to the sites

A component of the project that was built into the research design was an intention to feed our findings back to the organisations that collaborated with us. One way that this was done was in the third core group interviews in each site. We discussed broad findings with respondents, especially the usability tables in Chapter 7. Their responses in many cases confirmed our interpretations, though some useful clarifications also emerged. More formally, we fed back with both written reports and oral presentations to management. At Finlay we also presented a lunchtime seminar to a wide range of laboratory staff.

This feedback has again involved a learning process as the project developed. As the first research site in our staggered research programme, we fed back to Finlay first, both after the pilot (in order to secure permission to extend the project) and following the second core group interviews. At this second feedback session, we presented a written report to the Project Team, whose responses then fed into the content of the third core group interviews. We are not convinced that the Project Team themselves felt they gained much from all this feedback, but the wider group of staff who attended our seminar certainly appeared to appreciate the opportunity to learn finally why we had been interviewing them.

With Brodies, we undertook a number of different feedback strategies. Throughout the study we produced various paper reports for them on particular issues that had emerged which we thought they would find useful. We also undertook one feedback session with key Head Office staff where we presented our findings in a final report. Brodies' approach in this meeting took the form of 'give us the bottom line – does the system work or not?', which did not sit easily with our outlook on how technology becomes embedded within an organisation. Nevertheless, the exercise of presenting our work to this type of audience proved both useful and fraught. Our unease about producing a report for senior managers in such a large company meant that perhaps we overprepared ourselves, and provided them with too much information and analysis (the final report was over forty pages). Whether they took seriously the points we made about rethinking their approach to users is hard to judge. However, we felt this was a better approach than telling them what they wanted to hear. One regret is that copies of the final report were not passed on to store staff, since we were not granted permission from Head Office to send the report to stores.

Our feedback at Bancroft both built on our experience of feeding back in the other two sectors, and benefited from the fact that our research was by then complete. Consequently we presented to the IT Steering Group a less extensive overview of our findings in the university than we had elsewhere, but with a more comparative cross-sectoral element, covering the study as a whole. The intention was to respond to specific questions from our audience and then subsequently tailor our written report towards the issues raised in discussion. Of the three sites, our feedback to Bancroft was received the most positively, and involved the greatest amount of engagement with the issues we raised. This was a perhaps unsurprising result of both a greater receptiveness to academic research, and a concern to avoid making the same 'mistakes' again as they moved towards needing to choose a new MIS system.

Giving feedback to the organisations researched raises a number of questions over who are the 'users', organisational sponsors or organisational 'beneficiaries' of research (Rappert in preparation). In Brodies and Bancroft we fed back only to managers, despite the fact that a number of respondents in all three sites had engaged with our research topic and expressed an interest in learning about our results. The organisational structure and culture of Brodies, especially, made problematic the idea of bypassing management gatekeepers in order to follow up store staff's interest in the project. At the other end of the scale, the diffuseness of authority at Bancroft paradoxically would have made it difficult to bring our respondents together to hear our findings in the way that we did at Finlay. This situation is ironic given the focus of the project on 'users', and is an issue that increasingly faces researchers seeking to work with non-academic partners – which is anyway a requirement generally now of UK social science funding (ibid.).

In the field

To close this Appendix, we want to reflect a little on the experience of conducting fieldwork within an organisation. Whilst studying techno-organisational change 'in the making' (Latour 1987) is not the same as ethnography, it does share some of ethnography's characteristics, particularly in terms of the experience of doing research. Choosing to study a particular organisation requires an acculturation into both the organisation itself and its wider context, the sector it operates within. Our fieldwork therefore required, to begin with, getting to know a little about each site and its sector – the key issues for staff, what wider changes were taking place aside from a new MIS implementation, how the sector was organised, and what particular terminologies it used. This was helped by the fact that within the team we had previous or on-going experience of working in, or at least knowing others who worked in, each of the three sectors. But it also entailed reading specialist journals and magazines, speaking to people in the sector who might be able to give us information and perhaps further contacts, as well as initial discussions with gatekeepers in our three sites and site visits to set up the fieldwork.

All of this can be initially quite alienating to the outsider. For example, we had to learn very specific, and often very localised, sets of jargon within each organisation – at Finlay there was a whole realm of bacteriological language to become familiar with, whilst Brodies management were very fond of acronyms that could be quite baffling to an outsider. We were more familiar with the university setting, of course, although we work in an institution with a very different history and culture to Bancroft. To not understand one of Brodies' acronyms, or not to know what a particular medical phrase meant, could mean missing out on important follow-up questions in later interviews.

Understanding the way an organisation works, its routines, and the kinds of outlook staff might have was also important. How formally should we address the people we were interviewing? How should we dress? Could these things affect how different organisational groupings identified us – for example, if we dressed formally at the university, would academic staff assume we were aligned with management, and vice versa? Perhaps more crucially, giving a sense that we understood the ins and outs of organisational life and the dynamics of the sector could prove highly valuable in being treated with respect by both gatekeepers and respondents, because we would be perceived as treating *them* with respect. Hence we deliberately avoided trying to interview people at Brodies during the Christmas period (which runs from September to January for retailers), or people at Bancroft during the examinations or registration periods. Related to this point, establishing some shared interest on an individual level can often be crucial to the success of an interview, as we found on a number of occasions. Respondents might become far more forthcoming because a chance comment by the interviewer has touched on a pet topic, or because they have discovered the interviewer comes from the same town or supports the same football team.

As well as making individual contact, the experience, and benefits, of conducting fieldwork can vary a great deal according to the degree of the researcher's 'immersion', to use an anthropological term, within an organisation. Some of our site visits involved just a short journey, which meant we sometimes saw less of the 'backstage' (Goffman 1959) of organisational life than at sites which involved longer trips, where we would then group a number of interviews together, and even stay overnight. Having to spend time in an organisation whilst waiting for the next interview, or stay overnight (in the case of Bancroft this involved staying *inside* the organisation, in guest accommodation), puts greater stresses on the researchers, but also provided increased benefits to the research. A researcher might struggle to find somewhere quiet and unobtrusive to wait for an hour or two between interviews, perhaps even to the extent of having to wander around neighbouring streets. Spending a tea break within the organisation – during a period of observation – can also be highly disconcerting. Should one try to strike up conversations with strangers in this situation, or pretend to make notes in a notebook and try not to feel abandoned? Getting to know the space and dimensions of the site could also prove tricky, as can knowing which areas might be off-limits – for example, which parts of a laboratory contain dangerous bacteria.

Despite these disconcerting aspects of research, there are some important benefits from spending more time in an organisation. Enforced waiting times can provide an opportunity for observing organisational life and dynamics more casually than in an interview. It gives time to observe how staff mark out space and technology, and how they interact with each other outside the somewhat forced context of an interview. At Finlay, we noticed on our site visits before the new computer system had been installed that staff in the office where specimens were first registered had adorned their computer terminals with small furry toys, and photographs cut from magazines. Visiting the same office several months into the implementation of PBS, it was notable that the new terminals had not been adorned in the same way. At Brodies, there was a telling use of posters in the 'backstage' areas of the stores. Some reminded staff how to act once they moved 'frontstage', others conveyed company slogans, such as the poster on one store manager's wall that said:

Thought for the year:
Make it known
Make it happen
Make it stick

Some of the most interesting insights into organisational relations can come from casual observations that are made possible by chance aspects of research – an unplanned encounter during an interview, for example. At Bancroft, the telephone rang during an interview with one senior manager. The respondent was arguing about who should be producing a MAC report for another manager, whom he belittled, at the same time as criticising a third person, whom we were going to be interviewing later that day. This was helpful in illustrating how complex the organisational responsibilities and tensions had become since the new system had arrived, although it placed our researcher in a slightly awkward position regarding cross-organisational confidences. An even more insightful observation took place at Brodies, where a store manager received an unannounced visit from Area Office during our interview. Whilst expressing during this interview the equal relations between local and central management, and the informality of the organisation's management culture, the store manager was at the same time making himself 'presentable' – straightening his tie and so on. As he heard the Area Office manager approaching, our store manager was eating a Mars bar, which he then tossed behind a filing cabinet – obviously relations were not equal or informal enough to be seen eating by Area Office staff!

Perhaps the biggest challenge to the fieldwork dimension of the project was sharing and co-ordinating amongst ourselves the knowledge that was being built up, almost tacitly, through these chance occurrences, and through individual researchers' absorption of the details they observed as they conducted their fieldwork. In order to address this, we instituted a 'fieldwork diary', where we would note our impressions for each interview of the most important issues for that respondent. The objective here was to build up a progressive picture for each site, over the entire period of fieldwork, of the key issues around techno-organisational change, and to flag any themes which were emerging from the interviews. Any of the research team could then find out what questions had been raised during recent interviews, before transcripts became available. This system was not stuck to rigidly, but it was particularly effective for the sites where two or more people were interviewing different people over the same period of days or weeks.

Conclusion

As well as detailing the bare bones of our methodology, what we hope this Appendix has done is to give some of the flavour of conducting research in organisational settings, and to identify some of the particular characteristics of our own experience in this study. This project has raised, we feel, a wide range of generic issues about research, not all of which we have yet managed to resolve for ourselves, but which deserve consideration and further reflection.

It is also important to recognise, though, the way that researchers' own biographies feed into the issues and case studies they pursue and how they approach their investigation and analysis (Aldridge 1993, Cotterill and Letherby 1993, Clifford and Marcus 1986). The way we conducted our fieldwork was based on a combination of our own research training, our different research experiences prior to this project, and our contrasting disciplinary and research backgrounds. As a team, we could muster expertise from past experience in interviewing managers and more junior staff in a variety of organisations, policy-makers and bureaucrats in several fields, innovators and everyday users of a number of technologies. We also had considerable experience of trying to make sense of a range of documentary sources such as company archives, patents, technical documents and official publications. This broad expertise derives from a disparate set of disciplinary backgrounds, in sociology, anthropology, political theory and policy analysis, applied to a wide range of topics, such as health, development, social policy, gender relations, science policy and technical innovation.

Nevertheless, any new piece of research involves, in many ways, starting afresh. Each organisation is to some degree new to those researching it, however well they prepare themselves. This was certainly the case for us, since none of us, for example, had previously interviewed actors right across the range of positions within an organisation or, indeed, researched the organisational acquisition of IT. Our experiences from this project will not, then, fully prepare either us or anybody else for other experiences 'in the field'. We hope, nevertheless, that they have given a sense of some of the generic issues involved in social research, researching organisations and researching sociotechnical change.

Bibliography

Acker, J. (1990) 'Hierarchies, jobs, bodies: a theory of gendered organizations', *Gender and Society* 4, 2: 139–58.

Acker, J. (1992) 'Gendering organizational theory', in A.J. Mills and P. Tancred (eds), *Gendering Organizational Analysis*, London: Sage.

Ackroyd, S. (1996) 'Organisation contra organisations: professions and organisational change in the United Kingdom', *Organization Studies* 17, 4: 599–621.

Akrich, Madeleine (1992) 'The de-scription of technical objects', in Bijker and Law (1992b).

Akrich, Madeleine (1995) 'User representations: practices, methods and sociology', in Rip *et al.* (1995).

Aldridge, Judith (1993) 'The textual disembodiment of knowledge in research account writing', *Sociology* 27, 1: 53–66.

Aldridge, M. (1996) 'Dragged to market: being a profession in the postmodern world', *British Journal of Social Work* 26: 177–94.

Allen, D.K. and T.D. Wilson (1996) 'Information strategies in UK higher education institutions', *International Journal of Information Management* 16, 4: 239–51.

Anderson, M. (1992) 'Implementing an information infrastructure strategy: the University of Edinburgh experience', *University Computing* 14: 8–13.

Appadurai, A. (1986) *The Social Life of Things: Commodities in Cultural Perspective*, Cambridge: Cambridge University Press.

Ashmore, Malcolm and Evelleen Richards (eds) (1996) 'The politics of SSK: neutrality, commitment and beyond', special issue of *Social Studies of Science* 26, 2.

Badham, R. (1995) 'Managing sociotechnical change: a configuration approach to technology implementation', in Benders *et al.* (1995b).

Barnett, C. (1995) *Cyber Business*, Chichester: John Wiley.

Bartky, S.L. (1988). 'Foucault, femininity and the modernization of patriarchal power', in I. Diamand and L. Quinby (eds), *Feminism and Foucault: Reflections on Resistance*, Boston: Northeastern University Press.

Bauman, Z. (1998) *Globalisation: The Human Consequences*, Cambridge: Polity Press.

Bell, D. (1976) *The Coming of Post-Industrial Society*, Harmondsworth: Penguin.

Benders, J., J. de Hann and D. Bennett (1995a) 'Symbiotic approaches: contents and issues', in Benders *et al.* (1995b).

Benders, J., J. de Hann and D. Bennett (eds) (1995b) *The Symbiosis of Work and Technology*, London: Taylor and Francis.

Berg, M. (1997) 'Of forms, containers, and the electronic record: some tools for a sociology of the formal', *Science, Technology and Human Values* 22, 4: 403–33.

Bessant, J. (1993) 'The lessons of failure: learning to manage new manufacturing technology', *International Journal of Technology Management* 8: 197–215.

Bijker, Wiebe E. (1987) 'The social construction of Bakelite: toward a theory of invention', in Bijker *et al.* (1987).

Bijker, Wiebe E. (1992) 'The social construction of fluorescent lighting, or how an artifact was invented in its diffusion stage', in Bijker and Law (1992b).

Bijker, Wiebe E. (1995) *Of Bicycles, Bakelites and Bulbs: Toward a Theory of Sociotechnical Change*, Cambridge MA: MIT Press.

Bijker, Wiebe E. and John Law (1992a) 'General introduction', in Bijker and Law (1992b).

Bijker, Wiebe E. and John Law (eds) (1992b) *Shaping Technology/Building Society: Studies in Sociotechnical Change*, Cambridge MA: MIT Press.

Bijker, Wiebe E., Thomas P. Hughes and Trevor Pinch (eds) (1987) *The Social Construction of Technological Systems: New Directions in the Sociology and History of Technology*, Cambridge MA: MIT Press.

Bloomfield, B., R. Coombs and J. Owen (1994) 'The social construction of information systems', in Mansell (1994b).

Blume, Stuart (1992) *Insight and Industry: The Dynamics of Technological Change in Medicine*, Cambridge MA: MIT Press.

Blume, Stuart (1997) 'The rhetoric and counter-rhetoric of a "bionic" technology', *Science, Technology, and Human Values* 22, 1: 31–56.

Boje, D.M. (1995) 'Stories of the storytelling organization: a postmodern analysis of Disney as *Tamara*-Land', *Academy of Management Journal* 38, 4: 997–1035.

Boreham, P. (1983) 'Indermination: professional knowledge, organisation and control', *Sociological Review* 31, 4: 693–718.

Bourdieu, P. (1984) *Distinction*, London: Routledge and Kegan Paul.

Bowker, G. and S.L. Star (1994) 'Knowledge and infrastructure in international information management', in L. Bud-Frierman (ed.), *Information Acumen: The Understanding and Use of Knowledge in Modern Business*, London: Routledge.

Bowlby, S.R. and J. Foord (1995) 'Relational contracting between UK retailers and manufacturers', *International Review of Retail, Distribution and Consumer Research* 5, 3: 333–60.

Bradley, H. (1996) *Fractured Identities: Changing Patterns of Inequality*, Cambridge: Polity Press.

Braverman, H. (1974) *Labour and Monopoly Capital*, New York: Monthly Review Press.

Breaks, Michael (ed.) (1991) 'Information systems strategies', Special issue of the *British Journal of Academic Librarianship* 6, 2.

Broadbridge, A. (1991) 'Images and goods: women in retailing', in N. Redclift and M.T. Sinclair (eds), *Working Women: International Perspectives on Labour and Gender Ideology*, London: Routledge.

Brown, A. (1995) *Organisational Culture*, London: Pitman.

Brunsson, N. (1985) *The Irrational Organization*, Chichester: John Wiley.

Buchanan, D. and J. Storey (1997) 'Role taking and role switching in organizational change: the four pluralities', in McLoughlin and Harris (1997b).

Burgess, Robert G. (1991) *In The Field: An Introduction to Field Research*, London: Routledge.

Butler, J. (1990) *Gender Trouble*, London: Routledge.

Callon, Michel (1986a) 'Some elements of a sociology of translation: domestication of the scallops and the fishermen of St. Brieuc Bay', in Law (1986b).

Callon, Michel (1986b) 'The sociology of an actor-network: the case of the electric vehicle', in Callon *et al.* (1986).

Callon, Michel and Bruno Latour (1992) 'Don't throw the baby out with the Bath School! A reply to Collins and Yearley', in Pickering (1992).

Callon, Michel, John Law and Arie Rip (eds) (1986) *Mapping the Dynamics of Science and Technology: Sociology of Science in the Real World*, Basingstoke: Macmillan.

Campbell, C. (1987) *The Romantic Ethic and the Spirit of Modern Consumerism*, Oxford: Blackwell.

Casey, C. (1995) *Work, Self and Society*, London: Routledge.

Chabaud-Rychter, Danielle (1994) 'Women users in the design process of a food robot: innovation in a French domestic appliance company', in Cockburn and Fürst–Dilić (1994).

Checkland, P., S. Clarke and J.S. Poulter (1996) 'The use of soft systems methodology for developing HISS and IM&T strategies in NHS Trusts', *Current Perspectives in Healthcare Computing Conference Proceedings*, London: BJHC.

Chemistry and Industry (1985) 'Top industrialists predict biotech revolution', *Chemistry and Industry* 21 October: 669.

Clark, J. (1995) *Managing Innovation and Change: People, Technology and Strategy*, London: Sage.

Clark, P. (1987) *Anglo-American Innovation*, Berlin: Walter De Gruyter.

Clarke, Adele and Theresa Montini (1993) 'The many faces of RU486: tales of situated knowledges and technological contestations', *Science, Technology, and Human Values* 18: 42–78.

Clegg, S. (1990) *Modern Organizations*, London: Sage.

Clifford, James and George E. Marcus (eds) (1986) *Writing Culture: The Poetics and Politics of Ethnography*, Berkeley CA: University of California Press.

Cockburn, C. (1983) *Brothers: Male Dominance and Technological Change*, London: Pluto Press.

Cockburn, Cynthia and Ruža Fürst–Dilić (eds) (1994) *Bringing Technology Home: Gender and Technology in a Changing Europe*, Buckingham: Open University Press.

Cockburn, Cynthia and Susan Ormrod (1993) *Gender and Technology in the Making*, London: Sage.

Cohn, C. (1987) 'Sex and death in the rational world of defence intellectuals', *Signs* 12, 4: 687–718.

Collins, H.M. and Steven Yearley (1992) 'Epistemological chicken', in Pickering (1992).

Collinson, D.L. (1992) *Managing the Shopfloor: Subjectivity, Masculinity and Workplace Culture*, Berlin: Walter de Gruyter.

Collinson, D.L. and M. Collinson (1997) 'Delayering managers: time-space surveillance and its gendered effects', *Organization* 4, 3: 375–408.

Coombs, R., D. Knights and H.C. Willmott (1992) 'Culture, control and competition: towards a conceptual framework for the study of information technology in organizations', *Organization Studies* 13, 1: 51–72.

Cotterill, Pamela and Gayle Letherby (1993) 'Weaving stories: personal auto/biographies in feminist research', *Sociology* 27, 1: 67–79.

Cowan, Ruth Schwartz (1987) 'The consumption junction: a proposal for research strategies in the sociology of technology', in Bijker *et al.* (1987).

Cowan, Ruth Schwartz (1989) *More Work for Mother: The Ironies of Household Technology from the Open Hearth to the Microwave*, London: Free Association Books.

Czikszentmihalyi, M. and E. Rochberg-Holton (1981) *The Meaning of Things: Domestic Symbols and the Self*, Cambridge: Cambridge University Press.

Dant, T. and D. Francis (1998) 'Planning in organisations: rational control or contingent activity?', *Sociological Research Online* 3, 2 <http://www.socresonline.org.uk/socresonline/3/2/4.html>

Dawson, P. (1988) 'Information technology and the control function of supervision', in D. Knights and H. Willmott (eds), *New Technology and the Labour Process*, London: Macmillan.

De Certeau M. (1984) *The Practice of Everyday Life*, Berkeley: University of California Press.

Deetz, S. (1998) 'Discursive formations, strategized subordination and self-surveillance', in A. McKinlay and K. Starkey (eds), *Foucault, Management and Organization Theory*, London: Sage.

Delbridge, R. and J. Lowe (1997) 'Manfacturing control: supervisory systems on the "new" shopfloor', *Sociology* 31, 3: 409–26.

Dent, M. (1996) *Professions, Information Technology and Management in Hospitals*, Aldershot: Avebury.

Dobbin, F.R. (1994) 'Cultural models of organization: The social construction of rational organizing principles' in D. Crane (ed.), *The Sociology of Culture*, Oxford: Blackwell.

Dominelli, L. (1996) 'Deprofessionalizing social work: anti–oppressive practice, competencies and postmodernism', *British Journal of Social Work* 26: 153–75.

Douglas, M. (1992) *Risk and Blame: Essays in Cultural Theory*, London: Routledge.

Douglas, M. and B. Isherwood (1980) *The World of Goods: Towards an Anthropology of Consumption*, Harmondsworth: Penguin.

Du Gay, P. (1996) *Consumption and Identity at Work*, London: Sage.

Edgerton, David (1993) 'Tilting at paper tigers', essay review of MacKenzie, *Inventing Accuracy*, in *British Journal for the History of Science* 26: 67–75.

Elston, M.A. (1991) 'The politics of professional power: medicine in a changing health service', in J. Gabe, M. Calnan and M. Bury (eds), *The Sociology of the Health Service*, London: Routledge.

Elzen, Boelie (1986) 'Two ultracentrifuges: a comparative study of the social construction of artefacts', *Social Studies of Science* 16: 621–61.

Ewart, Wallace (1985) 'Managing information', in Lockwood and Davies (1985).

Ferguson, K.E. (1984) *The Feminist Case against Bureaucracy*, Philadelphia: Temple University Press.

Fine, B. (1995) 'From political economy to consumption', in Miller (1995b).

Fiorito, Susan, Elenor May and Katherine Straughn (1994) 'Continuous evolution: corporate configurations of information technology', in Mansell (1994b).

Fiorito, Susan, Elenor May and Katherine Straughn (1995) 'Quick response in retailing: components and implementation', *International Journal of Retail and Distribution* 23, 5: 12–21.

Fleck, J. (1994) 'Continuous evolution: corporate configurations of information technology', in R. Mansell (ed.), *The Management of Information and Communication Technologies: Emerging Patterns of Control*, London: Aslib.

Fletcher, J.K. and P.Y. Martin (1998) 'Doing gender in organizations: disappearing women's work and mobilizing masculinity', paper presented at the Conference on Gender, Work and Organization, Manchester, 9–10 January.

Fournier, V. (1997) 'Boundary work and the making of the professions', paper presented at the Conference on Professionalism, Boundaries and the Workplace, University of Derby, 1 February.

Freidson, E. (1988) *Profession of Medicine: A Study of the Sociology of Applied Knowledge*, Chicago: University of Chicago Press.

Freidson, E. (1994) *Professionalism Reborn*, Cambridge: Polity Press.

Fujimura, Joan H. (1992) 'Crafting science: standardized packages, boundary objects, and "Translation"', in Pickering (1992).

Gardner, John, John Fulton and Joanne Best (1993) 'Trends and tensions in IT policy in universities', *Higher Education Quarterly* 47, 3: 259–73.

Garnham, N. (1994) 'Whatever happened to the information society?', in Mansell (1994b).

Garsten, C. and C. Grey (1997) 'How to become oneself: discourses of subjectivity in post-bureaucratic organizations', *Organization* 4, 2: 211–28.

Gherardi, S. (1995) *Gender, Symbolism and Organizational Cultures*, London: Sage.

Giddens, A. (1990) *The Consequences of Modernity*, Cambridge: Polity Press.

Giddens, A. (1991) *Modernity and Self-Identity: Self and Society in the Late Modern Age*, Cambridge: Polity Press.

Gill, R. and K. Grint (1995) 'The gender–technology relation: contemporary theory and research', in Grint and Gill (1995).

Gilmore, Rosemary, Ian Nicholson and Roz Williams (1994) 'Powerhouse family perspectives', *Axis* 1, 2: 4–13.

Goddard, A.D. and P.H. Gayward (1994) 'MAC and the Oracle family: achievements and lessons learnt', *Axis* 1, 1: 45–50.

Goddard, J.B. (1992) 'New technology and the geography of the UK information economy', in K. Robins (ed.), *Understanding Information: Business, Technology and Geography*, London: Belhaven Press.

Goffman, Erving (1959) *The Presentation of Self in Everyday Life*, Harmondsworth: Pelican (1971 edn).

Griffin, S. (1978) *Woman and Nature: The Roaring Inside Her*, San Francisco: Harper and Row.

Griffiths, R. (1983) *NHS Management Inquiry*, London: DHSS.

Grint, K. and R. Gill (eds) (1995) *The Gender–Technology Relation*, London: Taylor and Francis.

Grint, Keith and Steve Woolgar (1995) 'On some failures in nerve in constructivist and feminist analyses of technology', in Grint and Gill (1995).

Grint, Keith and Steve Woolgar (1997) *The Machine At Work: Technology, Work and Organization*, Cambridge: Polity Press.

Gullestad, M. (1984) *Kitchen-Table Society*, Oslo: Universitetsforlaget.

Hall, W. (1995) *Managing Cultures: Making Strategic Relationships Work*, Chichester: John Wiley.

Handy, C.B. (1985) *Understanding Organizations*, London: Penguin.

Harlow, E., J. Hearn and W. Parkin (1995) 'Gendered noise: organizations and the silence and din of domination', in J. Newman and C. Itzin (eds), *Gender, Culture and Organizational Change*, London: Routledge.

Harvey, D. (1990) *The Condition of Postmodernity*, Oxford: Blackwell.

Hebdige, D. (1979) *Subculture: The Meaning of Style*, London: Routledge.

Hochschild, A.R. (1983) *The Managed Heart: Commercialization of Human Feeling*, London: University of California Press.

Hommels, Anique (1998) 'Changing cities: transforming obdurate artifacts and embedded structures', paper presented to the EASST Conference, Lisbon, 30 September–3 October.

Hughes, Thomas P. (1983) *Networks of Power: Electrification in Western Society, 1890–1930*, Baltimore MD: Johns Hopkins University Press.

Hughes, Thomas P. (1986) 'The seamless web: technology, science, etcetera, etcetera', *Social Studies of Science* 16: 281–92.

Hugman, R. (1996) 'Professionalization in social work – the challenge of diversity', *International Social Work* 39, 2: 131.

IGD (1998) *Retail Distribution 1998*, Watford: IGD Business Publication.

Itzin, C. (1995) 'The gender culture in organizations', in J. Newman and C. Itzin (eds), *Gender, Culture and Organizational Change*, London: Routledge.

Jackson, P. (1997) 'Information systems as metaphor: innovation and the 3 Rs of representation', in McLoughlin and Harris (1997b).

Johnson, G. (1988) 'Rethinking incrementalism', *Strategic Management Journal* 9: 75–81.

Johnson, J. (1972) *Professions and Power*, London: Macmillan.

Keenoy, T., C. Oswick and D. Grant (1997) 'Organizational discourses: text and context', *Organization* 4, 2: 147–57.

Kling, Rob (1992) 'Audiences, narratives, and human values in social studies of technology', *Science, Technology, and Human Values* 17, 3: 349–65.

Kling, R. and S. Iacono (1985) 'Computerisation as the product of social movements', in R. Gordon (ed.), *Microelectronics in Transition*, Norwood NJ: Abex.

Kling, R. and S. Iacono (1995) 'Computerization movements and the mobilization of support for computerization', in Star (1995b).

Knights, D. (1997) 'Organization theory in the age of deconstruction: dualism, gender and postmodernism revisited', *Organization Studies* 18, 1: 1–19.

Knights, D. and F. Murray (1994) *Managers Divided: Organisation Politics and Information Technology Management*, Chichester: John Wiley.

Kondo, D.K. (1990) *Crafting Selves: Power, Gender, and Discourses of Identity in a Japanese Workplace*, London: University of Chicago Press.

Latour, Bruno (1987) *Science in Action: How to Follow Scientists and Engineers Through Society*, Milton Keynes: Open University Press.

Latour, Bruno (1992) 'Where are the missing masses? The sociology of a few mundane artifacts', in Bijker and Law (1992b).

Latour, Bruno (1996) *Aramis, or the Love of Technology*, Cambridge MA: Harvard University Press.

Law, John (1986a) 'On the methods of long-distance control: vessels, navigation and the Portuguese route to India', in Law (1986b).

Law, John (ed.) (1986b) *Power, Action and Belief: A New Sociology of Knowledge*, London: Routledge and Kegan Paul.

Law, John (1987) 'Technology and heterogeneous engineering: the case of Portuguese expansion', in Bijker *et al.* (1987).

Law, John (1994) *Organizing Modernity*, Oxford: Blackwell.

Law, John and Wiebe E. Bijker (1992) 'Postscript: technology, stability, and social theory', in Bijker and Law (1992b).

Law, John and Michel Callon (1992) 'The life and death of an aircraft: a network analysis of technical change', in Bijker and Law (1992b).

Leflaive, X. (1996) 'Organizations as structures of domination', *Organization Studies* 17, 1: 23–47.

Leonard-Barton, D. (1991) 'The role of process innovation and adaptation in strategic technological capability', *International Journal of Technology Management* 6, 3/4: 303–20.

Liff, S. and H. Scarborough (1994) 'Creating a knowledge database – operationalising the vision or compromising the concept?', in Mansell (1994b).

Lockwood, Geoffrey and John Davies (1985) *Universities: The Management Challenge*, Windsor: Society for Research into Higher Education/NFER–Nelson.

Longhurst, B. and M. Savage (1996) 'Social class, consumption and the influence of Bourdieu: some critical issues', in S. Edgell, K. Hetherington and A. Warde (eds), *Consumption Matters*, Oxford: Blackwell.

Lown, J. (1990) *Women and Industrialization*, Cambridge: Polity Press.

Lunt, P.K. and S. Livingstone (1992) *Mass Consumption and Personal Identity: Everyday Economic Experience*, Buckingham: Open University Press.

Lyon, D. (1988) *The Information Society: Issues and Illusions*, Cambridge: Polity Press.

McCracken, G. (1988) *Culture and Consumption: New Approaches to the Symbolic Character of Consumer Goods*, Bloomington IN: Indiana University Press.

MacDonald, K.M. (1995) *The Sociology of the Professions*, London: Sage.

Mack, Pamela E. (1990) *Viewing the Earth: The Social Construction of the Landsat Satellite System*, Cambridge MA: MIT Press.

MacKenzie, Donald (1990) *Inventing Accuracy: A Historical Sociology of Nuclear Missile Guidance*, Cambridge MA: MIT Press.

MacKenzie, Donald and Judy Wajcman (eds) (1985) *The Social Shaping of Technology: How the Refrigerator Got its Hum*, Milton Keynes: Open University Press.

MacLeod, A.E. (1995) 'Hegemonic relations and gender resistance: the new veiling as accommodating protest in Cairo', in B. Laslett, J. Brenner and Y. Arat, *Rethinking the Political*, London: University of Chicago.

McLoughlin, I. and M. Harris (1997a) 'Introduction: understanding innovation, organisational change and technology', in McLoughlin and Harris (1997b).

McLoughlin, I. and M. Harris (eds) (1997b) *Innovation, Organizational Change and Technology*, London: International Thomson Business Press.

Mallard, Alexandre (1998) 'Compare, standardize and settle agreement: on some usual metrological problems', *Social Studies of Science* 28, 4: 571–601.

Mansell, R. (1994a) 'Negotiating the management of ICTs: emerging patterns of control', in Mansell (1994b).

Mansell, R. (ed.) (1994b) *The Management of Information and Communication Technologies: Emerging Patterns of Control*, London: Aslib.

Mansfield, E. (1992) 'Academic research and industrial innovation', *Research Policy*, 21: 295–6.

Martin, J. (1992) *Cultures in Organizations*, Oxford: Oxford University Press.

Martin, M. (1991) *Hello Central? Gender, Technology and Culture in the Formation of Telephone Systems*, London: McGill–Queen's University Press.

Mason, David, John Fielden and Allan Schofield (1998) *Management and Administrative Computing Initiative – Post–Implementation Review*, Report for JISC, the Joint Information Systems Committee of the Higher Education Funding Councils, Holmfirth: David Mason Consultancy.

May, T. (1994) 'Transformative power, a study in a human service organisation', *Sociological Review* 42, 4: 618–38.

Merchant, C. (1980) *The Death of Nature: Women, Ecology and the Scientific Revolution*, London: Wildwood House.

Miller, D. (1987) *Material Culture and Mass Consumption*, Oxford: Blackwell.

Miller, D. (1990) 'Appropriating the state on the council estate', in J. Putnam and C. Newton (eds), *Household Choices*, London: Futures.

Miller, D. (1995a) 'Consumption as the vanguard of history: a polemic by way of an introduction', in Miller (1995b).

Miller, D. (ed.) (1995b) *Acknowledging Consumption: A Review of New Studies*, London: Routledge.

Miller, D. (1997) *Capitalism: An Ethnographic Approach*, Oxford: Berg.

Miller, D. (1998) *A Theory of Shopping*, Cambridge: Polity Press.

Miller, P. and N. Rose (1990) 'Governing economic life', *Economy and Society* 19, 1: 1–31.

Misa, Thomas J. (1992) 'Controversy and closure in technological change: constructing "steel"', in Bijker and Law (1992b).

Moodie, Graham C. and Rowland Eustace (1974) *Power and Authority in British Universities*, London: George Allen and Unwin.

Morgan, G. (1997) *Images of Organization*, London: Sage.

Mort, M. (1995) 'Building the Trident network: a study of the enrolment of people, knowledge and machines', unpublished PhD thesis, Lancaster University.

Mort, Maggie and Mike Michael (1998) 'Human and technological "redundancy": phantom intermediaries in a nuclear submarine industry', *Social Studies of Science* 28, 3: 355–400.

Mumby, D. and L. Putnam (1992) 'The politics of emotion: a feminist reading of bounded rationality', *Academy of Management Review* 17, 3: 465–86.

NHS Executive (1995) *Implementing the Infrastructure*, London: NHS Executive.

NHS Executive (1998) *An Information Strategy for the Modern NHS*, London: NHS Executive.

Noble, G. and D. Lupton (1998) 'Consuming work: computers, subjectivity and appropriation in the university workplace', *Sociological Review* 46, 4: 803–27.

Nonaka, I. (1994) 'A dynamic theory of organizational knowledge creation', *Organization Science* 5, 1: 14–37.

Orlikowski, W.J. (1992) 'The duality of technology: rethinking the concept of technology in organizations', *Organization Science* 3, 3: 398–427.

Ormrod, S. (1995) 'Feminist sociology and methodology: leaky black boxes in gender/technology relations', in Grint and Gill (1995).

Pickering, Andrew (ed.) (1992) *Science as Practice and Culture*, Chicago: University of Chicago Press.

Pinch, Trevor (1993) '"Testing – one, two, three . . . testing!": toward a sociology of testing', *Science, Technology and Human Values* 18: 25–41.

Pinch, Trevor and Wiebe E. Bijker (1987) 'The social construction of facts and artefacts: or how the sociology of science and the sociology of technology might benefit each other', in Bijker *et al.* (1987).

Pollert, A. (1981) *Girls, Wives, Factory Lives*, London: Macmillan.

Pollock, Neil (1996) 'Enrolling users and translating "needs"', paper presented at the EASST/4S Conference on Signatures of Knowledge Societies, Bielefeld, Germany, 10–13 October.

Pollock, Neil (1998) 'Working-around a computer system: some features of a hybrid sociology', unpublished PhD thesis, Lancaster University.

Poster, M. (1990) *The Mode of Information: Poststructuralism and Social Context*, Cambridge: Polity Press.

Rachel, J. and S. Woolgar (1995) 'The discursive structure of the socio-technical divide: the example of information systems development', *Sociological Review* 43: 250–73.

Radnor, M. (1992) 'Technology acquisition practices and processes', *International Journal of Technology Management* 7: 113–35.

Rappert, Brian (in preparation) 'The uses of relevance: thoughts on reflexive sociology', submitted to *Sociology*.

Reed, M. (1996) 'Expert power and control in late modernity: an empirical review and theoretical synthesis', *Organization Studies* 17, 4: 573–97.

Reed, M. and M. Hughes (eds) (1992) *Rethinking Organisations*, London: Sage.

Rip, Arie, Thomas J. Misa and Johan Schot (eds) (1995) *Managing Technology in Society: The Approach of Constructive Technology Assessment*, London: Pinter.

Rose, N. (1989) *Governing the Soul: The Shaping of the Private Self*, London: Routledge.

Rosen, Paul (1995) 'Diamonds are forever: the socio-technical shaping of bicycle design', in Rob Van der Plaas (ed.), *Cycle History 5: Proceedings of the Fifth International Cycle History Conference, Cambridge, September 1994*, San Francisco: Bicycle Books.

Rosen, Paul (1998) 'Planning urban sociotechnical change: constructivism in the city', paper for International Workshop on Technological Futures – Urban Futures, Durham Castle, April.

Rosen, Paul (forthcoming) *Framing Production: Sociotechnical Change in the Bicycle Industry*, Cambridge MA: MIT Press.

Rosenberg, N. (1982) *Inside the Black Box: Technology and Economics*, Cambridge: Cambridge University Press.

Rothschild, Joan (ed.) (1983) *Machina Ex Dea: Feminist Perspectives on Technology*, New York: Pergamon Press.

Russell, Stewart (1986) 'The social construction of artefacts: a response to Pinch and Bijker', *Social Studies of Science* 16: 331–46.

Sahlins, M. (1976) *Culture and Practical Reason*, Chicago: University of Chicago Press.

Saks, M. (1995) *Professions and the Public Interest*, London: Routledge.

Scarborough, H. (1997) 'The social construction of strategic information systems', *Journal of Management Studies* 34, 2: 171–90.

Schmidt, Susanne K. and Raymund Werle (1998) *Coordinating Technology: Studies in the International Standardization of Telecommunications*, Cambridge MA: MIT Press.

Sclove, Richard (1995) *Democracy and Technology*, New York: Guilford Press.

Seaton, R.A.F. and Cordey Hayes (1993) 'The development and application of inter-action models of industrial technology transfer', *Technovation* 13, 1: 45–53.

Senker, P. (1992) 'Automation and work in Britain', in P.S. Adler (ed.), *Technology and the Future of Work*, New York: Oxford University Press.

Sillince, J.A.A. and S. Mouakket (1998) 'Divisive and integrative political strategies in the IS adaptation process: the MAC Initiative', *European Journal of Information Systems* 7: 46–60.

Silverman, David (1985) *Qualitative Methodology and Sociology*, Aldershot: Gower.

Silverstone, R. (1994) *Television and Everyday Life*, London: Routledge.

Silverstone, R., E. Hirsch and D. Morley (1992) 'Information and communication technologies and the moral economy of the household', in R. Silverstone and E. Hirsch (eds), *Consuming Technologies*, London: Routledge.

Singleton, Vicky and Mike Michael (1993) 'Actor-networks and ambivalence: general practitioners in the UK cervical screening programme', *Social Studies of Science* 23: 227–64.

Skinner, D. (1992) 'Technology, consumption and the future: the experience of home computing', unpublished PhD thesis, Brunel University.

Slater, D. (1997) *Consumer Culture and Modernity*, Cambridge: Polity Press.

Spelman. E. (1993) 'Reproduction of mothering', in J.A. Kourany, J.P. Sterba and R. Tong (eds), *Feminist Philosophies*, London: Harvester Wheatsheaf.

Star, Susan Leigh (1989) 'Layered space, formal representations and long-distance control: the politics of information', *Fundamenta Scientiae* 10: 125–54.

Star, Susan Leigh (1991) 'Power, technology and the phenomenology of conventions: on being allergic to onions', in John Law (ed.), *A Sociology of Monsters*, London: Routledge.

Star, Susan Leigh (1992) 'The Trojan door: organizations, work, and the "open black box"', *Systems Practice* 5, 4: 395–409.

Star, Susan Leigh (1995a) 'The politics of formal representations: wizards, gurus, and organisational complexity', in Star (1995b).

Star, Susan Leigh (ed.) (1995b) *Ecologies of Knowledge: Work and Politics in Science and Technology*, Albany: SUNY Press.

Star, Susan Leigh and James Griesemer (1989) 'Institutional ecology, "translations" and coherence: amateurs and professionals in Berkeley's Museum of Vertebrate Zoology', *Social Studies of Science* 19: 387–420.

Stehr, N. (1994) *Knowledge Societies*, London: Sage.

Sturdy, A. (1998) 'Customer care in a consumer society: smiling and sometimes meaning it?', *Organization* 5, 1: 27–53.

Tancred, P. (1995) 'Women's work: a challenge to the sociology of work', *Gender, Work and Organization* 2, 1: 11–20.

Terry, J. and M. Calvert (1997) 'Introduction: machines and lives', in J. Terry and M. Calvert (eds), *Processed Lives*, London: Routledge.

Thomas, Robert J. (1994) *What Machines Can't Do: Politics and Technology in the Industrial Enterprise*, Berkeley CA: University of California Press.

Timmermans, Stefan and Marc Berg (1997) 'Standardization in action: achieving local universality through medical protocols', *Social Studies of Science* 27: 273–305.

University Grants Committee (1989) *Report on the Management and Administrative Computing Initiative*, Cheltenham: UGC.

Wajcman, Judy (1991) *Feminism Confronts Technology*, Cambridge: Polity Press.

Wajcman, Judy (1993) 'The masculine mystique: a feminist analysis of science and technology', in B. Probert and B.W. Wilson (eds), *Pink Collar Blues: Work, Gender and Technology*, Melbourne: Melbourne University Press.

Wajcman, Judy (1998) *Managing Like a Man*, Cambridge: Polity Press.

Walby, S. (1997) *Gender Transformations*, London: Routledge.

Walsh, V. (1993) 'Demand, public markets and innovation in biotechnology', *Science and Public Policy* 16, 4: 224–32.

Walsham, G. (1993a) 'Reading the organization: metaphors and information management', *Journal of Information Systems* 3: 33–66.

Walsham, G. (1993b) *Interpreting Information Systems in Organizations*, Chichester: John Wiley.

Webster, A. (1994) 'UK government's White Paper (1993): a critical commentary on measures of exploitation of scientific research', *Technology Analysis and Strategic Management* 6, 2: 189–201.

Webster, F. (1995) *Theories of the Information Society*, London: Routledge.

Webster, J. (1993) 'Women's skills and word processors', in B. Probert and B.W. Wilson (Eds), *Pink Collar Blues: Work, Gender and Technology*, Melbourne: Melbourne University Press.

Webster, J. (1996) *Shaping Women's Work*, London: Longman.

Whitley, R. (1992) 'The social construction of organizations and markets: the comparative analysis of business recipes', in Reed and Hughes (1992).

Williams, Brian (1995) *The MAC Initiative: Final Report*, Manchester: NCC Services.

Williams, R. (1983) *Keywords: A Vocabulary of Culture and Society*, London: Fontana.

Winner, Langdon (1977) *Autonomous Technology: Technics-Out-Of-Control as a Theme in Political Thought*, Cambridge MA: MIT Press.

Winner, Langdon (1986) *The Whale and the Reactor: A Search for Limits in an Age of High Technology*, Chicago: Chicago University Press.

Winner, Langdon (1993) 'Social constructivism: opening the black box and finding it empty', *Science as Culture* 3, 3 (No. 16): 427–52.

Witz, A. (1986) 'Patriarchy and the labour market: occupational control strategies and the medical division of labour', in D. Knights and H. Willmott (eds), *Gender and the Labour Process*, Aldershot: Gower.

Witz, A. (1992) *Professions and Patriarchy*, London: Routledge.

Wood, S. (ed.) (1982) *The Degradation of Work*, London: Macmillan.

Woolgar, Steve (1991a) 'The turn to technology in social studies of science', *Science, Technology, and Human Values* 16: 20–50.

Woolgar, Steve (1991b) 'Configuring the user: the case of usability trials', in John Law (ed.), *A Sociology of Monsters*, London: Routledge.

Wynne, Brian (1988) 'Unruly technology: practical rules, impractical discourses and public understanding', *Social Studies of Science* 18: 147–67.

Zuboff, S. (1988) *In the Age of the Smart Machine*, Oxford: Heinemann.

Author Index

Subject Index